CHANGE OF COURSE

CHANGE OF COURSE

Sailing into Love & Adversity
on Caribbean Shores

REGINA PETRA MEYER

Published in Australia in 2022 by Regina Petra Meyer,
www.reginapetrameyer.com

Copyright © Regina Petra Meyer, 2022
The moral rights of the author have been asserted

A catalogue record for this work is available from the National Library of Australia

ISBN: 978-0-6489053-8-7 (Paperback)
ISBN: 978-0-6454445-4-4 (Ebook)

All rights reserved. Except as permitted under the *Australian Copyright Act 1968* (for example, fair dealing for the purposes of study, research, criticism or review) no part of this book may be reproduced, stored in a retrieval system, communicated or transmitted in any form or by any means without prior written permission from the author. All enquiries should be made to the author: connect@reginapetrameyer.com

Produced by Broadcast Books, www.broadcastbooks.com.au
Cover and text design by Hazel Lam
Typeset in Bembo Std 12.5/14 by Hazel Lam
Cover photograph portrait from the collection of Regina Meyer
Cover photograph yacht by Don Hebert Photography
Author photograph by Blue Sky Photography
Map by Maryia Foteva
Proofread by Puddingburn Publishing

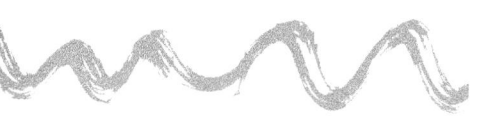

To all the curious dreamers.
May you find the courage to take the first step.

And to my dad.
He preferred to stay put.

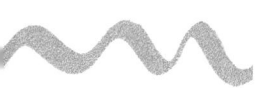

AUTHOR'S NOTE

This is a true story of my wanderings in the Caribbean, my passion for sailing and the unexpected, of love lost and found, and my search for freedom. It is my most genuine attempt to recount my experiences as close as possible to how they transpired all those years ago. But even after the last words have been typed, edited and printed, *Change of Course* simply holds this: recollections of my personal perspective and its subjective truth.

The years depicted in this book cover a stimulating and turbulent period in my life. These situations and stories are etched deep into my soul and have allowed me to access vivid memories: some make me laugh out loud, some leave me squirming in my chair, while others highlight surprisingly brave and daring moments. During the writing process, I had personal photos to fall back on (and occasionally lose myself in), plus passport stamps, old notes, and emails to help me stay on track.

To protect the privacy of those who have influenced this work, I have changed all the names of the people and some locations in my story. Except for Sven. He chose to be himself.

CONTENTS

Preface		1
1	Conjuring up Adventures	5
2	Caribbean Ahoy!	11
3	Sunday Follies	26
4	A Balancing Act	42
5	Reflections	57
6	Swept Away	73
7	The Chips are Down	89
8	Decision Time	102
9	All Things Delicious	118
10	Aquamarine Immersion	132
11	A Quick Turnaround	150
12	New Beginnings	161
13	Exposing Truth	176
14	Turbulence Ahead	191
15	Crash and Burn	201
16	Savouring Revenge	214
17	Embracing Uncertainty	225
18	Chasing Sunsets	240
19	Manifesting Ambitions	254
20	Cleaning, Cooking, Racing	265
21	Fun and Frivolities	279
22	Jumping Ship	293
Yachting Glossary		309
Acknowledgements		313

Antigua

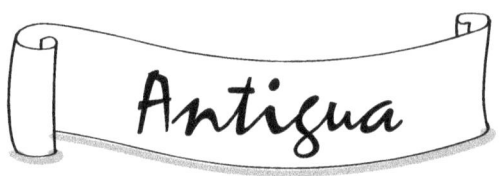

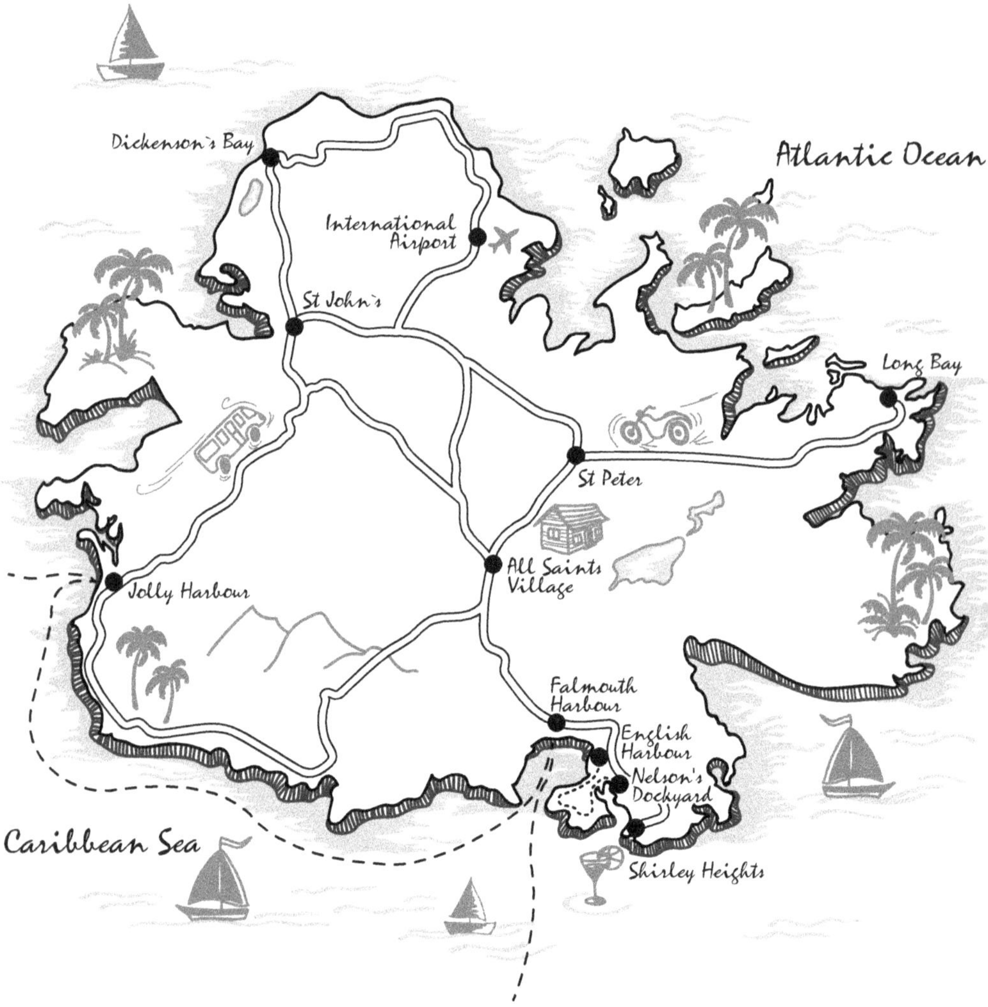
Dickenson's Bay
International Airport
Atlantic Ocean
St John's
Long Bay
St Peter
All Saints Village
Jolly Harbour
Falmouth Harbour
English Harbour
Nelson's Dockyard
Caribbean Sea
Shirley Heights

PREFACE

My goal was never to live an ordinary life. From an early age I'd felt a niggling presence, a fear almost, of getting stuck in a situation or place. Something drove me to challenge and question this persistent irritation. I had a stubborn determination to break free from the confines of my upbringing. My rebellion was not so much about the way my parents raised me, but more about the confines of my culture and the accumulative pressures of a traditional society. Switzerland is a stunning country and I count myself lucky to have been born and raised there. These days I love to go and visit, and I fully appreciate my origin, because I have since found a home in myself and am no longer dependent on a people or culture to define me. But as a young woman, I found my home country stifling and constricting. I associated the place with phrases like, 'You are just a cog in the wheel' and 'We all must fit in and play our part.' I could not stand these sayings, nor the people peering out from behind closed curtains and openly judging my unconventional choices. I was one of the first 'divorce children' in my community. The label 'divorce child' was used regularly in conversations in my childhood and it confused me. Somehow, I understood that it meant I was flawed, my future doomed and possibly I was destined for failure. So I set my sights on a different kind of horizon.

Years later, when I asked my mother about the origins of my insatiable wanderlust, she chuckled. No, this desire to travel was not inherited, she said. None of my ancestors appeared to have ventured far from home. Instead, she recalled catching me walking down the road with a little suitcase in hand when barely three years old. I digested this information and for the first time felt a deep sense of acceptance for that indescribable urge lodged deep within my soul. This desire to seek, learn and uncover had always been with me. What if *this* was the purpose I had been seeking for years?

In my teens I rebelled against the conservative culture in Switzerland by colouring and reshaping my hairstyle on a fortnightly basis. I spoke my opinion at school openly, often challenging teachers and school friends with my unpopular ideas, like the time when refugees first arrived in my hometown and some of them took shelter in our local church. During an art class my friends expressed disgust at the refugees' actions and when I challenged their racist comments the room fell silent. When deliberating my career path, my father suggested a certificate in administration. At the time, he reckoned university education was unnecessary for a woman who was only going to end up married. I had been picturing myself as a kindergarten teacher or social worker. However, I did not want to burden either of my divorced parents with the cost of my ongoing education and yearned to be free and independent as soon as possible. As a compromise, I settled on a business diploma, but chose to specialise as a travel

Preface

agent in a last grasp at defiance. This job became the launch pad for my explorations of the world around me.

I had barely completed my diploma before reconnecting and becoming romantically involved with a school friend. We developed a nourishing and harmonious relationship, travelled the world together, feeling enriched in each other's company. But after twelve years, our union was beginning to reveal cracks. A gnawing doubt was making me question myself and the relationship. A haunting emptiness was threatening to swallow me; there was a pain that I couldn't yet identify. Something wasn't right, but though I tried, I was failing to understand what it was, or the meaning of my life. Who was I and what was my purpose?

While not knowing the answers, I did know how to respond to my yearning for adventure. At the age of ten my father had introduced me to boating life aboard his little yacht, docked at the shores of our neighbouring lake in Switzerland. Thereafter, during my occasional visits, we sometimes ventured out on what was a modest sailer but which to me was the most beautiful yacht in the world. I was certain I wanted more of these treasured moments. Why did sailing ignite my passion? It spoke of ultimate freedom – the simplicity of being at sea with life defined by weather, watch rosters and mealtimes, and being isolated from people, society and everyday pressures, was appealing.

Self-reliance was essential when exposed to the forces of nature, while navigating the high seas on a long-range passage or cruising among island groups. Sailing, for me, appeared as a meditative and environmentally friendly mode of transport, offering unbridled adventure beyond the reach of an eagerly extended bow.

Aside from adventuring, this story is about my journey of self-discovery. Propelled by restlessness, I was driven to seek truth and understanding through travel, and through relationships with men. I had to learn to claim responsibility for myself. Each choice affected everything on my path: the people I encountered, the connections I made or broke, the directions I sailed and where that put me emotionally. This journey was exciting on the outer, the physical level, but profoundly confronting and challenging to my inner world. Physically and emotionally isolated, I had to make decisions I sometimes did not feel ready to take. At times I felt deeply lonely and vulnerable, harshly exposed to the uncertainty of my unfolding path.

Always, however, I let myself be guided by my moral compass, my integrity. This was the quality I treasured above all and if my personal standards slipped, it hurt the most. It did not matter whether my path was clear, or if I took a wrong turn, as long as I stayed authentic and true to myself. I had to leave the safety of my home, and later of my relationship, so I could explore, discover, and learn for myself.

'A ship in harbour is safe, but that is not what ships are built for.'
J.A. Shedd

1

CONJURING UP ADVENTURES

I could feel the sun caressing my skin and could taste the salty air on my lips. Closing my eyes, I saw palm trees fringing picture-perfect tropical beaches and sailing boats anchored in serene bays. Excitement and anticipation rushed through my being, yet here I was, facing a bleak reality. The long winter in New Zealand was cold and damp. Not tempted by the outdoors for once, my favourite pastime was sitting rugged up in front of the meagre gas heater, devouring book after book. Ignoring my dripping nose, I clumsily opened another thick volume with my frosty hands. These were quiet and lonely days in our new home, in yet another new country. Seeking refuge from my harsh and dreary circumstances, I became engrossed in adventurous sailing tales that I found in the local library. My body was stiff from the cold, but my mind did not notice, for it was escaping to hot and exotic places. I began to dream of extraordinary journeys.

Accidentally I stumbled upon crewing websites and was immediately hooked by this tantalising world hovering at my fingertips. Since first stepping foot on my father's yacht in my childhood, my wonder and fascination had remained palpable. On the yacht, my heartbeat accelerated in proportion to the boat gaining speed, its sails proudly billowing in the breeze. As the boat moved along, making a soft whooshing sound, I was mesmerised by our wake splashing and curling the water's surface behind us. Sometimes we would drop the sails mid-lake and sit motionless for a while. I loved listening to the gentle sound of the waves lapping against the hull and the feel of the soft sun caressing my face. Over the years I had repeatedly tried to convince my partner to take up a sailing lifestyle, but he suffered from terrible seasickness and, hence, we never pursued my dream. But on these webpages, I reasoned, I could at least get a taste of other people's exciting life choices and adventures. Thrilled, I learned that anyone could apply to join private yachts for a stint at sea. In exchange for a holiday on board their vessel, the yacht owners requested help with sailing, the onboard chores and possibly a small financial contribution. This information was entirely novel to me and I felt inspired by its possibilities.

Sitting cross-legged on the floor in front of the warming gas flame, I reached for my laptop and googled 'crewing opportunities'. Delighted to find reputable sites, I immediately set up a profile on several of these online communities. With this task completed, I made a cup of tea. Holding the warming cup in my hands and sipping the steaming liquid, I closed the computer and shut my eyes. I felt an energetic tingling through my body and realised I had opened a door to potential adventure. I wondered where it might lead.

Shortly after posting my profile, offers started flowing into my inbox. They were plentiful and diverse, each seeming more exotic than the last. Should I join a sailing boat on its voyage from Thailand to Africa, or cruise comfortably on a catamaran in the Caribbean? Maybe I could explore the Pacific with a young family, or venture into the grey and stormy Southern Ocean on the way from New Zealand to Chile.

These quick and unexpected offers were tempting, but I felt too immersed in my current reality to accept any of them. Instead, with my partner and best friend of twelve years, Sven, we decided that life in New Zealand was not working out the way we had imagined and arranged to relocate back to Australia. Sven could transfer with his job to a rural and coastal area south of Adelaide. For a while I forgot about this alternate sailing lifestyle. We settled into a tiny village by the sea. This quaint little community was surrounded by undulating hills on one side and the ocean on the other. Most of the houses were holiday homes, bestowing the place with a ghostly energy, and living there proved to be eerily quiet.

Sven started his new job and I tried to secure employment. However, in a village of minute proportions this was difficult. Chatting to the few locals, I quickly learned that aside from one sizeable resort there was only a pub, a coffee shop, a small grocery store and a post office, all of which were family-run businesses. I lodged an application with the resort and was pleased when I was invited for an interview a few days later. As the manager and I sat on a sofa facing each other I felt hopeful.

'Regina, thank you for coming in. I have to be honest though, we do not have any positions vacant at the moment, but I was intrigued by your colourful CV and wanted to meet you for a chat,' he said, with a sheepish smile.

For a moment I felt baffled by his confession and then burst out laughing. This was not what I had anticipated. I took it as a positive sign that someone at least valued my life experience and after a stimulating conversation I left the resort. The days were starting to seem long and lonely with no work and no friends. Eventually I stumbled across a morning coffee circle of retired folks who, although twice my age, welcomed me into their midst. Day by day we conversed over coffee, while my life trickled by. No matter how hard I tried to ignore it, the niggling voice within persisted and kept pushing me towards an adventure. Living quietly and comfortably was not for me. Trying to satisfy this growing wanderlust, I found the local library and devoured more yachting sagas. But these short-lived, second-hand experiences only stoked my fire. I wanted more.

The first step was to learn how to sail. A local sailing school offered a basic training course and, without thinking twice, I enrolled. From the first moment I loved being on board a wind propelled yacht. I loved learning how to raise and trim the sails to improve performance. I could not hear enough about storm tactics and increasingly I was visualising thrilling adventures on sleek yachts and sailing to exotic and wondrous locations.

While Sven and I had spent many harmonious years together and had travelled and lived in several countries, we felt our relationship had stalled in recent years. On one of our many walks along the local coastline, we finally agreed that we needed time apart, to figure out what each of us wanted from our lives and whether our relationship was a part of that future. As I was still without work and desperate to fulfil my dream of a sailing adventure, we decided that I would crew on a yacht while Sven remained at home in his job.

Immediately, I revisited the online crewing sites. This time I looked up the profiles in earnest and considered which boat and experience would suit me best. I chose a boat located in the Caribbean. The South African skipper, a man in his late sixties with lifelong ocean-going experience, was planning a final sail to Australian shores with the hope of finding a suitable buyer for his treasured old wooden sailing boat, and then he'd return to his home country. The photos showed a well-maintained yacht with beautiful lines. Being an older vessel, the interior was rustic, confined and less spacious and private than the more recent builds. The boat was an ex-racing yacht, had an array of sails and the deck was crammed with winches and lines. The combination of this yacht, together with the knowledge of the captain, seemed a fantastic opportunity. I knew that time on board would increase my sailing ability in leaps and bounds and decided that I would happily forfeit comfort and privacy in exchange for this learning experience. The trip was planned to take three months. Starting from Antigua a crew of five would sail through the Panama Canal, stopping over in the Galapagos and at all the Pacific Island nations on the way back to Australia. Enthusiastically I signed on and booked myself a one-way ticket to the Caribbean.

A few weeks later I stood in front of the airport's passport control, my hands damp and shaking with nervous anticipation. I took one last look into Sven's kind, deep blue and so familiar eyes. We embraced tightly, I kissed his lips, and made myself turn and walk towards the gate. Halfway, I looked back, seeing my beloved man of many years walk away, his head downcast, and wondered if I was making the biggest mistake of my life. A sudden burst of tears threatened to escape. I took a deep breath, re-centred and walked determinedly towards the plane and my future.

Once in the air, my thoughts focused on my destination. My much-anticipated adventure was about to start, and I was eager to sail the big, open oceans. I visualised blue skies, dolphins playing in our wake, days of moody clouds and towering waves. I saw myself swimming in crystal clear water, visiting stunning beaches, enjoying good company with lots of laughter, and fulfilling interactions with local people. Most of all, I looked forward to gaining clarity.

Everyone around me seemed to know exactly what they were doing and what their purpose was. On the contrary, my life seemed slightly derailed, lacking direction and purpose. I wanted to address that unsettling restlessness that had bubbled inside of me for a long time now. And the time had come for Sven and me to bring clarity to the nature of our relationship.

My life was on the verge of taking a sharp and unexpected turn. Armed only with courage and the desire for adventure, I leapt into the unknown, immersing myself in the waves of life.

2

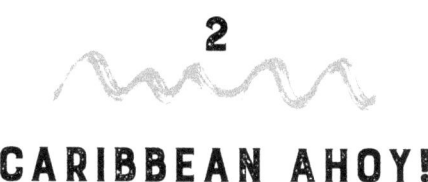

CARIBBEAN AHOY!

Peering through the elliptical window beside me, I saw a small island emerging from the seemingly endless ocean and sky. The tiny dot gradually grew bigger as the plane approached. As the green hills and rust coloured rocky outcrops of the island took shape, their rugged forms contrasted sharply with the soft hue of the surrounding ocean. As the plane descended, tantalisingly beautiful beaches became visible. Antigua. This was where my one-way ticket would end and my adventure was set to begin.

I was overcome with feelings of deep gratitude and certainty that this island would be a favourable and hospitable destination for me. Excitedly, I stepped onto the tarmac and, for the first time, breathed in the hot and fragrant air of the Caribbean.

At the immigration counter, a formidable officer eyed me with a stern, somewhat disapproving look. Had my captain not forewarned me about the immigration procedures, I would have quavered under her relentless gaze. Instead, I confidently pulled out the crewing confirmation letter the skipper had sent me and passed it to the officer, who promptly stamped me in for the next thirty days. Relieved I proceeded to Baggage Claim, hauled my heavy backpack onto my shoulders, declared the many nuts and seeds I had packed to augment the boat's provisions, and was swiftly waved through.

Outside the busy terminal a taxi driver was waiting to whisk me away in a comfortable van. The pothole-riddled ride took us almost across the entire island. We drove through little villages hiding from the street behind lush growth. I glimpsed small wooden houses with curtains blowing through open windows in the afternoon breeze, occasional bare brick houses awaiting a coat of paint, ramshackle food stalls shaded with sun-faded umbrellas tiredly advertising a local beer, and semi-finished brick buildings with rusty iron bars reaching out of the walls, looking forlorn.

As we slowed, I noticed a group of young children by the side of the road. They were running around in bare feet laughing and teasing each other, engrossed in their play. Each was sporting a creative and uniquely braided hairstyle. Dressed in hand-me-downs that were faded and hanging off their lanky frames, they appeared completely carefree and joyful.

A few sickly looking dogs were roaming the gravel paths, scavenging for a tasty piece of rubbish. Groups of plump women were chatting animatedly on a verandah while small clusters of grey-haired men sat quietly in the shade of a tree, watching the world go by. A stunning young woman dressed in tight pants and a tiny top was confidently sauntering down the street. I opened the window so I could smell and hear and immerse myself more fully, soaking up the atmosphere.

The driver turned in to a dirt driveway and stopped in front of the small marina. I paid for my ride and nervously gathered my bags. This was it! What if I did not like the owners of the boat?

What if I did not like the boat? What if I did not like my crew mates? What if …

But, too late. I tried to calm my nerves and started to walk down the narrow dock towards the yachts, neatly lined up one after the other. As I approached, an old man with a slight limp walked towards me. He had the distinct look of an old sea salt: dishevelled grey hair, gangly bowlegs, weathered wrinkly skin and clothing that had been extended well past its use-by date. His T-shirt and shorts bore holes the size of a grown man's thumb and were covered with stains from long hours spent maintaining an equally old vessel.

'Regina?' I was not surprised to be greeted by a hoarse, bordering on croaky, voice. It matched his appearance. I smiled as we made eye contact. His eyes were slightly faded from age but shone with a glint of humour and spirit that I immediately liked.

'Yes, that's right. And I presume you are Henry from *Zephyr*?'

'Indeed, I am. Welcome to Antigua, Regina. Nice to meet you.' His outstretched hand firmly gripped mine. 'Come along this way,' he said, pointing down the finger dock. '*Zephyr* is right up there.'

As we walked towards the yacht, I silently assessed Henry, my skipper for the next three months. He seemed older than I'd expected and his gait was quite frail. His skin was like leather, hanging off his frame as if he somehow had shrunk over the years. His posture was slightly bent forward, and his hands and fingers were strong and calloused, bearing the signs of a lifetime of physical labour.

'This is it. Welcome on *Zephyr*, Regina.'

I took a moment to measure the boat. Externally, she was as beautiful as portrayed in the images Henry had sent me. The hull was clean, and reflections of the water's surface sparkled on the immaculate paintwork. The bow proudly pointed towards the dock and the teak deck elegantly extended all the way back to the stern of the boat. Henry stepped stiffly across the railing at the bow and indicated to me to hand my bags over. Clearly, he was a man of few words.

First, I handed him my heavy backpack, followed by the small carry-on, and finally I stepped onto *Zephyr* myself – my new home. Carefully I walked towards the cockpit in the back, willing myself to be graceful and appear like a seasoned mariner. During our preliminary contact I had not pretended to possess a lot of experience, but I wanted to leave a positive first impression and start this new chapter on the right foot.

Henry dropped my bags down below and introduced me to his wife, Maude. She smiled and appeared friendly. Her piercing blue eyes were set in a soft and wrinkled face, framed with shoulder-length wavy grey hair. Compared with her skinny husband, she was stocky and had a grandmotherly air. Her greeting was pleasant, and I felt relieved that the people I had chosen seemed genuine and welcoming. Choosing a boat far from home with an unknown captain and crew had been a gamble. The perfect host, Maude had already boiled the kettle in anticipation of my arrival. The three of us sat down in the cockpit, sipping cups of tea and getting acquainted.

The retired couple told me about their joint life working on luxury sailing yachts around the world. Henry had been a professional yacht captain for most of his career, while Maude had worked in other roles on board. Having enjoyed a nomadic and childless life throughout their working years, they had chosen a similar retirement life by acquiring *Zephyr*. For the past few years, they had been mostly stationed at this marina in Antigua. Maude quietly confessed to being tired of the ocean-going life and was yearning to return to her family in South Africa. Henry gruffly mentioned plans to sell the yacht soon due to his health concerns and was hoping to attract more affluent buyers in Australia.

Once we finished our drinks Henry beckoned me to go below deck, so he could give me a tour and an introduction into the finer details of the yacht. 'You see, Regina, this is not a spacious interior.'

I nodded and thought that it indeed appeared rather cosy.

To my right, I could see a small galley, the yacht's kitchen. On the left was a cubicle with a door, which I presumed was the shower and toilet. Ahead in the cabin there were two benches, one elevated above the other, on either side of the hull, and a narrow passageway in between. Up front I found the bow cabin, the bed covered with heavy sail bags. At the back I could see two bunks on either side of the engine and a small navigation station behind the shower room. To my astonishment, aside from the head – the bathroom on board – there were no doors, no privacy, whatsoever. The interior was fitted out in varnished wood. It was gleaming and well maintained, but made the cabin look dark and enclosed. I swallowed and tried my best to look enthused. I was excited, but the lack of privacy was something that I would have to adjust to.

'It's homely and you have maintained it well,' I said, highlighting the positives. 'It's smaller than I thought. But I will adapt,' I added with more conviction than I felt.

Henry nodded. 'Yes, I know. Compared with the new boats this is small. But it is a great boat. *Zephyr* took part in the Sydney to Hobart Yacht Race back in the '70s, you know.'

Both Maude and Henry proceeded to give me detailed descriptions on how to operate the levers on the toilet correctly. I was instructed not to use hair conditioner, so the shower pump would not clog up, and to open and close the fridge sparingly and only when cooking, to save energy. The couple were obviously fond of their boat and set in their ways. Fair enough, I thought, after all it was their home. Henry pointed at the four benches and mentioned that one of these would be my designated bunk. Two other crew, a Scottish couple, would join *Zephyr* shortly and I was given the first choice. Looking at the bunks I saw that the lower ones were slightly wider than the elevated ones.

'I'll pick this top one here.' I preferred the bigger bunk, but picking the smaller one meant I would not have anyone sleeping above me. The lesser of two evils, I thought.

'Sure. How about you unpack, then we'll go for a beer?' Henry had already clambered up the small wooden staircase into the cockpit.

I opened the lockers next to my bunk and was relieved to find them empty. Unpacking my bag, I tried to fit everything in a logical order for convenient access. I was pleased when all my belongings easily fitted into the small compartments without having to cram them in. This was going to work quite well, I decided, feeling content with my situation and the streamlined gear. I closed the lockers and zipped up the empty backpack. I had arrived.

We walked to the bar, which was integrated into the main marina building, and ordered a cool beer. When unpacking earlier I had noticed the cabin was very warm and attributed this to the lack of windows and hatches. Greedily I took a gulp of the beer and felt myself relax. Henry and Maude were busy chatting to other boaties about their day-to-day challenges and I was able to absorb the atmosphere. Our group had gathered around a large table and were happily talking, comfortable in each other's company. Most of the yachties were either retirees or professional skippers and their crews. A mixed bunch, many came from Europe, the United States, Australia or South Africa. They were dressed in daggy old clothes and shared the same sunburnt look. The conversation was friendly and occasionally I was eyed with interest and asked a question.

After our drink we wandered back to *Zephyr* where Maude prepared dinner for the three of us. As we sat in the cockpit, they started talking about the neighbouring boats.

'Do you see that boat over there?' Henry pointed at a stately new yacht on the other side of the dock.

'Yes, what about it?' I asked, scanning the standard looking cruising yacht.

'Poofter boat. That's not proper sailing.' He snarled dismissively.

I could not believe what I had just heard and did a doubletake to see if this was a joke. Henry was frowning and after a bitter laugh he growled, 'Lazy morons that invent something like that. Furling sails and powered winches. No understanding of real sailing.'

'Oh, okay. But I guess that's a sign of the times, right? Things change. I mean, furling sails are handy with shorthanded crew?' I tentatively probed.

'No, that's not proper sailing. You can never trim correctly and overstretch the sails. It's for lazy bastards,' Henry barked, and

I decided the best course of action was to keep my mouth shut for the time being.

'And see that boat over there. They have just replaced their engine. Have no clue how to do any maintenance, but enough money to throw around. Stupid! And, by the way, Regina, beware of the local people, especially the men – they are out to take advantage of you. Be on guard, will you?'

I was stunned by the anger and judgment in Henry's speech. I had not come across someone so harsh in a long time and wasn't sure what to do. Was it my place to challenge his old-fashioned and righteous opinions, or was it better to remain silent for now? This was my first day and I was yet to find my feet on this boat. I decided to wait and see how things would develop.

Over the next few days, I learned to sit and listen with detachment. Both Henry and Maude were unpleasantly outspoken, and I quickly discovered it was best to sport a non-committal look and nod my head occasionally. They clearly did not approve of late model yachts, how those vessels were equipped, or how the younger skippers ran their boats. They continually enlightened me on fellow yachties' mistakes and to my disgust the couple were also very vocal about their dislike for the local population.

Holding on to old and rigid values gave Henry and Maude plenty to talk about, but they did not seem happy. Neither within themselves, nor as a couple. Their faces were carved with deep, angry-looking lines and they appeared stuck in the past. I didn't share their opinions and occasionally tried to give them a gentle nudge, especially relating to their racist comments. I kept mentioning my positive experiences and hoped to at least sow a seed. But largely I tried to avoid such conversations and hoped that my fellow crew mates would be more companionable.

Clare and Andy arrived from the United Kingdom a few days later. A professional couple in their late thirties, they were taking a sabbatical to fulfil their own sailing dream. Being only a few years older than me, I was overjoyed to have their company. I was hopeful the atmosphere would lighten up now we had three positive and happy people on board.

Over the next few weeks, we started preparing the lovely old *Zephyr* for the big ocean passage back to Australia. We worked long days in the blistering sun, carrying out our delegated chores. I loved Clare and Andy's company. They were laidback and between them, had considerable sailing experience. We were all excited about our upcoming Pacific adventure and kept visualising what our time at sea would be like.

Henry mentioned that we would sail to Dominica for a few days so we could get sailing experience on *Zephyr,* and extend our entry permits for Antigua upon our return.

To keep my luggage to a minimum, I was travelling without a laptop. I had planned to keep in touch with Sven via internet cafes but discovered they were scarce in Antigua. Cautiously I approached Henry and asked if I could borrow his computer to make a Skype call before we left for the short trip. The skipper handed me his device, cautioning me to be careful with it, and I went to the bar to access the wi-fi. After a few tries I got a connection. Overjoyed to hear Sven's familiar voice, I told him about *Zephyr,* describing the yacht in minute detail. I mentioned Henry and Maude, including their challenging personalities, the arrival of my pleasant crew mates Andy and Clare, and the sailing we were about to do. Sven listened patiently and passed on his news from his daily life in Australia. Hanging up I felt happy and recharged and was looking forward to my first sail on *Zephyr*.

Back at the yacht Henry told us about the various colour-coded lines that connected the sails to the boat and were relayed with numerous blocks and pulleys on deck to their end position. He went on to explain the function of each of the dozen manual winches on deck and, as he continued his instructions, I strained to remember what each line was used for. Once he finished the induction, Henry turned on the diesel engine and proudly stood behind the wheel. Precisely as briefed, we released line after line and slowly glided out of the harbour, weaving our way carefully through the anchored yachts. Once we reached the mouth of the bay, Henry assigned each crew member to a specific position. I stood beside the mast, alert and ready. I could feel the adrenaline in my body as I waited for Henry's instructions.

'Hoist the main!' A resounding bark by the old salt kicked us all into gear.

We rushed to raise the sail as quickly as possible. Henry shouted instructions in rapid succession and we scrambled to carry out the tasks on the rocking deck. Once the main sail was proudly bulging in the breeze, we had to clamber to the foredeck and hook the jib onto the forestay. Hoisting the smaller sail on the front was slightly easier, but soon my arms were on fire from the exertion. When the two sails were up and trimmed to perfection, we breathlessly gathered in the cockpit.

'Well, there's a lot of room for improvement, that's for sure. Regina, at the mast you are responsible for relaying all messages between the helmsman and bowman, so make sure you speak up. Andy, you picked the wrong line, make sure next time you get it right. Clare, you were too slow on the winch, that has to improve.'

We sat there sombre and slightly stunned. As this was the first time we'd sailed on this yacht, Henry's harsh feedback left me deflated. I had looked forward to sailing on his beautiful yacht and yearned to do myself and the skipper proud. Henry did not waste time and ordered us back to our posts. He proceeded to hammer us with nonstop tacks and gybes so we would gain experience. We all were focused, wet from the spray, and worked tirelessly to please our unforgiving skipper. The atmosphere plummeted. Gone were the happy smiles from earlier, instead we were now labouring with pinched faces, straining our untrained muscles and impatiently yelling instructions at each other. In the short breaks between manoeuvres we sat morosely bunched together in the cockpit. Andy, Clare and I would occasionally give each other an encouraging nod, while listening to Henry and Maude recount glorified stories from their sailing careers.

Nothing could dampen my spirits for long, however, and by the end of the day I was feeling exhilarated. The wind pushed our boat relentlessly through the disturbed seas and I enjoyed watching the waves splashing over the bow, washing all the way back to the cockpit, and drenching us. I did not mind getting wet – it made me feel alive and invigorated. I loved to see the sails filling with wind and, taking advantage of the weather, we made the yacht gain speed as we adjusted the trim. I was surprised how fast *Zephyr* was moving through the waves and found myself completely absorbed in the sailing. My world was the boat and the ocean beyond.

My arms started to feel heavy and drained from the hard, physical labour and my hands were wet and wrinkly from the constant exposure to salt water. On my right hand I felt the painful sting of a big blister. In our last sail change of the day it burst during one of the tacks, where the rope had been pulling on the flesh. I felt a searing pain and momentarily wondered if this trip had been a good idea. Would it be this hard for the whole trip? Surely not. I firmly pushed that thought away.

Once we arrived in Dominica, Henry went to clear customs for us all while Maude prepared a vegetable and chicken curry with rice, and a small rocket and tomato salad. We ate our meal overlooking a quiet bay and a lush and mountainous tropical island. Taking in the sights, I felt rewarded after the day's stresses. This moment suited my image of cruising life on a yacht.

Tired from our day's efforts, we quickly retreated into our narrow bunks. As my body started to relax, I found myself being gently rocked to sleep by the sound of waves softly lapping against the hull.

The following morning, Henry and Maude surprised us by announcing we would stay in this anchorage for another night. When they said we could take the day off the mood lifted immediately. Shortly after, Henry ferried us ashore in the faded grey inflatable dinghy.

Andy, Clare and I took a quick walk around the tiny settlement. Aside from a few drab looking restaurants that were advertising the local brew and plain seafood dishes, there was not much to explore. For something to do, we hired a young tour guide so we could trek further afield, through lush tropical rainforest, to the Salton Waterfalls. The guide showed us a local cinnamon bark tree and harvested a cocoa seed on the way. Reaching our destination, we saw a steep and impressive moss-covered cliff, surrounded by dense growth of ferns, shrubs, dangling lianas and enormous trees with far reaching roots.

Water was rushing over the edge and thundering into the small pond below. I inhaled the moist air and tiny drips of the humid mist settled on my face. Sitting on mossy boulders next to the swimming hole, we snacked on nuts and fresh bananas and, after a refreshing dip, the worries and doubts of the previous day fell away.

The next morning, we rose early and helped ourselves to a quick breakfast of oats and tea. While I washed the dishes, the others securely stowed our belongings in the dedicated spots, so nothing would tumble around the cabin during our sail back to Antigua. Henry and Maude eyed our progress like hawks, making sure we followed their instructions to the letter. Clare, Andy and I occasionally shared a conspiratorial glance and rolled eyes at their pedantic requests.

Once *Zephyr* was prepared, we lifted the anchor and set off, leaving the lush little island of Dominica behind us. We were greeted by a fresh breeze and a vast blue sky, with only an occasional puffy cloud. Perfect sailing conditions! We hoisted the sails and the yacht started to move effortlessly through the deep blue water. The boat was pushing along at a great pace, creating a perfectly curved bow wave at the front and we sat listening to the gurgling sound of our wake.

We relaxed, enjoying the moment. The tension that had risen again during the sail manoeuvres eased off and we shared stories and engaged in light banter. Maude prepared the usual 9am tea and passed everything up from below deck. As she handed a mug to me, she had a sparkle in her eyes that I had not seen before and quietly said, 'Regina, this cup needs to be thrown away once you finish it. It's cracked and has reached the end of its life.'

'Okay,' I replied, 'I shall give it an appropriate burial!'

Once I had finished, I waited for a gap in the conversation and loudly announced, 'You need to know, I've had enough of this. That's it from me!' With an exaggerated theatrical gesture, I launched the retired mug overboard, far into the ocean, where it immediately disappeared from our view.

Henry's jaw dropped and he looked at me in shock. He was at a loss for words for once, which satisfied me immeasurably. Trying to process my comment, he was slowly coming to terms with the fact that he had just witnessed me chucking a perfectly good mug into the sea.

'Regina! What the heck is going on? Why did you throw the cup away?' was all he could get out.

I cracked up, exploding with laughter. Turning to look at Maude, I saw her peeking up from downstairs with a sheepish look on her face. Suddenly everyone was in stitches and we experienced our first truly exuberant moment together.

As we reached the northern end of Guadeloupe, which we had been slowly passing on our right side, we changed our course back towards Antigua. With the favourable wind angle gone, the waves were coming at *Zephyr* from an awkward direction, making our passage bouncy and wet once again. The wind picked up and Henry called me to his side, saying he would show me how to put a reef in the main sail.

I stood on the rocking cabin top, trying to keep track of the different steps and knots involved. After explaining the procedure once, Henry told me to perform it on my own. I fumbled and frowned, trying to remember the correct sequence. Once I finished, pleased with my result, I looked at him expectantly, hoping to receive his approval. Instead, Henry glared at me and at the top of his lungs yelled, 'You stupid bitch. You got it wrong!'

I froze. Nobody had spoken to me like this before. Previously when Henry had been harsh or disrespectful, I had brushed it off as a minor, isolated incident. But this was more than a mere comment, this was his bitter personality, so I decided to stand my ground.

'Henry! Stop right there. How dare you talk to me like that? This is unacceptable! If you do not change, I will leave the boat straight away. I did my best with the task you set, and this was my first time doing it.'

Henry quickly back-pedalled and grovelled. 'Ah, Regina, I did not mean it like that. It won't happen again.'

I gave him a bone-chilling look to convey how serious I was. As he met my gaze, I knew we had reached a silent, mutual agreement. From that moment, Henry treated me with more respect and started giving me more sailing responsibilities.

When we got back to Falmouth Harbour, we docked *Zephyr* back in her spot and started to clean her. The decks and hull needed to be soaped and rinsed. The jib needed to be unhooked from the forestay and dried, folded and stowed. The lines were carefully rolled up and hung in neat coils at the bow rail. Once the boat was cared for, we sat in the cockpit and relaxed with a hot cup of tea.

3

SUNDAY FOLLIES

'Today is Sunday.' Henry was stating the obvious but I had lost count of the days. Appreciating the reminder, I nodded my head in acknowledgment.

'Well, on Sunday evenings we usually go to Shirley Heights, a historical locality on top of that mountain over there,' he said, pointing up. 'It's on a cliff edge overlooking both English and Falmouth harbours, the hills of Antigua and the Atlantic Ocean, plus we get to see a beautiful sunset. A Caribbean steel drum group plays first, followed by a local band. We can buy a barbecue dinner, rum punches and other drinks at the bar and there is usually a lot of dancing. In short, it is a fun night out. Would any of you like to join us tonight?'

'Yes, I'm in,' I replied as soon as Henry put his question. Clare and Andy were also keenly nodding.

We had showers at the marina building and quickly dressed and got ready. Soon enough we piled into a taxi, slowly weaving our way up the hill, caught in an impressive traffic jam for such a small island. This seemed the place to be on a Sunday evening. Getting out of the car we were immediately greeted by a captivating rhythm and the distinct metallic sound from the steel pans in the distance. Instead of walking along the carpark towards the entry gate, however, Maude and Henry directed us to an opening in the prickly shrubbery next to the paved area. Puzzled, we trudged behind them along a tiny goat trail, while Henry urged us to stay out of view from the road.

'Henry, why don't we just walk up the road like everyone else?' I asked.

'Because of stupidity, that is. They started charging an entry fee a couple of months ago and it never used to be like that. God knows what they use the money for. But anyway, we found a way to get around paying.'

I thought that Henry was being stingy and a snigger escaped my lips. The irony of watching our group stumbling single file along a barely visible dirt track, trying to avoid being scratched by the thorny shrubs, only to save a few bucks, was amusing. I decided that I would happily support the local economy on future visits.

Once we inconspicuously entered the grounds from the rear, we found ourselves in an old military complex, which I later learnt dated from the late 1890s. We wandered around what remained of the once majestic stone buildings to a small square in the centre. A steel band was playing on a small covered side stage and the musicians were beating their drums with focus, creating the rhythmic and melodic tunes. I could feel my feet starting to tap and a grin began to stretch from ear to ear. This was my kind of fun!

I left the safety of the group to explore the small area alone. An outcrop with massive boulders sat on the edge of the cliff.

Scrambling onto a rock, I could see right down into English Harbour and the adjoining historic site of Nelson's Dockyard. As my eyes roamed, I took in the mountainous landscape of Antigua in the background, a glass-shaped bay filled with anchored yachts leading out into the ocean, an occasional white cap highlighting the vast sea. Excitedly I identified the inlet as Falmouth Harbour, the home of *Zephyr*. The sun was already dipping low and within moments the entire scene became bathed in a golden glow. The sky turned various shades of red and amber as the sun slowly disappeared beyond the horizon. I admired this beautiful spectacle of nature and was filled with deep appreciation. I was on holiday on a tropical island in the Caribbean and feeling happy and free.

On the way back to the square I walked past a man who was weaving hats, fans and animals out of palm fronds. As I stopped to have a look, he smiled and swiftly wove a rose, handing it to me with a charming gesture and a cheeky wink. I wandered on and grabbed myself my first rum punch.

The steel band was finishing their set and I could see another band was getting set up on the main stage. Soon enough their music was blasting out of the large speakers and the rhythms started heating up. The music was pumping and people began to move onto the dance floor. Everyone seemed to be up and dancing, having fun. The energy was electric.

Swaying from side to side, I was not comfortable enough to dance just yet. I was scanning the crowd, adoring seeing so many people enjoying themselves, when my eyes fell upon a tall man. He was dancing nearby and his fluid moves were mesmerising. He had short, stubbly dreadlocks, which bobbed rhythmically as he danced and jumped to the beat. Dressed in a pair of loose jeans and a crisp white sleeveless shirt that revealed muscular, well-toned arms, I could not take my eyes off him. He looked strong, sensual and agile as he moved with the rhythm. Suddenly he raised his head and looked straight at me. My heart dropped a beat and I nervously smiled at him. His eyes sparkled and a smile lit up his face. Then he stopped dancing and sauntered towards me.

'Hi. Would you like to dance?' His voice was deep and warm, and the corners of his lips lifted.

'Ahh … Mmm … No, I think I'm okay, thanks,' I stammered. My throat was dry and my hands damp. My, oh my, I was in way over my head and promptly remembered Henry and Maude's warnings about the local male population.

'Okay. No problem,' he said, giving me a friendly smile.

Feeling rather deflated I watched him walk away from me.

A moment later Henry came up to me and said, 'Regina, I just want to let you know that that young man is Jeremiah, Jay for short. He is actually all right. We know him well. He comes here every week to dance, so feel free to dance with him if he asks again.'

Bummer, I thought, wishing I'd known that earlier.

I sipped my drink, trying to inconspicuously watch the handsome guy dancing. He must have felt my eyes lingering on him, as he suddenly turned and walked towards me.

'Hi again.' Another breathtaking smile. 'Are you sure you don't want to dance?'

'Oh … Okay. That would be nice,' I quickly added. I emptied my drink, disposed of the cup and followed him onto the dance floor.

Confidently he walked into the centre of the square until we were surrounded by dancing bodies. We stood in front of each other with the sound of the music filling the air and the bass resonating in my chest. I lifted my gaze, immersing myself in his silky, golden-brown eyes, and in that moment, all the noise and commotion around us seemed to fade away. Suspended in profound stillness, my heart fluttered. One look and I felt I had touched the depths of his being. In the same instant, I had a glimpse of the most sublime human beauty.

'Are you ready to dance?' His husky voice catapulted me back to the dance floor, and somewhat dazed, I nodded.

I had always been a staunch sceptic when it came to 'Love at First Sight' stories. But suddenly my world had turned upside down. Something, yet to be defined, had shifted. Shaking off any thoughts, I let myself be swept up in the moment. I loved dancing, but in the past few years I'd had little occasion to. As if needing the prompt, I noticed in the crowd a man with a T-shirt in big letters announcing, 'Dance Like No One Is Watching You!' Throwing my head back, I laughed. The electrifying music moved my body as if it had a mind of its own. I soaked up the energised atmosphere on the dance floor, while the night slowly took over the sky above us. Throughout, my senses were fully alert to the presence of this delightful stranger.

Jay was close to me, very close. I watched him dancing with his eyes closed and lips gently parted. He appeared completely absorbed in the music and I greedily took advantage, secretly scanning this intriguing man. His movements were in sync with the sound, fluid and almost painfully sensual. I noticed his sculpted muscles flexing as he lifted his arms and saw a few pearls of sweat appearing on his attractive dark face.

I was dancing, jumping and winding my body to the Caribbean tunes. Every now and then Jay moved behind me, his torso demandingly pressing against mine. Immediately my body tuned into his and we began moving as one. Whenever Jay's hand brushed the bare skin on my arm it triggered shivers down my spine. There was an electrifying current in the air around us and at times I stepped away, needing to ease the tension. Jay always met my gaze with a little smile, wrinkles forming in the corners of his eyes. His lips looked soft and tantalising and I had to consciously avert my eyes to distract my vivid imagination. I felt alive and intoxicated.

Once the music started to wind down, I spotted Henry and Maude. They were standing on the edge of the square and were eagerly signalling me. Guiltily, I wondered how long they had been trying to gain my attention.

I tugged Jay on his shirt. 'Jay, I'm sorry I have to go now. Look, my captain and his wife are waiting for me.' I smiled shyly. 'Thank you so much for the dancing. It was wonderful!'

'Are you coming back next Sunday?' He looked hopeful.

'I am not sure, but I will try to come again,' I said, already aware that I would move heaven and earth to return in a week's time. 'Good night.'

I slowly turned away, sincerely hoping to meet this man again.

Clare and Andy giggled as I approached them. On the way back down the hill in the taxi, they enjoyed teasing me.

'Girl, what was with the intense winding and grinding on the dance floor?' Andy lifted his eyebrows suggestively. 'You two could have burnt down a house.'

'Good on you for having fun!' Clare chipped in. 'All said and done, he certainly is easy on the eyes. Well done, girl.'

For a moment I felt self-conscious and guilty about the intense attraction I felt for this stranger and how intimately we had danced together. A mental picture of Sven flashed before my eyes, but I quickly reminded myself that I had not done anything wrong. I was feeling so happy and energised by the experience, nothing could dampen my perfect mood.

Over the next couple of days, Henry and Maude kept us busy on *Zephyr,* preparing the yacht for the big ocean passage. We had not used the spinnaker yet and Henry instructed us on how to correctly bind the massive, lightweight sail to prevent it from tangling during the hoisting process. He then took out the bosun's chair and explained that we would have to learn how to sew sheepskins onto the shrouds, so the sails would be protected from constant chafing during our voyage. Carefully Henry taught us all how to hoist a person up the mast and impressed on us that the second person who was stationed on deck, lifting and lowering the suspended colleague as needed, was never to lose focus or stray from their post. I had never spent much time dangling from a rope, let alone on a yacht, and was looking forward to being hoisted up.

Once I was strapped into the simplistic chair made from durable car seat straps and a small wooden board as a seat, Andy assisted me to climb up the mast by pulling me with the halyard. At the top I briefly enjoyed the sweeping bird's eye view across the yachts and the bay. With a sigh I swung myself carefully out to the shroud and tried to lock myself into a spot so I would not dangle around too much. Gingerly I took out the sheepskin, the chunky needle and thick thread, strapped the sewing protector onto my right hand, and went to work. It looked rather easy on the dock, but with every puff of breeze, the mast and I wiggled.

I had to constantly wrap my feet around a rope or a piece of the mast in an attempt to maintain my position. At the same time, I was tightly folding the patch around the wire, so it would remain in place, and began pushing the needle through the tough skin. The sun was burning. Soon, sweat was pouring down my face and my hands became slippery. I had classified this task as a minor job, 'just a little bit of sewing', but now that I was labouring, I realised that it would take days rather than hours to complete. Meanwhile, Andy was uncomfortably shuffling on the teak deck, keeping a close watch on my progress. After lunch we swapped positions and persevered until dinnertime.

The days were excruciatingly hot, especially with the jobs that needed to be done on deck and up the mast. Despite wearing sunproof clothes, hats and sunscreen, we felt like we were sizzling. Henry and Maude, comfortably settled in their well-worn routine, liked to get up around 7:30am, followed by breakfast at 8am and were ready to start the day once the 9am VHF marine broadcast was finished. After that we worked for about an hour, until ordered to stop for a mid-morning tea break. The afternoons, in contrast, were long and painfully hot, interrupted only by yet another tea ceremony. We repeatedly pleaded with Henry and Maude, asking if we could start working at sunrise, when the air was still cool, and finish earlier in the afternoon. But the old couple insisted on sticking to their routine and we grudgingly and dutifully complied.

Despite the heat and the hard physical work, day in and day out, my mind constantly drifted back to that previous Sunday. The handsome face with the big smile, surrounded by the cheeky little dreads, kept flashing before my eyes. Ashamed, I would push the image aside, willing my thoughts back to Sven in Australia.

I could not explain why I felt so drawn to this man. Regardless of the guilt, I kept hoping to see him again next Sunday.

One morning, as we sat drinking our tea in the cockpit, Henry suddenly announced that he was changing our crew positions. Being an old captain, he still ran his boat like a professional yacht and instead of rotational jobs he preferred to assign specific positions to each crew member. When Henry and I had communicated prior to the trip, he'd said that due to my limited sailing experience I would be the designated cook on board.

His statement came as a total surprise. He explained that he had decided to relieve me of the cooking and instead promoted me to be the bowman on board. The bowman (or woman) was responsible for all tasks on the foredeck and hierarchically is second in charge after the captain. Andy had held this position and looked absolutely crushed, understandably, as he had far more sailing experience and certifications than me. So far, I had only completed a basic sailing course and managed to accumulate ten days on a yacht. Henry's decision was unexpected and although flattered by his trust in my sailing abilities, I did not understand the need of assigned positions for a cruising passage. As far as I was concerned, we were a team and the overall aim was to sail the boat safely from the Caribbean to Australia.

Henry, oblivious to the emotions he'd unravelled, bluntly went on, 'Andy, you will now be stationed at the mast and Clare will handle the winches and cook.'

Andy's frown deepened and leaning forward he challenged Henry immediately. 'I don't see why we need a designated cook.

On any other passages and trips I have taken part in, we've always shared the cooking among the crew.'

I quickly jumped in. 'I totally agree with Andy. I don't mind doing some cooking, that way it's not a massive chore for one single crew member. Between the three of us we can share the catering on a rotating basis.'

'No. We will have a set cook. I am not letting anyone tell me how to run my boat.' Henry slammed his cup down, rose from his cockpit seat and heaved his gangly body onto the deck. With a stubborn look he barked, 'About time we got back to work.'

That night, as Andy, Clare and I sat in the local bar, our spirits were at their lowest and none of us spoke for a while. Henry's moodiness and Maude's righteousness had started to wear me down and I was wondering how the other two felt. As crew, the three of us got along well, but I had noticed Henry treating Andy, and Clare in particular, with harshness and impatience.

'What are you guys thinking?' I said, finally breaking the silence, not liking their grave expressions.

'Well, frankly, Henry's a prick!' Andy thundered, as if he had been waiting for a prompt to allow him to unleash his frustration. 'I don't understand why he's so bloody stubborn. Surely it's not a big deal if we all agree to cook. Why does he act so ridiculously authoritarian? And I can't stand the way he talks to us – especially you, Clare!'

'I feel like I am absolutely useless, you know.' Clare's eyes filled with tears, as she quickly continued, 'Before we came here, I took a long sailing course and we circumnavigated the UK with the sailing school. I loved the trip. It was fun and challenging at times. At the end they told me that I'd done really well. But this,' she said, indicating with her hand towards *Zephyr*'s berth, 'is unbearable. He nags about every little thing I do wrong and I get nervous and make more mistakes. Now I am questioning if the UK sailing school was crediting me wrongly, or if Henry really is a mean old sod.'

'Oh, Clare, I am so sorry that you are feeling like that. There is nothing wrong with your sailing abilities,' I said. 'He is nit-picking and probably frustrated about something else altogether. Regarding the cooking, I don't see why we can't agree to share the chores among ourselves anyway. Why should he care who is preparing the meals, as long as we all fulfil our other duties, too?'

'Yes, I think that's the best we can do. I am happy to go along with this plan,' Andy said. He seemed composed again and Clare nodded, a tentative smile lighting up her face.

Nursing our cold drinks, we began to discuss the missing crew situation. Throughout our email communications, Henry had mentioned he'd wanted a total of five crew for the passage. Four crew members, plus him as a captain. Since Maude refused to do the trip, we technically remained a crew member short. Henry had not touched on this situation during our chats and that left us wondering about his plans.

That's when Patrick strolled into the bar. He was one of the professional skippers on a yacht that was docked a few berths down from *Zephyr*. Unlike other vessels with multiple crew, Patrick was running the boat on his own. He was in his early fifties, his hair short and surprisingly neat for a mariner, and he sported a comfortable little bulging belly, most likely due to his passion for good Italian food and wine. He was a casual and friendly guy and in recent days had made a conscious effort to welcome the three of us. Patrick questioningly indicated towards the empty chair and we all enthusiastically nodded.

'Well, you lot don't look overly happy. Is the cranky old bastard getting to you?'

I nearly choked on my drink hearing his blunt statement. Suddenly everyone spoke as we tried to tell him what had been going on.

Patrick shook his head. 'Guys, you can't let him get to you. Look, they are my friends and essentially, they are nice people. But they have been stuck with each other and this boat for a while. They are too old to physically sail their yacht on their own. That's how they got stuck in Antigua.' Patrick looked around our group and I started to feel sorry for the old couple when I thought about their predicament. Patrick continued quietly, 'Now Maude desperately wants the boat gone, while Henry doesn't really want to sell it.' He took a gulp from his drink. 'You should know that you guys aren't the first crew they've had here. There was a whole group here last year and I am sorry to say that in the end he didn't follow through with the trip.'

Shocked, I absorbed this information. Perhaps Henry was not as committed to sailing to Australia as he made out to be. We were not a full crew and, so far, Henry had not mentioned the missing member of our team. Did he have someone in mind or was he deliberately not looking, I wondered? Or did he subconsciously plan to sabotage our trip in this manner? My heart ached at the thought of our trip not happening, and I could not imagine abandoning my dreams at this stage.

I could understand that selling *Zephyr* would be a painful choice for Henry. A professional captain all his life, he would not only say goodbye to his passion, the yacht, but also to a way of life. He would have to make the transformation from a sea nomad to a landlubber. I felt a pang of compassion for his situation. Henry had mentioned that he was on blood pressure tablets and various other medications. Aside from his temper, which was positively fiery, he was a frail old man. He was lost in the past, endlessly recounting stories and staunchly believing in how much better things used to be. He was desperately trying to hold on, while knowing it was already gone.

And Maude, his professional offsider and wife of many decades, had spent most of her adult life at sea. Whether the ocean-going lifestyle was something she chose deliberately, or if she only remained in it due to her marriage, I did not know. We knew that in recent years she had been longing for a steady home on land and wanted to enjoy more time with her family in South Africa. Henry and Maude had been spending these past few years wishing for different outcomes. Instead of looking for a solution that suited them both, they each had projected their bitterness and anger onto the people and situations around them.

Patrick had given us a new perspective into the circumstances of our skipper and his wife, and for a while we sat quietly in front of our drinks, contemplating the situation. Before leaving the bar, we agreed that we were all committed to proceeding with the planned passage and wanted to focus on learning more about sailing *Zephyr*. We decided to support each other as a team and confront Henry if his behaviour got any worse.

The remainder of the week was relentless. We worked all day Saturday, and on Sunday Henry and Maude gave no indication of allowing us a break. We were too timid to speak up and, albeit half-heartedly, completed our tasks. Andy was splicing some ropes and Clare and I were alternating with the dreaded sewing on the shrouds. My arms and legs were sore from the constant balancing act in the bosun's chair and the heat of the sun was getting to me. Clare looked equally worn out from assisting me from her post on deck.

'It's a pretty hot day today. You've done good work, team!' Henry tried his best to sound cheerful as we sat slumped over our plates. 'I reckon after lunch we will clean up our work stuff, give the deck a quick hose and finish for the day. Sound good?'

We perked up a bit and nodded in unison.

'Who's up to going to Shirley Heights later this afternoon?' I asked, trying not to look too excited.

I looked expectantly at Clare and Andy, who were whispering to each other.

'No. We are not coming today. We will enjoy a little downtime with just the two of us.' They looked relieved at having created some space for themselves and we all launched into the clean up with new enthusiasm. We were done in no time and went our own ways. Henry and Maude took a nap. Andy and Clare wandered off. I borrowed Henry's laptop and unsuccessfully tried to call Sven.

At four o'clock on the dot, Henry, Maude and I stood ready at the mouth of the marina. Once on the mountaintop, not wanting to upset the couple, I obligingly trudged behind them along the goat trail with the prickly bushes. I didn't mind this time, as long as I got to dance.

'Already looking forward to seeing Jay again, Regina?' Henry asked.

I blushed and laughed nervously, unsure how to respond. Of course I was looking forward to seeing him. Jay had dominated my thoughts all week.

Once in the compound I left Henry and Maude to themselves. As with everything else, they maintained a routine and always sat in their usual spot. I got myself a sweet rum punch and assessed the situation. Not seeing my handsome stranger, I wandered across to the steel band, closed my eyes and started moving to the catchy tunes.

'Hello. You came back!'

I felt lips brush against my earlobes and my heart missed a beat. I turned and immediately lost myself in those silky eyes. What was it with this man? I wondered. He was irresistible.

He smiled and asked, 'You want to dance?'

The evening was a blur. Just like the previous week, the place was packed with people and the atmosphere was fun and full of energy. Jay and I danced with our bodies closely connected. Eyes closed, I absorbed the sounds, the movement of my body against his and the quivering sensations when our bare arms connected. I was intoxicated, not from the rum, but from my heightened senses. I felt incredibly happy and alive.

'What's your name?' Jay placed his hand on the small of my back and gently guided me to the lookout area during a break.

'I'm Regina. You're Jeremiah, right? Jay for short, if I remember correctly?' He already felt so familiar, it was strange to do the introductions now.

'Yes. Jay, the invincible,' he said with a cheeky wink and I promptly blushed. His smile broadened. 'Regina. That's a nice name. My dancing queen.'

I was not used to flirting and his intense looks threw me off guard. Although not prone to blushing, this man had a knack of making my face flush, and my body responded with waves of tingling.

I loved to dance and to my surprise, I particularly enjoyed the sensual Antiguan dance style. Jay mostly danced behind me, his body connected with mine. Moving as one to the loud music, the intimate touch and moves were new territory to me, yet seemed natural. My body was loving the freedom of the movements and on the dance floor my mind switched off entirely. I was in the moment, enjoying the sensations and letting the energy flow. I noticed an occasional disapproving glare by a contemptuous holiday maker and was unsure if this was due to our interracial interaction, or the sultry dancing. Probably both. I cared about neither.

When I was once more abruptly summoned by Henry and Maude, I had to leave the party in a hurry. Turning to go, I looked into Jay's eyes and felt a magnetic pull towards him. I could not understand how he managed to get under my skin, but I knew I would find a way to return the following week.

4
A BALANCING ACT

The next morning our new work week commenced and having had only one day off since we joined the boat, the mood was subdued. During a quiet moment Clare confessed that she and Andy were thinking about moving into accommodation ashore. As a couple they struggled with the lack of privacy aboard and, along with the interpersonal challenges with Henry and Maude, they longed for a space of their own. They had not found anything yet but were continuing to look for a suitable place. Also, we suspected that we might set sail later than Henry had initially promised and we were preparing for a long wait.

Later that evening the three of us concluded that we had to confront Henry and Maude about our working days on board. The agreement we accepted pre-trip was that we would be given free food and accommodation in exchange for our labour, to help get *Zephyr* in shipshape condition for the trip. But so far Henry had pushed us hard and we were working full days, with hardly any time off. During our nightly beer at the bar we decided this arrangement was not sustainable.

'I don't understand Henry's plan,' Andy muttered. 'We should have been well under way by now. If we are staying longer in Antigua, he can't expect us to work nine to five, seven days a week.'

'I agree, Andy. This is our holiday, too!' I said, not liking our entrapment. 'We freed up our time and paid to fly in from different parts of the world and we don't even get time to explore and experience this beautiful island.'

'I would rather buy a meal here and there and get more time to myself in return. We've got ourselves in a strange situation,' Clare said, and shook her head, probably wondering how she and her hubby had landed in such a predicament. I could relate to her feelings and hoped we could negotiate better terms with Henry.

With our confidence boosted and our intentions clear, we finished our drinks and headed back to the boat. We clambered aboard across the bow rail, and in single file, tiptoed down the narrow side deck. Stepping lightly down into the cockpit, we stepped, one by one, down the companionway into the cabin.

We had to take turns preparing for bed as the interior was pokey and too small for the five of us to move around at the same time. I sat on the bunk and let everyone have their turn in the little bathroom, using the moment to take stock of our situation.

I thoroughly enjoyed living on a boat. Each night I fell asleep to the sound of waves lapping against the hull and to the gentle rocking motion of the yacht. I loved the physical aspect of sailing, the work on the boat itself, and the exhilaration while we were at sea. There was something magical about being on the ocean and I felt in my element. This lifestyle suited me perfectly and already, in this short time, the yacht felt like home.

Zephyr was considered an old yacht. Built in the early 1970s, her 46-foot length and beautiful wooden construction meant she was a decent size sailer. Since coming on board a few weeks ago, I had adjusted to the somewhat glum and cramped interior and was content with my little bunk.

The bow cabin was filled with bulky sail bags and spare ropes. The head on the boat consisted of one shower and a hand-pumped toilet. Opposite the bathroom cubicle was a gimballed stove, a deep chest fridge and cupboards containing the galley goods. In front of Henry's bunk was his cluttered navigation station, including the VHF and HF radios and minimal marine electronics.

In my opinion, *Zephyr* was an oldie, but a goodie. Initially designed as a cruiser racer, she featured more than a dozen tailing winches on deck. Two people were needed to work a winch – one to grind the winch handle, tightening the rope that fed into the barrel, and the other to pull the line away from the cylinder, keeping it taut. With that many winches and ropes we had to be constantly focused and ready to perform several jobs in quick succession.

Also on deck and strung along the mast was an abundance of different sheets. During our first sail, Henry had explained the purpose of each one. Whenever I had a spare moment, I would sneak back on deck to remind myself of the name and use of each line. I wanted to learn as much as I could, so I could quickly become a valuable crew member. This was a great yacht on which to learn and improve my sailing skills, and I was intent on giving my best.

Despite Henry's gruff and grumpy attitude, he seemed to respect my enthusiasm and the way I stood up to him. So, unlike Clare and Andy, who continued to experience his ill-tempered ways, I started to see a Henry who loved sailing and was as excited as each of us about our big trip ahead.

I could not wait for our journey to commence.

A Balancing Act

The following morning, as we sat in the cockpit drinking strong coffee and crunching on fresh bread rolls, I cleared my throat. Yesterday, Andy, Clare and I had agreed that we needed to discuss and face our situation with Henry, whatever the outcome. Since I got along best with him, I was elected as our spokesperson.

'Henry.' I waited until he met my gaze and looked him in the eyes. 'We would like to chat with you about our situation on board,' I stated calmly.

'You want to have a D&M?' he asked, with a slight twinkle in his eyes.

'What does that mean?' I said, caught off guard.

To my surprise he roared, a proper belly laugh. 'A deep and meaningful, Regina. That's what you want?'

'Yes! Yes, exactly. Is it a good time now?' Rather surprised by his light-hearted response, I looked at him closely, trying to gauge his state of mind.

'Okay … Shoot.' Henry smiled and indicated for me to begin.

'Henry, as you are aware, the three of us have been working hard here on *Zephyr*, every day with hardly any time off. We flew in from different parts of the world and spent a lot of money to get here. Plus, we all took leave from our jobs to take part in this adventure with you. We understood that the initial agreement was that we would work in exchange for food and board, to get *Zephyr* ready for the voyage. But you also led us to believe that we would depart Antigua within a week or two of our arrival. We've been stuck on this island for longer than anticipated.' I took a breath, hoping the message was coming across in a positive way. 'Considering that instead of sailing we are spending weeks ashore, we would like to propose a new arrangement. We are happy to work during the week, but request days off on the weekends, so we can explore and enjoy time off, during what are essentially, our holidays. And ... ' I looked at Henry. He nodded, indicating for me to continue.

'We are all excited about the trip and keen to learn as much as possible, but we also want to make this an enjoyable experience. We want to share the chores, especially the cooking, among the three of us. This is an amazing trip we are about to embark on, and we feel that at times you have been unduly harsh toward us crew. Henry, we do expect to be treated fairly and with respect.'

The old skipper looked surprised at my frank statement. I did not give him the opportunity to interject, but quickly soldiered on.

'We are also concerned that you still haven't communicated anything about the final crew member. Can you give us an update on this situation? We ask you to keep us informed regularly on new developments in that area.' I laughed nervously, wondering how Henry would receive the huge download. 'That's it – for now at least!'

Henry briefly exchanged a look with Maude, while the three of us fidgeted anxiously in our seats. He took a breath and began his reply.

'I understand that you are on holiday and your proposal for days off seems fair. So, let's agree that weekends will be free time and weekdays will be workdays. If you want more days off, let me know and we will work around it. Is that acceptable?'

I looked at Andy and Clare and we nodded our heads in unison.

'So, that's settled then. Now, we've discussed the chores before. If you insist on sharing the cooking then you can arrange a roster between the three of you, providing you are fit and ready on time for your scheduled watches. Deal?'

Again, all heads bobbed in agreement, with small, tentative smiles forming on our lips.

'Now, regarding the last crew member. I have been in contact with several people. Only last week a guy committed to joining us and then cancelled at the last minute. I have also had a chat with a skipper on the dock – you know, the young chap on the racing yacht. His mother is interested in joining us and I emailed her yesterday. Hopefully, if all goes well, she will be here soon. I will keep you updated as I learn more.' He paused, then said, 'Let me say one last thing.' He sounded sincere and looked at each of us before he continued. 'I appreciate that you approached me in this calm manner for this D&M chat. It is important that we don't let anything fester. So, in the future if there is anything else, please let's discuss it in this way again.'

With these words, I felt my tension ease, not realising how anxious I had been about having this conversation.

'Now, are we all good?' Henry finished with a chuckle.

'Yes!' we exclaimed together. We were laughing and relieved, each of us much happier with the new agreement. The sun suddenly seemed brighter and I felt empowered by the experience.

'Right, let's get back to work until Friday. Then you can enjoy your first full weekend off. Sounds good?' Henry said with a chuckle.

'Yes, let's do it!' I beamed at him and my crew mates, already planning my days off.

The rest of the week passed quickly. With our new agreement in place and more days off to look forward to, I felt more relaxed and my spirits lifted. I indulged my constantly wandering mind, which persistently veered off to Jay, the gorgeous warrior man, his soft velvety eyes and beaming smile. I was hoping to see him again on Sunday.

I loved the atmosphere up on the mountain, the stunning sunsets and, of course, the dancing. But my main motivation to return had more to do with my infatuation with Jay. I wanted to see him and dance with him again, feel our bodies connect and move as one. The mere thought of our physical closeness had me trembling in anticipation, yet I also felt ashamed of my intimate thoughts and physical reaction towards a man other than my partner. I valued integrity and honesty – qualities I was determined to live by – yet felt I was standing on the edge of a slippery slope.

When it came to Jay, I couldn't control my thoughts or feelings. My guilty conscience was the only dampener on my vivid imagination. Sven had been my lover, partner and loyal companion for years. I didn't understand my infatuation with Jay but could not seem to dismiss it either. I had no clarity on the situation, instead it hid behind a thick veil of tangled emotions and confusion. Wanting a distraction from this mental struggle, I focused on sightseeing instead.

I was excited about exploring the island. St John's, Antigua's capital city, was a thirty-minute bus trip from the marina, and I wanted to buy a new pair of flip-flops in the duty-free zone at the cruise liner terminal. Maybe I would also indulge in a coffee or ice cream to celebrate.

Come Saturday morning, Andy and Clare walked off, light on their feet. I waited on the roadside until a tired-looking minibus came bumping along in my direction. Confidently I flagged it down and got on.

'To St John's?' I hesitantly asked the driver.

'Yeah, gal. Get on,' he replied with a broad smile.

I smiled and took my seat, and then a young boy collected the modest fare. Settling into my spot, I looked around. The van had seen better years. Its seats were torn in many places and had lost most of their cushioning. The paintwork was peeling off the body and some windows were fully open, while others appeared jammed in random positions. The air blew sticky and hot through the vehicle as we rattled along. Loud music blared out of the metallic speakers, and I overheard a few passengers debating about the costumes of two rival carnival troupes. Soon I observed that I was the only tourist and, for the first time in my life, the only white person on a bus. No one took notice of me and I sat back, relaxed, soaking up the atmosphere.

The minibus rumbled into an old and dusty area. The bus terminal's traffic islands were bustling with people and its roads jammed with buses in varying states of disrepair. I hopped out of the van and set off to explore the island's capital. Across the street I spotted a fresh goods market and could not resist having a look. It was crowded with Saturday morning shoppers. Built of bare concrete, the hall was spacious, and accommodated many stalls. Simple wooden benches were laden with tropical produce, including bananas, pineapples, eggplants and cucumbers. I also saw sweet potatoes, rocket salad and a few bruised tomatoes. The selection was modest but fresh, and I was reminded that I was indeed on a small island. With a population of fewer than 90,000 spread across the two islands of Antigua and Barbuda, St John's felt more like a country town than a capital city.

Anything that was not grown locally had to be either flown or shipped in.

Leaving the market, I continued up the narrow main road. Cars and people were weaving their way along the busy street. Old people slowly shuffled among the crowd. Young guys with solid boots, oversized pants and baseball caps bounced their way up and down the sidewalk. Pretty young women with skin-tight pants and sexy tops strutted along confidently. Most shops advertised their wares through huge speakers out front. Following the flow of pedestrians, I began to step along to the reggae, calypso and soca beats. There was no mistaking that I had landed in the heart of the Caribbean. I was loving it!

Roaming through St John's, I walked a couple of blocks away from the ocean, up a steep hill, and found a cemetery and small park. Wandering back downhill, I came out at the cruise liner wharf. Towering high above the local buildings, a gigantic ship was connected to the dock with enormous ropes, as if caught in an oversized spider's web. Near the wharf I strolled along an unusually clean and well-maintained shop-lined alley. This area, a short stroll from where the cruise ship was docked, was clearly designed to showcase a quaint Caribbean look, but to my mind, it lacked the lively atmosphere of the real island life of a few streets back. I quickly purchased my flip-flops and resumed my explorations.

In a small side street, I found a roti shop. Far removed from the regular tourist haunts, the modest restaurant was pleasantly quiet. I devoured a soft roti wrap filled with scrumptious chicken and vegetable curry and considered my next adventure.

Not wanting to waste a moment of my precious day, I walked back to the bus terminal and asked for directions until

I found the Jolly Harbour bus. This was the other main marina on Antigua, and I'd heard mention of stunning beaches nearby. A short ride on another dilapidated vehicle and I was dropped off outside a shopping centre. The fresh façade intrigued me and browsing the aisles I was surprised by the variety and selection of the largely imported goods. I had a look around the neat marina at the centre of Jolly Harbour, checked out the notice board there and walked by the adjoining upscale resort. While this area was far more exclusive than other parts of the island that I had visited, I was not overly inspired and decided to jump on yet another bus. I asked a few people if there was a way to return to Falmouth Harbour via a different route. A young man assured me that I could take the local bus via Old Road to Swetes and from there I could connect with another bus to my base.

The directions sounded easy enough, so I boarded the local bus and sat on a torn seat that had been covered in plastic in an attempt to prevent further damage. Soon sweat was dripping down my torso and legs and I was glad all the windows were open, to provide at least some airflow. I sat by the window, breathing in the hot, blossom-laden air. As we careened along the road, I spotted a particularly stunning frangipani tree draped in lush burgundy blooms, a striking contrast to the tree's green foliage and the deep blue ocean in the background. We passed picture-perfect, surprisingly empty beaches, and wove through tiny villages of plain wooden houses with rusty, corrugated-iron roofs. Fishing nets were drying in functional front yards. The rustic dwellings spoke of simple livelihoods. Next we passed a palm tree plantation nestled at the foot of a mountain.

Suddenly the road became unbelievably steep and winding. The old bus was revving high in first gear, heaving its weight uphill at a painfully slow pace. Both sides of the road were framed by lush and dense rainforest and I felt like we had entered a different world. Dwellings were sparse and by now, only a few passengers remained on board. Among the unfamiliar scenery, I began to feel uneasy, concerned about finding my way back to the yacht. Noticing my uncertainty, the friendly bus driver smiled and told me not to worry. A short while later he stopped the bus at an intersection and patiently explained where to hail the next bus back to Falmouth Harbour.

Standing on the road, waiting for my transport, I began to recall the many warnings about Antigua. I had heard tales of holiday makers being mugged or violated, locals cheating tourists, and the stories of so-called innocent young women being exploited by local men. Reflecting on my day, I felt appreciative of the many residents who had helped me to find my way around. I wondered if any of the yachties, who so liberally spread negative gossip and frightening stories, had ever immersed themselves in the local culture. My initial impression was that the Antiguan people were friendly, open and willing to assist. Occasionally I was aware of a cheeky wink or a tease from a passing male, but as long as I did not engage, nothing further happened. The same behaviour could easily occur anywhere in the world, and I disliked the yachties' fear-mongering attitude.

I returned to our dock humming with excitement and enjoying my new familiarity with this island country. As a child and teenager in Switzerland, I had been immersed in a predominantly white society. I had not been exposed to any form of black culture and found myself falling in love with the local Antiguans. The people I had encountered were cordial and welcoming. They radiated a warmth and joyfulness that was irresistible. I adored their beaming smiles and could not get enough of their amazingly creative hairstyles. The women and girls proudly wore elaborate braids, colourful wigs and stunning hair creations that rivalled Queen Amidala's in *Star Wars*. The men and boys appeared to prefer short cuts, with only the occasional fashionable hairdo or fanciful braids.

Wanting to avoid Henry and Maude's gruff company after such a great day out, I wandered over to Patrick's boat.

'Hey, Regina, nice to see you! Come aboard. I was about to open a bottle of wine. Would you like a glass?' he asked with his usual twinkle in his eyes.

'Sure. That would be lovely,' I replied and followed him onto the deck.

We sat in front of the mast. Patrick poured us each a generous glass, and we toasted and savoured the first sip.

'It's Italian. Chianti. Italians have the best food and wine,' Patrick said with a dreamy look.

I chuckled, having already heard about his slight obsession. 'Thanks, Patrick, it is a lovely drop and even nicer sharing it with you,' I said, sincerely appreciating his company and generosity.

'So, what have you been up to? I haven't seen anyone working on *Zephyr* today.'

'Well, remember the day you joined us in the bar and we told you how unhappy we were?'

Patrick nodded.

'After you left, we decided to confront Henry about the situation, and he agreed that some time off was in order. From now on, no more work on weekends! Today and tomorrow, I am as free as a bird.' I laughed and Patrick raised his glass, smiling broadly.

'Wow, well done you lot! That's reason for a celebration.' Gaily we clinked glasses.

'Would you like to stay for dinner, Regina? I am planning a simple Italian pasta, and you are welcome to join me.'

I happily accepted the invitation and we sat for a while on the deck, looking out over the other yachts, with the sun slowly setting. The bay became bathed in a warm golden glow and sitting there, in good company, I felt incredibly grateful. In a short time I had experienced many wonderful and enriching moments. This trip was turning into the adventure I had envisioned.

I quickly updated Patrick on the *Zephyr* news since our last chat. Then he asked about my day and I proceeded to recount my explorations and encounters. Grateful for someone to confide in, I mentioned my partner Sven in Australia and my fateful encounter with the handsome Jay at Shirley Heights.

'Oh, Regina, stay away from the local men. They will sweep you off your feet and break your heart. It usually doesn't end well,' Patrick said, giving me a sympathetic look as he stood up.

Wine glasses in hand, we relocated below deck, where he pointed towards a settee and invited me to sit down. As he got busy with making dinner, I thought about his comment. I felt troubled and saddened that I continued to encounter people, well-travelled and supposedly of broadened horizons, who walked through life with such closed minds and hearts. I disliked stereotyping and vowed to myself to always treat every person as an individual and an equal. I aimed to meet each with respect, friendliness and curiosity. I had travelled the world extensively and my encounters with people from different countries and cultures had been nothing but inspiring and enriching. I promised myself to continue living life open-heartedly, to stay receptive to new experiences and allow more rewarding moments to touch my soul. Most of all, I wished to maintain my positive perspective on people and on life.

Next morning, I rose early and sat alone in the cockpit for a while. The sun was low and the sea was calm. I could hear the waves caressing the hulls, the occasional clanging of a sheet against a mast, and distant bird song. The sun's early warmth gently touched my face and I closed my eyes to savour the moment.

Another sunny day was on the way and I contemplated my options. I would certainly go to the Sunday event at Shirley Heights tonight. I could not resist Jay's immense pull and was determined to recreate the fabulous time I'd had last week.

I shared a quick breakfast with Henry and Maude, who seemed in brighter spirits. They said that yesterday, Andy and Clare had announced that they had found accommodation ashore but would still work on *Zephyr* and do our sail trainings in preparation for the big trip. Since they had already mentioned this plan to me, I was not surprised and was happy that they had found a better solution for themselves. Maude and Henry started pottering around on the boat and I borrowed Henry's laptop, taking it to the bar.

I logged into the temperamental wi-fi and took a deep breath. I had only been able to connect with Sven a couple of times since my departure. Today the connection was crackly and the speech often distorted and delayed, resulting in a broken and hesitant conversation. I spoke to Sven about the trip to Dominica on *Zephyr,* about the delay of our departure, the recent upheaval around our working days, and the missing crew member. I told him about the sunset parties on Sundays and how I loved dancing up there, omitting any mention of Jay. During the call I was riddled with guilt and struggled to make sense of my infatuation. Why, out of the blue, did I harbour this intense attraction for a stranger when I had a loving and dedicated partner at home? Distracted by my emotions I barely listened to Sven's news. My ears only picked up upon hearing that he would soon travel to India for training for his work. Sounding happy, he said he had been able to tack on a few weeks of leave, which he planned to spend in our hometown in Switzerland.

After the call, I sat for some minutes in silence. Hearing Sven's familiar voice had reminded me of the deep bond we shared. I was overcome with shame that I had not told him about my strong feelings towards Jay. Sven was my long-term partner, my rock and my closest friend. I completely trusted him, yet I was not sharing with him what I most needed to.

In a sombre mood I quietly packed away Henry's laptop. The wife of the marina owner passed by my table. She had hovered in the bar throughout my call and, without doubt, had overheard parts of the conversation.

She threw me a piercing look. 'You better watch your dancing up there at Shirley Heights, if you want to keep your relationship going.'

Although it was painful to be on the receiving end of her scornful message, I could not blame this woman for her judgment. Already, my Sunday shenanigans had provoked gossip and controversy within the small yachtie community. On my way back to *Zephyr* her words kept running through my mind and my heart felt torn.

5

REFLECTIONS

'Who would like to take Sven's homework to him, so he can catch up on today's class?'

No sooner had the sixth-grade teacher finished speaking, than several hands eagerly shot in the air. But mine was waving most assertively and, with a firm shout of 'Me!' I secured the assignment.

Sven was one of the popular boys in our class and I had a crush on him from an early age. He had beautiful, deep blue eyes, a straight nose and full lips that were often curled upward in a small smile. His face was framed by a thick mop of wavy light brown hair that touched his shoulders. He was athletic, intelligent and independent. Unlike the other guys in the class, he was composed and mostly disinterested in the other boys' mischief. He chose not to hang out with anyone his age but preferred the company of his older brother and his friends. To us girls, Sven had the air of a more mature and desirable male. He was either unaware of our adoration or simply not interested in females in those early teen years. He was friendly with everyone but appeared aloof. His mates, music, soccer and paragliding were his main interests.

Fast-forward a couple of years, and after finishing my apprenticeship as a travel agent, I packed my bags for my first backpacking adventure and travelled through Central America for three months. I returned enriched and invigorated. Looking forward to reconnecting with friends and share my memories, I walked into Mr Pickwick, a popular local pub, in high spirits. Walking in, I noticed Sven, his brother Frank and a few of his mates leaning against a high set table. I ordered a drink and went over to join them.

'Hey, how are you? I haven't seen you in a while,' Frank said.

'Yes, well, I've been backpacking in Central America for three months!' Excitedly, I launched into relating tales from my travels.

'And what have *you* been up to?' I said, turning towards Sven, immediately aware of his mesmerising blue eyes.

'I finished my apprenticeship as an electrician and I'm about done with the compulsory army training.' He paused, as if unsure how to continue.

'And on the personal front?' I prodded.

'Well, I still live at home with my parents and spend a lot of time with my mates and paragliding. Next November we're planning a motorbike trip through Algiers and Tunisia, which should be fun!' His eyes lit up.

We continued chatting for a while. Before I left, we agreed to catch up again soon, in the way that old school buddies do.

Over the following weeks we happened to run into each other more and more. Mostly they were informal and accidental encounters, although secretly I would check out the pubs and bars beforehand, only entering when I was certain he was there.

I got along well with Sven's brother and his mates and we had a good time joking and talking together. The longer I spent in Sven's company, the more I was drawn to him. I was attracted to my school friend. It was weirdly wonderful.

One night, as we were sitting around a table in the local pub, Frank turned to me and said, 'Hey, we are going to France on our motorbikes over Easter for a few days. Why don't you join us?'

The invitation was welcome but unexpected. I hesitated, then said, 'I will think about it, but I guess it would be nice!'

Secretly I had been hoping that Sven, and not his brother, would invite me on a date one day. I wondered if I had sent out a wrong signal, or if Sven was not interested in me.

Later that night as we were saying our goodbyes and I was about to walk home, Sven offered to give me a lift. I hopped into the passenger seat and we drove off. When we arrived at my home, Sven parked the car and we sat in silence for a moment until he turned to me with a serious look.

'Reggie,' he said, using my nickname and looking me straight in the eyes. 'I would love if you came to France with us. But I would prefer if you rode on the bike with me.'

'Yes, that's my preference, too,' I said with a relieved smile, quickly adding, 'Sven, I am relieved you said that.'

Over the next weeks we spent more and more time together and we enjoyed each other's company. Eventually we became lovers. I decided to move out of my parents' place, found a little flat, and within a few days Sven came to live with me.

We worked, saved money, and managed to fund several extended trips exploring countries on most continents. We took on the world, met people from across the globe, experienced wonderful landscapes and immersed ourselves in different cultures and ways of life. Together we braved occasional challenges but mostly had an adventurous, fun and harmonious time.

∼∼∼

After one trip that lasted well over a year, we returned to our home in Switzerland. We were sitting at the dining table after a meal when I said, 'Sven, what do you think about living in Australia or New Zealand?'

He looked stunned. 'Why? We've only just settled back in after being away.'

We had found a lovely little house to rent – a rare treat in Switzerland. Straight away we had decorated it with IKEA furniture and created a warm and comfortable home.

'I have been thinking about it,' I said. 'We are both turning thirty this year and people in our age bracket are awarded the most points for the skilled migration visa.' Aware that my idea probably sounded absurd after our long absence and having just put down roots again, I added, 'So, if we ever wanted to live in either of those countries, now is the time to try.'

'Mm … It's an interesting idea. But I am not really convinced, Reggie. I like it here. The house is great and my new job is working out well. But for a moment, let's run with the thought. Which country are you talking about – Australia or New Zealand?'

Over the next few weeks, we went back and forth on the idea, talking about the benefits of applying for such a visa or staying at home. We debated which country was better, easier and more suitable for us. As the discussion went to-and-fro the idea solidified and after much consideration, we decided to apply for a permanent residency visa for Australia. We reasoned that our chances of being issued a visa might be slim, but we would try rather than just dreaming about it. If successful, we would give living in Australia our best shot.

Once we had made our decision to proceed with the visa application, I promptly set to work. A few months later we sent two neat folders containing our applications and required documents to the Australian Embassy in Berlin. We did not expect to hear back from the embassy for at least a year and went on with our lives. Then, only a few months after the application, Sven unexpectedly received an appointment for a phone call with the ambassador. We assumed they required further information about our case, so neither of us thought much about the call.

I sat by the phone with Sven while he answered the ambassador's questions. After a little while, the ambassador excused himself to review his documents. We patiently waited, unsure what to expect.

'Sven, are you still there?' he asked.

'Yes, I am here.' I could hear the nerves in Sven's voice.

'All right. I am satisfied with the information you have provided and am granting you the visas. You can send in your passports at your earliest opportunity so we can issue the documents.'

What? Had we heard correctly?

'Excuse me, I don't understand. What do you mean? Don't you have to get approval from Australia to issue our visas?' Sven stammered and I could hear the ambassador chuckling.

'No. I have full authority to grant your visa. Like I said, I am happy with your information and therefore I will issue the visas. Please, send me your passports.' He laughed again. 'Congratulations and welcome to Australia!'

Sven ended the call, stunned. We looked at each other and both burst into laughter. This was a total surprise! Only six months had passed since submitting our application and we had not even started saving money yet. Now, with the visa granted, we were obliged to arrive in Australia within the year, otherwise the visa would be void. This was an exceptional outcome, and we decided then and there to go with the flow, embrace the opportunity and make the most it.

Yet another adventure began as we sold most of our belongings in Switzerland and got ready to establish ourselves in Australia. There was much to organise. Bank accounts and insurance had to be sorted, our paperwork needed to be minimised and delegated to someone in our absence. We had to prepare a final tax report, give notice to the landlord and resign from our jobs. Then came the final goodbye party and we were off to a new life!

∿∿

Several months later, we arrived in Australia as skilled migrants, and with our backpacks and a tent, took up temporary residence in a campground in Perth. As we got to know people in the caravan park, they expressed surprise that we had immigrated with so little luggage and only a small camping shelter. Everyone was supportive. We had help finding the right car, were given advice on how to set up bank accounts and car insurance without a permanent address and received many tips on how to ease our transition into this country.

Nevertheless, I was in shock after our arrival and felt like we had made a big mistake. During the preparations I had focused on our visa applications and forgotten to prepare myself emotionally for the change ahead. Sven was my rock at that time. Free of the paperwork, he had instead mentally visualised our new chapter and once we arrived, he slowly and steadily kept soldiering on.

Fulfilling Sven's long-standing dream, we purchased a second-hand Landcruiser Troop Carrier and started kitting it out. In Switzerland we had decided to transport a few treasured items by ship: our two high-end mountain bikes, our dive equipment, extra clothing, and personal memorabilia. Along with the camping gear, everything had to fit inside our 4WD and be easily accessible. Back in Switzerland, Sven had spent hours drawing and planning the interior of this vehicle, trying to optimise the space. In Australia, a few months later, we were soon regulars at the local hardware store, acquiring the building materials Sven needed to construct the interior of our soon-to-be mobile home.

When our shipment arrived in Perth, we picked everything up at the commercial port. Unloading our gear in the campground, we ended up with a massive pile of boxes that stood higher than our miniature tent. We were amused, looking at our treasured belongings, everything we had carefully selected to accompany us in this new chapter, all piled up in a one large heap. Fortunately, the weather was favourable. Sven completed the finishing touches on the shelving and started loading the car with care and precision. Everything fitted perfectly. We found a second-hand rooftop tent in great condition and mounted it to the truck. Within three weeks of our arrival we were ready to head off.

Slowly we travelled north, enjoying our freedom and the amazing landscapes. And the locals welcomed us wherever we went. After travelling cross-country for 6,000 kilometres, we arrived in Cairns and decided to look for work. After an informal interview I landed my first job in Cape Tribulation, Far North Queensland, as a horse-riding tour guide. Though it was as far removed from Switzerland as one could be, we quickly adapted to life in this small settlement of fewer than one hundred residents. We were living in the tropics and bordering not just one, but two, World Heritage listed areas: the Great Barrier Reef and the Daintree Rainforest.

I loved my job on horseback and was stoked to be doing something wildly different from the administration positions I had held in Switzerland. This was new and out of my comfort zone, just as I had visualised. As a child I was wild about horses and from age eleven, would spend countless hours at stables, sweeping them out, grooming the animals and, of course, riding ponies and horses as much as I could. In this new job, I was fulfilling a childhood dream. After a few days of networking in the tiny community, Sven gained employment at the local resort in the maintenance department. We moved into staff accommodation and were proud to be earning our first Australian dollars. This felt like a massive achievement and we enjoyed our new lifestyle and the slow pace of this remote settlement, nestled at the foot of Mount Sorrow and bordering a multitude of tropical beaches.

After a few weeks, an opening arose for a dive instructor on the resort's day trip vessel. Sven and I had completed our dive instructor training a few years prior and I was excited to be given the chance to gain experience. The crew worked harmoniously as a team, and I was taught all there was to know about boat handling. I loved being out on the ocean all day and working physically. On my days off I went horse riding for leisure. Feeling energised with this life balance, I was excited about our future in this country.

Several months later, my mother and her second husband came for a visit and Sven and I quit our jobs to explore Australia's east coast with them. The four of us travelled in two 4WD vehicles and slowly made our way south, searching for new adventures and exciting landscapes.

In Brisbane, after travelling together for five weeks, we said our goodbyes. Several days later, a heartbreaking call came from Richard, a friend we had met in Perth. Richard and his wife, Sarah, had been travelling around Australia with their two little girls. They had just purchased a property in northern New South Wales, having decided to put down roots for a while. We had been planning to head towards their place and reconnect with them when I answered Richard's call.

'Regina, I am sorry to tell you this way, but Sarah died in an ultralight plane crash yesterday afternoon. It was a freak accident.' The silence was deafening, and I took a moment to absorb the gravity of his message.

'Oh my god.' I was in shock and lost for words. 'Richard, I don't know what to say… I am so terribly sorry to hear this. Listen, we can leave today and stay with you and the girls and help with anything that is needed. Provided you would like that.'

'Yes, please, come. I don't fully believe it myself yet. It's so terrible.'

We left immediately and spent the next six weeks with Richard and his adorable daughters, Emma and Lisa. I quickly slipped into the role of the carer and came to love these precious and innocent little beings. We spent a lot of time with Richard's neighbours who also became close friends.

After several weeks, Emma and Lisa repeatedly kept looking at me and asking, 'Regina, can you become our new mum?'

The comment tore at my heart and I knew the time had come for us to move on. As much as I loved and cared for the girls, I could not take on the role of their mother and the longer we stayed, the harder the separation would become. Coincidentally we were living close to Byron Bay, the yogic navel of Australia, and I had been contemplating doing yoga teacher training. Browsing the internet later that day, I stumbled upon an advertisement for a nine-month, full-time teacher training course. It was comprehensive and of a high standard and, to top it off, classes were to commence the following week.

The next day Sven and I drove to Byron Bay. We entered the yoga school just as they were starting the opening event for the upcoming training. Prior to her speech, I briefly hijacked the school's owner and explained my last-minute desire to join the training. She asked me about my yoga experience and, satisfied, agreed for me to join the course the following week, to allow us time to relocate.

Immediately, Sven and I found ourselves immersed in an alternative and wholesome lifestyle, with people engaged in a wide variety of holistic practices. Sven quickly found a job as an electrician in a nearby town, though despite having more than ten years of domestic and commercial experience in his trade in Switzerland, he was required to attend the local TAFE college, complete selected subjects, and pass an exam to gain a local licence. For the time being he was given a trainee wage, and as I was not earning any money either, we were surviving on a meagre income.

Reflections

The nine months of my yoga teacher training in Byron Bay were inspirational. I learned about yoga philosophy, the physical postures, anatomy and nutrition, and was challenged with self-inquiry. I felt I had been waiting for this opportunity to engage in self-reflection and gain a better understanding of my inner world, and immersed myself in the curriculum with great dedication.

Sven showed interest in the course as well. Despite the lack of funds, we were content. I felt excited about meditation and becoming more in tune with myself, and found joy in being silent and connecting with nature. We rode our mountain bikes in the hills and went for long beach walks. On weekends we went camping in our 4WD, and we tried surfing, but mostly got pummelled by the iridescent waves. It was a wholesome, peaceful and happy time.

At the end of the training my fellow trainees returned to their homes, scattered around Australia and the world. Sven and I were among the minority who remained in Byron Bay. Sven finished his required subjects at TAFE and was awarded full employment while I started my own yoga classes.

Around that time, our relationship experienced its first tremor. During a call, my mother mentioned that she had given our phone numbers to Barbara and Samantha, two young women from Switzerland, who were travelling in Australia. Sven did not know them well, but I had spent many years in my childhood exercising and looking after their ponies. We had lost touch in recent years, and I was looking forward to company from Switzerland, the opportunity to speak Swiss German and catch up on news from home.

Barbara and Samantha appeared on our doorstep, intending to stay for a day or two. However, we had a delightful time and they stayed with us for a week. They were our age, raised in the same village and we had much in common. They would explore the area during the day and in the evenings, we would share a meal, recount stories, and laugh often and from the heart.

I was sad to see them leave as I enjoyed their company and loved hearing their news from home. As we were lying in bed on the eve of their departure, Sven was unusually sombre.

'Sven, what is going on with you?'

Silence.

'Come on, Sven. Please, talk to me,' I gently probed. 'Tell me. Did you fall in love with one of the girls?' I asked and tried to read his face.

Much to my surprise, Sven's eyes started welling up with tears. After a while he quietly said, 'Yes, I think so. I feel strongly connected and drawn to Barbara. I cannot help it. I'm sorry.'

Taken aback by his admission, I took a moment to digest the information. I tuned in to my heart and in that instant, I knew what I needed to do. If this feeling were mutual, I would not stand in the way. I would release Sven from our relationship and wish them happiness. Barbara was a woman of integrity and beauty, inside and out. But first I had to find out whether the feelings were reciprocated.

'Okay. Does she know about it?' I felt surprisingly calm and centred.

'No. It's just in my head, nothing has happened.' His voice quivered and I could sense the emotional turmoil he was going through.

'Sven, it's okay. I am not angry with you and there is no reason yet for sadness. I understand that you have developed feelings for Barbara. I have already arranged to meet them for a yoga class tomorrow. My suggestion is to ask them to return one more time tomorrow night. I want you two to sit down. You need to communicate your feelings and find out how she feels. We need to know, one way or another. If the attraction and feelings are mutual, I would rather have this out in the open now, than have it drag on. I will support you however this unfolds.' I took a deep breath before I continued. 'So, if I ask them to come to our place for dinner tomorrow, will you be okay with that?'

Sven looked at me, his eyes soft with vulnerability and gratitude. 'Yes, I think that would be a good idea.'

The next day, sitting in a small cafe after our yoga session, I mentioned Sven's confession to Barbara. Genuinely shocked, she immediately insisted the feeling was not reciprocated, and said she wanted to speak with Sven to clarify the situation.

The sisters agreed to return for a final and, as it turned out, somewhat subdued dinner at our place. Sven and Barbara were able to talk in private. They agreed they shared a unique connection and wished to maintain a friendship for that reason. I could see that they both were relieved and at peace at the end of the evening. I felt reassured and was pleased with the outcome and openly supported Sven to continue to cultivate a meaningful friendship with this exceptional woman.

Over the next two years, however, when Sven heard from or made contact with Barbara, his infatuation resurfaced. While I fully supported their friendship, Sven's prolonged obsession with her was beginning to tire me. I felt he was comfortable in our relationship but was not sure what would happen if Barbara ever became available. I did not feel very desired. We also started to disagree on where we should live. After two years of permanent residency we had obtained our Australian citizenship and were free to leave and re-enter the country as we pleased.

Sven wanted to return to Switzerland, at least temporarily, as he felt homesick. For my part, I was heavily opposed to returning home. At the time I felt a strong resistance to my roots and anything Swiss in general. This was largely due to my frayed relationship with my parents. We had hardly any contact, sometimes months would pass without a call, and we had been unable to reach a point of peace in our connection. Staying apart seemed easier. My choices, subconsciously influenced by this dissonance, were likely the reason why I ended up living on the opposite side of the globe.

Eventually, Sven and I agreed to return temporarily. A little over two years since we had left, we arrived in our hometown. Sven slotted back into his old job as an electrician, whereas I struggled to find even temporary employment, and only scored an occasional yoga class here and there. I was fortunate, though, to spend time with my grandfather, as it transpired that these would be the last months of his life.

Around Christmas time, approximately six months since our return, I felt saturated by all things Swiss and desperately yearned to move back to the Southern Hemisphere. I explained to Sven that in the New Year I intended to move to New Zealand and invited him to join me. He considered this carefully and eventually decided to come too. Shortly after the New Year we set off.

Upon arriving in New Zealand, we had to set ourselves up from scratch again. We bought a van and explored the country while Sven applied for work. Within a few months he gained employment in Palmerston North, in the wind turbine industry, and adored his job. I found casual work in a Toyota warehouse and in disability care. Winter came and in my free time, during those cold, wet months, I sat for many hours in the hot spa of the local public pool, reading any exciting and adventurous sailing book that I could get my hands on.

Several times over the past two years, Sven and I had casually discussed the possibility of ending our relationship. We were exceptional friends but lacked passion and vision for our life together, and did not have any specific goals for our future. Neither of us were passionate about having children, or getting married. Our relationship was based on our great connection and friendship. Our talks were amicable but somewhat odd, as we openly discussed a possible separation, contemplating the best solution for each of us. These conversations were always trusting and non-threatening, and sometimes we would laugh about it.

Overall, we never felt that we had enough reason to break up. Yes, there were aspects of our relationship that were not as good as they had once been, but mostly we felt that we shared a wonderful friendship and were a great team. Sven was my closest and dearest friend. We had experienced a tremendous amount together and I trusted him completely. But I could not shake off the unsettling question in the back of my mind, persistently asking, 'Is this it?'

After nine months and not fully satisfied with our situation in New Zealand, we decided to move back to Australia, and fortunately Sven could transfer within his company. Again, we packed up our belongings, sold what was of no use, and boarded a plane bound for Adelaide. We found a rental home in Carrickalinga, a tiny, quaint holiday village on the coast, an hour south of Adelaide. The move took our thoughts off the relationship issues for a while, but once we settled into our everyday routine, the niggling disquiet about our future returned.

One day, after mutual consideration, we agreed that we needed time apart, allowing us each to contemplate our expectations and wishes for the future. As Sven was firmly entrenched in his job and I had already been conjuring up a sailing adventure, we agreed that I would crew on a yacht and fulfil my dream as part of our trial separation.

Shortly before I flew out on my planned voyage we were walking along the local beach when a conversation came up. 'Sven, what are your thoughts relating to affairs or flings for both of us during my time away?' I asked.

Sven looked startled but thoughtfully considered my question. 'Well, how about we don't go looking for it, but if it happens, it's okay?' he calmly replied, raising an eyebrow.

'Okay.' I nodded. 'That sounds fair. And if all goes well and we choose to be together when I return from this trip, we will get married, all right?'

Sven looked at me and chuckled. 'Sure, why not,' he said, and contentedly we continued our walk along the seashore.

6

SWEPT AWAY

After my upsetting call to Sven, I slipped Henry's computer on the navigation table and quietly grabbed my daypack. Not wanting to answer any probing questions, I quietly snuck off the yacht and decided to visit a local beach to lift my spirits.

The coastline of Antigua was diverse and often breathtaking. Pristine, powdery white beaches contrasted with clear turquoise water. Tucked away coves surrounded by rugged cliffs beckoned me to take a private skinny dip. I could not wait to go for a swim. By contrast, the water in Falmouth Harbour was cloudy and a muddy, green-brown colour. I had asked Henry about the suspect water quality a few days earlier and he wearily shrugged his shoulders, lamenting that this was most likely due to yachts 'dumping their shit' into the bay. According to his accounts, the bay was crystal clear during the hurricane season. This was a sobering fact, especially since I had considered sailing to be an environmentally friendly sport.

I packed my day bag and set off for English Harbour. The heat was rising from the bitumen and after a few minutes I was dreaming about a cold drink. I crossed the path in front of a handful of ladies on their way to church, decked out in their best Sunday attire and seemingly unfazed by the heat. Animatedly discussing a recipe, their heads were bobbing, each adorned with an extravagant and elaborate hat. Ambling along I occasionally heard a fraction of a song carried by the breeze or caught a waft of delicious home cooking.

Arriving at Nelsons Dockyard, I appreciated the shade of the market's entrance and lingered, browsing through its many stalls. The traditional souvenirs and T-shirts were neatly displayed, and I was repeatedly coaxed to 'Come and have a look.' Quickly tiring of the shopkeepers' insistence, I continued my walk, going down a narrow alley. Passing a well-maintained stone building, I entered an open cobblestoned area with pretty little flower gardens and frangipani trees covered in blossoms. Several historical buildings clustered around the square and were surrounded by a man-made wharf, which was part of the ancient English naval base. Along the curved stone dock, beautiful yachts were lined up neatly, one after the other. There were a few modern vessels, but classic wooden yachts were predominant. Their varnish glowed proudly in the sun and the pattern of the water's surface reflected on their spotless hulls.

I strolled past the row of boats, appreciating their different builds, shapes, ages and looks. Feeling thirsty after the prolonged exposure to the sun, I entered a quirky little bar tucked away from the main buildings. Inside, it was dark and rustic, the walls decorated with boat memorabilia and the remaining space was filled with scribbled notes and simple drawings of yachts, palm trees and oceans. Sipping my Coke, I read some of the messages. They included commentaries about yachts that had passed through, crews expressing joy about a successful passage, mentions of love and loss – a story behind each mark. My excitement rose; soon I would be part of a similar adventure.

After finishing my drink, I walked past the timeless and graceful yachts once more and observed the professional crews on board. They looked smart and sophisticated in their uniforms. I smiled at them and wondered what life would be like, working on board such a yacht.

I followed the boats around the harbour and soon located the dreadlocked guy who ran a small boat shuttle service across to Galleon Beach. He promptly ferried me across the bay and dropped me off just outside the resort. Spreading out my towel in the semi-shade under a palm tree, I was looking forward to a relaxing afternoon. As I leaned back, resting on my elbows, I appreciated the breathtaking view in front of me. A pristine beach extended into the distance with a gentle curve and the transparent, aquamarine water was softly lapping onto the fine sand. White yachts quietly bobbed to the swell, and rugged, rocky outcrops framed the background. It was a serene, picturesque haven, a sailor's sanctuary from the open ocean beyond the bay's mouth. Here, my world was safe and calm.

Grabbing my book, I began to read, but struggled to focus. My thoughts persistently returned to the party that night at Shirley Heights, and my mind started to dream up exciting scenarios. I repeatedly had to suppress my fantasies and force my attention back to my novel. Eventually I decided to cool off in the ocean and immersed myself in the near transparent water. Floating weightlessly on the surface, I relaxed. Drifting along, I looked up at the azure sky, contrasted by a few puffy white clouds passing through my field of vision.

Later that afternoon on my way back to the boat, feeling calm and content after my day out, a taxi pulled up beside me. The driver wound his window down and, curious, I looked at him.

'Gal, you shouldn't be walking on your own. Where are you going?' The driver had a serious and concerned air about him.

'I'm on my way to Falmouth Marina. People have cautioned me before about venturing out alone, but I prefer to walk. I don't need a taxi today, thank you,' I answered politely, assuming he was looking for business.

'No, gal. I am not offering you my service. I already have customers in the back. Come on, hop in. I am giving you a lift.' He gave me one of those trademark Caribbean smiles and with his head indicated that I should get into the passenger seat.

Not feeling I had anything else to counter, I accepted the generous offer and got in the car.

'Thank you. That's very kind of you.'

'No problem.'

Without any fuss he pulled back onto the road and, as promised, dropped me outside the marina turn off. Yet again, I felt that I was experiencing a different side of Antigua. My positive, friendly and helpful encounters seemed in stark contrast to the negative perspectives that others had tried to prime me for. Well, I chuckled to myself, if my reality was like this, I would happily choose mine over everyone else's.

Back on the boat I had a quick rinse off. The compact cubicle housed a shower, a tiny sink and the hand-pumped toilet. I hung up my clothes to keep them dry and cleaned off the salt and dust as best as I could. Henry and Maude were ready to go when I came out. I quickly put on cargo pants and my favourite V-neck top, so I could shake it off without the restraints of a dress.

I bounced well ahead of Henry and Maude on the goat trail, bursting with anticipation and impatiently waiting for the old couple to keep up with me. We were welcomed by the fresh and lively sound of the steel band, and I was amazed at the synchronicity among the players. It was incomprehensible to me, how each band member pounded their pans with intense focus, yet still managed to occasionally look up, laugh and bop along as they played. But Jay was not there!

Disappointed, I turned back to the steel band and let my body gently move to the engaging rhythms. Soon, I was dancing boldly in a small gathering of tourists. The cobblestoned square was filling with holiday makers and a few locals and the energy was picking up.

I was dancing with my eyes closed, occasionally sipping my drink. Suddenly someone brushed up behind me and a deep voice whispered into my ear.

'Regina, you came back again!'

Hearing the warm voice with the charming Antiguan accent, I stopped dancing.

'Hello, Jay! It's great to see you!' I said, feeling my world was suddenly much brighter.

'You want to dance with me?' he asked.

Those dark brown eyes locked into mine and I went weak at the knees. No wonder I could not get him out of my head. I took a breath and nodded. We began to dance and, more familiar with each other's moves now, continued where we had left off last week.

The dancing became more sensual and intimate. Jay's muscular body pressed against mine from behind. Our movements fell into unison as we were swaying, stomping and seductively rotating our hips. Occasionally I turned to face him, his eyes were on mine, and I felt everything else disappear. At times, the intensity caused me to step away and briefly dance alone to gather my breath and senses. My feelings were supremely delicious and thrilling, but a little scary.

I had never felt this way before.

'Do you want to come for a walk?' Jay's lips brushed against my ear, and a tingling sensation resonated through my body.

Walk? What exactly did he want? No. I could not go. But how would it feel to kiss his luscious lips?

'No… NO. I can't go. I'm sorry, I prefer to stay here,' I said and stepped away from him.

What was wrong with me? I had a loving partner at home. I went to the bar and bought us both a drink. We sat on the curved rocks, by the cliff's edge.

'So, all I know about you is your name, Jay. Can you tell me something about yourself?' I probed.

'All right. I live in All Saints. I work delivering fruit and vegetables in a van. I have my own little house because I don't like paying rent and I come to Shirley Heights every Sunday to dance.'

'That sounds nice. Do you enjoy your job?'

'Yes, my boss man is okay, and I like the driver. We are a good team.' Jay smiled at me.

Understanding his strong local accent was challenging, so I tried to partially lip read to help me absorb the information. But watching those lips was proving distracting and my mind began to create a life of its own.

'Jay, how old are you?' I nervously asked. His age was hard to gauge. He had a fresh-looking face but some visible lines. He was both joyfully young and mature.

'I am twenty-eight,' he said, beaming.

I was taken aback by his reply, as I thought he was probably my age, not six years my junior. My ego soared, smugly relishing the fact that I had attracted a beautiful young man. Then the voice of reason thundered in, reprimanding me. Pushing all thoughts aside I searched for more answers.

'So, Jay. Tell me, do you come here to pick up tourist girls for fun?' I eyed him suspiciously.

'No. Me, I am not like that. You see that guy over there? That's exactly what he does. I come here because I like to dance and, one day, I would like to find someone special. Someone like you, maybe.'

His deep brown eyes radiated softness and sincerity. I swallowed and nodded. Fair enough, I thought, not everyone fits the stereotype. I remembered the promise I'd made to myself a few days ago that I would ignore generalisations and would treat every person as an individual.

I smiled at Jay and took the last sip of my drink. Then, as I was taking in the joyful scene on the dance floor, I saw Henry and Maude waving from the back, indicating they wanted to leave. I looked at Jay and pointed at my skipper and his wife and explained that I needed to go.

'Will you be here next Sunday?' He looked at me hopefully.

'Yes, I will. See you next week, Jay.'

We stood up and for a moment we lingered awkwardly. Our eyes connected, the atmosphere sizzled, and I yearned to be kissed, at the same time not wanting this next step to happen. Instead, I gave Jay a quick hug, blushed self-consciously and escaped towards Henry and Maude. I ignored their disapproving looks and headed for the exit, my body and emotions united in turmoil.

I knew I was falling in love. And there was no doubt I was sexually attracted to Jay and preparing myself emotionally to have an affair. But I was also afraid of the judgment from people around me and was in conflict with myself about my developing feelings. A quick fling, maybe. Yet deep down I knew I was not the kind of woman that could enjoy an affair. For me, sex had always resulted in emotional attachment. In truth, the concept of an emotionally detached affair had never been more than an enticing illusion. My feelings were already entwined with Jay. This had not been part of my plan and I was struggling to face the reality: I loved one man and was in love with another. I felt torn and insecure and was judging myself for my straying attraction and feelings, for being dishonest and disloyal to Sven.

Monday started with the usual routine of breakfast followed by the 9am broadcast on the cackling VHF radio. All was well in the bay, winds a gentle 10–15 knots, and the sun was out. A good day to do more sailing practice, Henry announced.

Andy and Clare arrived looking refreshed and relaxed. They were sharing a house with an English couple who had been living and working on the island for several years. The accommodation was simple, functional and reasonably priced. Most importantly, they had their own four walls until we departed on our sailing trip.

Henry started calling orders to get the boat ready to sail. Below in the cabin, everything had to be stowed. On deck the jib needed to be hooked onto the forestay, sheets tied onto the sail and fed back correctly into the cockpit. Henry wanted to do spinnaker practice today, so Andy and I got busy setting the ropes up on the foredeck.

We released the bow lines leading to the dock and lifted the stern anchor. Slowly motoring out of the bay, Henry briefed us on our positions. I was stationed on the foredeck. Andy was posted on the mast and Clare would handle the lines in the cockpit. Henry, as usual, was at the helm.

The skipper talked us through his preferred series of steps for a correct hoisting and dropping of the spinnaker, and we listened with full focus. I had never sailed on a boat with this massive lightweight sail, so I was both excited and daunted by the manoeuvre. I hoped I would not make a mistake and expose myself to the wrath of our temperamental captain.

As we entered the open ocean, the swell started to increase. We hoisted the main sail, then the jib, and settled into a comfortable groove. Occasionally a wave would crash against the bow. The disturbed water was violently sent on a trajectory towards the cockpit. Landing on our faces and bodies with an unexpected splash, we were simultaneously laughing and spluttering. Although soaked, I was feeling energetic and alive.

As we gained distance from the rocky island, Henry asked us to take our positions and to prepare for the spinnaker trial. I was standing at the front of *Zephyr*, leaning against the guard rail to keep my balance. Suddenly a large wave lifted the bow far out of the water, as if the yacht was reaching for the sky. After a moment of suspension mid-air, the boat tilted forward, smashing its bow deep into an oncoming wave. A surge of water rushed across the foredeck, submerging me waist-high in the frothing ocean, and I gripped the rail. After a moment *Zephyr* lifted itself back up, the water gushing off the deck as the boat climbed up another wave.

Being exposed to the elements was thrilling and I didn't mind getting wet. The day was hot and the water provided a welcome relief. But I had not anticipated getting drenched and desperately needed to change my gear.

'Okay, ready to hoist?' Henry called out from the back.

'Stop!' I yelled back at the top of my lungs.

'What the heck is the problem now?' he growled.

I strode back to the cockpit, stopped in front of Henry and looked him square in the eyes.

'Look, Henry, I wasn't aware that I was going swimming up there. So, let's say I was a little unprepared. If you must know, my pad is soaked and about to fall out. So, I reckon before that happens, I ought to do something about it.'

'Oh…Okay. I guess you better take care of that,' he mumbled and looked away.

Despite the embarrassment of having my personal predicament publicly exposed, for a moment I relished humbling this self-assured man. Inwardly chuckling, I went to take care of my business.

The remainder of the day was thrilling, educational and physically challenging. We proceeded to hoist and drop the spinnaker several times, until we worked like a well-oiled machine. I became semi-submerged in water several more times during the sail changes, feeling the waves pull at my clothes and limbs. I loved the taste of salt on my lips and my mind and body were fully absorbed in the tasks at hand.

When the colourful spinnaker was flying proudly, we each had the opportunity to steer the boat. The motion was unusual and unsteady as *Zephyr* was rolling from side-to-side while the swell passed underneath her hull. A strange quiet came over the yacht, and the wind seemed to have died down. No, not the case, Henry informed me. It seemed that way because we were now travelling with the wind and the boat speed was negating the wind force. Henry explained the apparent and true wind calculations and taught us how to helm the boat with the spinnaker as well as steering to a compass course. When my turn came, the boat started swaying from one side to the other like a slow pendulum, until it felt unstable and completely off course. Henry displayed surprising patience and assisted until I got the hang of it. Once I perfected my skills, the task seemed easy and natural. I was tuning in to the boat, looking up at the sails, feeling the breeze brush the back of my head while *Zephyr* was dancing along with the swell. I loved the interaction of boat, wind and ocean, and felt in my element.

Henry, wanting us to practise one last time, ordered us back to our positions. My muscles were tired and weary, but my mind was ready and willing for one more go. The spinnaker went up and one cotton string after the other started popping. The enormous sail was bulging with air when I heard a loud bang. Looking up, I saw the spinnaker pole directly above come crashing down towards me. Instinctively I lifted my arms and as the metal pole rushed towards my head, with all my might I used its momentum to push it away from myself and as far overboard as I could. The spinnaker pole slammed into the guardrail with a grinding sound and the tip of the pole reached into the ocean. With the worst averted, we quickly assessed the situation. The spinnaker was violently slapping around and the sail looked ready to wrap itself around the forestay.

Henry's voice rose to a new level as he yelled, 'Drop the spinnaker. *Now!*'

Rushing into our positions, Andy and I reached for the gigantic sail as it was plunging onto the deck and threatening to go overboard. Once we had all the fabric gathered and under control, we lifted the spinnaker pole back on board. On inspection we noticed that the pin of a shackle had been sheared off, rendering it useless. A simple case of wear and tear had caused the havoc. Adrenaline pulsed through my body and I felt lucky that none of us was harmed. Grateful for a valuable lesson, we returned to the marina.

We got back late in the afternoon with sun-kissed cheeks and salt-crusted bodies. My muscles were limp from the exertion, but I felt elated and empowered. This had been the best day of sailing for me so far. I loved my position on the foredeck and enjoyed the exposure and occasional immersion in the sea. After docking *Zephyr,* we struggled to muster the energy to do the meticulous clean-up demanded by our skipper.

This involved hosing, scrubbing, drying, folding, coiling, and stowing away. Half-heartedly we ticked off Henry's list and perked up only when we were at the bar clutching a refreshing beer. What a day. I savoured that first sip of the crisp, cold liquid and scrutinised the mixed bunch around my table. How interesting to be thrown into this random adventure with these strangers, fused only by our shared vision and dream. Within three weeks we had become close, created memories together, navigated our differences and overall, had become an integral part of each other's lives.

Henry showcased his signature grumpy attitude as he kept muttering about the maintenance that needed to be completed and how expensive each day of sailing was for him. Clare was sitting pensively, staring into her drink. Throughout the day Henry had again treated her in a condescending and harsh manner. On the way to the bar, she had quietly mentioned to me that she had been feeling increasingly insecure. I understood her doubts and urged her to stand up to Henry. Andy had ever so slightly cooled towards me since Henry had promoted me to be bowman. I could relate to his disappointment but, happy and hungry to absorb as much as I could, I ignored these underlying dissonances in the tribe.

Lying in my narrow bunk that night, my thoughts wandered back to Jay. I could not get him out of my mind. I replayed the softness of his skin, his strong and beautifully toned arms, and the feeling of our bodies brushing against each other. A flutter of energy rushed through my being. Reliving the warm timbre of his voice and his lips skimming my ear, I drifted off into a restless sleep packed with lucid dreams.

'Dammit! Fucking hell!'

The expletives continued and I looked up to see what the commotion was about.

Henry was on the dock behaving like an enraged goblin. He was stomping up and down furiously, with fists clenched, punching the air. His face was scrunched up and flushed scarlet. I had no idea what had upset him and gingerly walked up to the bow.

'Henry, what happened?'

'Ah, fuck! Someone didn't tie off one of the sheets properly and when I climbed onto the dock it dropped into the bloody water!' he roared. 'Now I've got to buy another bloody rope and spend more fucking money at the chandlery.'

'Okay. Well, how about I retrieve it for you?'

Looking down at the murky and soiled water, I was certain that I could drop in, dive to the bottom and recover the cursed item in a matter of seconds. I could rinse off in the shower immediately after. No big deal, I thought.

'No. You won't find it. Look at the bloody muck. You can't see past your eyeballs in that shit,' he growled.

'All right, Henry. What if I bet you a beer that I will find it?' I grinned with confidence and looked at him inquisitively. For a moment Henry seemed stunned, almost forgetting his anger.

'All right. Up to you,' he grumbled, somewhat calmer.

I took off my clothes on the dock, already wearing my bikini underneath. Inhaling deeply a few times, I narrowed down the spot and confidently plunged into the water. I briefly opened my eyes, to find myself surrounded by a muddy cloud. Unable to see, I closed my eyes and swam to the bottom. With my hands I started patting the silty ocean floor around me. *There*! One hand came up against a solid structure and upon moving closer I could easily distinguish the shape of the coiled-up rope. Quickly I grabbed it and pushed myself towards the surface. I broke the water with a splash and inhaled deeply. Henry was peering over the side of the dock. I couldn't wipe the grin off my face as I held up the rope.

'You owe me a beer, Henry,' I called teasingly, enjoying my moment of triumph.

Henry grumbled and even muttered a 'thank you' for my efforts, and I could not stop chuckling as I disappeared into the shower.

The whole day I revelled in my victory and kept teasing Henry whenever I could. He was a sorry loser, which made my achievement even more satisfactory. By the end of the day the whole bar knew that Henry had lost a bet and had to buy me a drink. Discreetly a few of the other yachties gave me a thumbs up or congratulated me on my cheeky attitude toward the old salt.

As time passed, we learned that Henry had gained a reputation on the dock. He and Maude would often complain about one thing or another, and were not considerate when it came to helping out or cooperating with neighbouring yachts. Over time they had managed to alienate most people with their unforgiving attitude and opinionated statements, and ended up with many acquaintances but few friends.

Many of the yachties, professional crew and leisure sailors alike, had treated the *Zephyr* team hesitantly at first, but as time went on, they were warming to our company and started to include us more in their circle. By now we had been in Antigua for nearly four weeks and I had settled in and was feeling comfortable and at home.

Over our beers, Henry finally shed some light on our missing fifth crew member. He had enlisted the mother of the young professional skipper in our marina and confirmed that she had booked a flight and would arrive the following week. Suddenly the trip was looking more promising and I was working with renewed vigour. We still had some sewing to finish, the black water tank needed to be flushed and cleaned, the food stores sorted, and navigation charts needed to be purchased.

Later that day, Andy and Clare approached me in private and mentioned that they'd made enquiries at the local crewing agency. With many professional boats around, there was plenty of short-term work available. Since Andy held the required certificates to skipper a yacht, they were considering other options should our trip fall through altogether, or if Henry's attitude deteriorated further. This information shook me to the core. Just as I had started to regain trust in our sailing project, suddenly everything seemed in jeopardy again. However, the thought of grabbing an opportunity to work on a professional vessel in this gorgeous environment did sound attractive. Antigua was a major hub for superyachts, both sail and motor.

With the weekend approaching, I thought more and more of Jay. We hadn't had a chance to spend much time together and part of me was yearning to get to know him better. I realised that my feelings were already deeply entangled with this man.

My emotions were in conflict with the ethical values I upheld for myself, and I kept pushing Sven and the unyielding guilt about my lack of loyalty to him from my mind. For the first time in our relationship, I could not, or rather had chosen not to, share everything with him and felt reluctant even to contact him. My irrational reasoning was, if I did not talk to Sven, I did not have to hide anything from him. Suddenly, I recalled our beach walk prior to my departure. Strolling barefoot along the waterline, we had discussed the possibility of one of us having an affair during our separation. We had agreed it was acceptable if we did not chase it. At the time I had not expected to meet anyone but now, replaying this conversation in my mind, it provided some peace. I could not deny my feelings for Jay and resolved to let the circumstances evolve naturally, without resisting or attempting to influence the outcome.

7
THE CHIPS ARE DOWN

On Saturday I went to Pigeon Beach and later took a stroll around English Harbour. Following my crew mates' lead, I ventured into one of the crewing agencies and had a tentative chat with the manager. She confirmed that plenty of work was available, both day jobs and charter contracts. All I would need to get started was a current CV and she would then try to find suitable employment for me. This sounded temptingly easy, I thought, as I meandered down the street, crossing paths with a shaggy looking Rastafarian man riding on a tired looking donkey. The Rastafarian's dreadlocks, of varying lengths and thicknesses, protruded from his head like octopus tentacles. A thick hemp rope was tied around the donkey's neck but instead of serving as a lead, it lazily trailed along the bitumen. To my amusement, both man and donkey seemed to know where they were going.

After two days of relaxing at the beach, observing local people and tourists frolicking in the ocean, I was ready for the much-anticipated weekly catch up with Jay. I was waiting for

Henry and Maude to call the taxi, but to my surprise the couple were not dressed to go out. When I asked if they were coming, Henry gruffly said that they were not planning to attend the party that night. I was baffled, as this was their established Sunday night custom. I briefly considered my options and decided to walk up the mountain to save the taxi fare.

When I arrived, Jay was already dancing in the square. My heart jumped and I headed to him. I had not eaten dinner yet, so I offered to buy some juicy barbecue chicken and salad. We found a quiet spot and sat down with the food and two rum punches. Sharing stories about our week, we savoured the food and most of all, each other's company. The atmosphere between us was charged and eye contact alone, or an innocent brushing of our hands, set my body aflutter.

I told Jay about my exciting sailing practice and how much I loved being on the water. I mentioned the tension on board and how I hoped that the trip would not fall apart. Jay talked about being busy at work and doing substantial overtime, with the Antigua Classic Yacht Regatta coming up. I had heard about this prestigious racing event of vintage yachts and I'd already noticed gorgeous old-timers sailing into the marinas. Jay went on to speak about the Antigua Carnival, which was separate from the regatta events, and I could tell he was excited. In the middle of hurricane season in July, with tourism at its lowest, Antigua's population stopped for over a week to participate in the carnival celebrations, including dance and music competitions. Seeing Jay's joy made me keen to stay and experience it too. Our light-hearted conversation was helping me to feel more comfortable.

I drew a deep breath, needing to be honest with this man.

'Jay, you need to know something. I have a boyfriend at home, but I am not sure if our relationship will continue. That's part of the reason why I came on this holiday.'

'Okay,' he replied, waiting for me to continue.

'I really like you. But I struggle with my feelings for you. I am afraid.' Words tumbled out, and I looked pleadingly at him, hoping he would understand my predicament. He gently held my hand in his.

'No problem, Regina. I understand. Take your time. I like you a lot. You are beautiful outside and in here.' He tapped his chest with his fist, his gaze focused on me.

Later, when we were dancing, we were closer than ever. The dance floor was crowded but I felt cocooned in our little world. Jay's hands gently explored my body as we moved to the music. Every now and then he gently pushed aside a strand of my hair, bending low to whisper in my ear. I felt close and connected and, tired of my emotional struggle, finally surrendered, unable to resist my feelings any longer. I was in love.

When the band finished playing, I was eager to find a taxi. Jay insisted that he could get me a lift and went to the lead singer of the band. The burly guy cordially agreed, and we wandered off to a quiet corner while the band packed up. I was sitting on a rock wall with Jay proudly standing in front of me. He was facing me, and I could feel the heat radiate off his body. We were talking quietly when he slowly bent forward and gently kissed my lips. I felt him exploring my mouth, time suspended, and I fell deeper into his spell.

The trip down the mountain in the band's vehicle was quick. Pressed against each other on the backseat, Jay and I exchanged glances and stolen kisses. As promised, the musician dropped me off right outside the marina entrance. Jay quickly gave me his phone number, asking to see me before next Sunday. After another passionate kiss, I said goodbye and dizzily sauntered back to the boat. Quietly I sneaked aboard the sleeping yacht.

The final crew member for our passage arrived in time to start the new week. Yana spoke with a strong eastern European accent. Aged in her early fifties, she was warm and friendly, and we hit it off from the start. She had little sailing experience but was a keen cook and eager to experience ocean travel and learn more about her son's way of life.

Throughout the week it became apparent that despite Yana's arrival, the situation on board was deteriorating daily. Henry continued to criticise Clare. She was in tears from the constant abuse, and Andy's aggravation mounted. Maude added to the tension with her persistent nagging, while I was preoccupied with my infatuation and lingering guilt.

In recent weeks, Patrick had become my commiserating buddy. I began the habit of dropping in occasionally to see him on his yacht. He was a jovial guy, seemed always happy with my company and I felt I could trust him. Over a decent bottle of red we would spend evenings talking about our days, the latest situation on *Zephyr* or resolving the issues of the world at large. Eventually I trusted him enough and confessed my growing feelings for Jay. To my surprise, rather than judge, he replied with compassion and understanding. I was deeply grateful for his acceptance in this otherwise unforgiving environment.

The Chips are Down

Despite the unease on *Zephyr* the week passed quickly and my focus was firmly set on the weekend ahead. Saturday morning, I took out my phone and nervously punched in Jay's number. Before we parted last Sunday, we had agreed to meet on Saturday afternoon and Jay had asked me to call to arrange a time and place to meet.

The phone rang and I anxiously gripped the mobile.

'Hello.' I was relieved to be greeted by his familiar voice.

'Hi, Jay. It's me.'

'Regina!' he called out happily, pronouncing my name with his unique Caribbean accent, making it sound like *Rah-gee-nah*. 'You want to come and visit me in All Saints today?'

'Sure, why not. What time suits you and how do I find you?'

He gave directions to his workplace, which I struggled to follow. However, I figured that if I'd managed to safely travel around the world, surely I could locate this place. A little before 4pm I caught one of the local minivans and asked the driver to pull up in All Saints. A modest community for local residents, it was also where several roads on the island intersected. When I alighted, a few people looked at me in surprise and one lady even asked if I knew where I was. I smiled, saying I was in the correct location and waved the bus off. Here I was, standing alone on the main intersection of All Saints. Not exactly a tourist destination; then again I was not here to sightsee.

I assessed the four directions of the road and decided to follow a smaller road leading down a hill. Suddenly a car stopped beside me. The driver, a vivacious and slightly eccentric yachtie I had met a few times in the bar, was shooting me a puzzled look.

'Girlie, what the heck are you doing walking around here?' he said, confusion written all over his face.

'Exploring. Going for a walk,' I lied, too self-conscious to admit my true cause. I did not know him well and was not ready to share my life with everyone on the dock.

'Chick, get in the car. You're going to either get mugged or raped. You shouldn't be wandering around here.'

'No, I am fine. Please, just let me do my thing,' I replied.

To my surprise, the guy shrugged his shoulders, called out a short, 'Best of luck to ya,' wound up the window and hurtled off.

I took the next turn to the right and proceeded along a small gravel path with overgrown weeds and shrubs on either side. A derelict house, a burnt-out car and some little wooden houses bordered the track. Uncertain which way to go next, I walked towards a group of teenagers. As I approached, they stopped talking, openly ogling me. Feeling a little uneasy I picked up speed and heard them call out as I passed.

'Oy, whitey! Want to come home with me?' This was followed by a wolf whistle.

Way out of my comfort zone, part of me was feeling threatened by the youths' presence, while another part was inwardly chuckling. Teenagers, I thought, are the same everywhere.

When I approached the next small intersection, I saw more colourful and modest houses along the roads to my left and ahead. On the track to my right, a bit further up, I spotted a truck parked in front of a building. That had to be the produce distribution business. Slowly approaching the premises, I recognised Jay standing in the courtyard and felt both nervous and relieved to see him. He was chatting to a man while several other guys were loading the truck. Suddenly I felt apprehensive and exposed, realising how removed I was from my known world. Luckily, I had no time to hesitate as a voice called out, 'Jay, your gal's here.'

The men turned and looked at me. Tentatively I smiled and waved at the man who was dominating my thoughts.

'Hi. I found it,' was about all I could say in front of this crowd.

'Regina! Welcome to All Saints!' Jay gaily called out, making me laugh.

He rushed to my side and introduced me to his colleagues. Sensing that I was shy, he bought two cold drinks and indicated for us to go on a walk.

As we strolled through his little village, he pointed out a few landmarks and houses of relatives and friends. Most of the buildings were simple and made with timber or bricks. Many dwellings were unpainted and looked like they were waiting to have another room or floor added to them. The yards were neat, adorned with fruit trees and occasional veggie gardens. A few of the houses emanated a decidedly poor air and looked ramshackle. Some had mismatched windows and doors, curtains made of torn and stained cloth billowing in the breeze, and rusty roofs reinforced with faded plastic tarps. These small shacks were built from recycled materials, haphazardly hammered together and barely provided basic shelter.

Eventually we stopped in front of a neat little house with greenish walls. Paint was flaking off in parts, barely disguising reclaimed wooden panels of wildly varying shapes and sizes. Old, reused windows were mounted into each sidewall. The frame of the hut and the corrugated roof, however, looked sturdy and solid. Curtains were fluttering through the windowpanes and banana plants and flowery shrubs framed the front of the building.

'This is my house,' Jay said proudly, looking at me expectantly.

'It looks lovely,' I replied, and meant it. The house was small but had the appearance of being loved and well looked after.

Jay invited me inside. Hesitantly I stepped onto the miniature verandah and across the threshold into a narrow room void of furniture. There were a few pictures on the wall, an old battery-operated radio on the floor and a pair of shoes by the door. A small and simple kitchen to the right was home to a rusty stove connected to a big gas cylinder. A rickety shelf held two pots, a few forks, a knife, two spoons, some natural bowls, and a cup. There was no sink or fridge. As far as I could tell the house had no electricity or running water. Jay ushered me to the other room on the left. It was almost entirely occupied by a double bed, covered with crumpled sheets. Next to the bed, heaped on the floor, was an enormous pile of clothes.

Seeing the pride in Jay's eyes, I was touched that he felt comfortable to share his home with me. I could not help but quietly compare it to what I had grown up with and been accustomed to throughout my life. This standard was far removed from my world, yet Jay was visibly happy and pleased with his accomplishment.

I smiled and looked at him. 'You have built a lovely home for yourself, Jay. You can be proud of yourself.'

'Thank you, Regina. I want to paint the outside next.' Thoughtfully he eyed me. 'What's your favourite colour?'

'Yellow. I love it because it is warm, bright and happy.'

'I will paint the house yellow for you,' he said and reached for my hand.

Made speechless by his touching promise, I placed my palm in his and he softly pulled me closer.

'Come here, babes,' he murmured, pressing his delicious lips on mine.

I leaned against his body, feeling his taut torso against my thumping chest. Slowly reclining on the bed, his touches and kisses gained more insistence. Suddenly panic rose in my throat.

'Jay, please stop. I can't do this. I am not ready.'

'Okay,' was his simple but not unkind response, and he moved a little away from me, giving me space.

'Jay, I am sorry. I do really like you. But this is all so new. I think I need to go home now,' I spluttered, standing abruptly.

Jay embraced me and placed a gentle kiss on my forehead.

'Don't worry, babes. It's no problem,' he whispered, and in that moment I loved him for his gentleness and understanding.

The following evening, I was not surprised when Henry and Maude chose not to go to Shirley Heights. They looked at me disapprovingly whenever I mentioned Jay's name. Clearly, they had meant that it was okay for me to dance, but not fall in love, with him. Not concerning myself with their thoughts, or judgments, I anticipated their absence and planned my trip up the mountain alone. This time, I would walk to English Harbour, take the little water taxi across to Galleon Beach and trek up the steep trail to the top. It would take ninety minutes, but I was up for a brisk hike before dancing.

The physical work on the boat and our training sails were having a noticeable effect on my body. I was leaner, my muscles had become defined and I felt fitter. I loved the changes in my physique and was grateful to feel strong and healthy. Having always been a tomboy, I had never put much thought into my looks or style. These days, however, I was feeling more feminine.

Something had awakened within me and I observed the changes with curiosity. I wondered whether this transition had occurred because of my attraction to Jay, or rather, the regular dancing that seemed to liberate me in a new way. Maybe, I mused, it was because of the many males within the yachting world. Hugely outnumbered, females tended to get more attention and appeared more valued in the boating circles. Perhaps, it was simply the right time for me to recognise, embody and appreciate my femininity. Whatever the reason, I felt splendid, energised, and embraced this transition.

On Sunday afternoon I put on my running shoes, my favourite black cargo pants and a sparkly figure-hugging top and took off for Nelsons Dockyard at a good pace. Although I had a fair hike ahead of me, I felt unstoppable. I loved feeling my body working and warming up with the exercise. The same Rastafarian ferried me across to the beautiful Galleon Beach. Shirley Heights towered far above the sandy shore where I was dropped off and I practically jogged uphill.

Out of breath and feeling the heat, I arrived at the familiar historical site. Not spotting Jay immediately, I went to grab myself the usual barbecue dinner and one of those sweet and tangy rum punches. Having spent every Sunday evening there for the past month, some local people were already beginning to recognise me. The lady at the bar with the gorgeous long braids waved and smiled, some of the steel band players nodded in my direction during their break, the man weaving his palm frond creations called out to me and quickly produced another rose. I was starting to feel at home.

I stood on the rocky outcrop enjoying the view, occasionally eavesdropping on a conversation. Tourists were happily snapping their holiday memories. Newlyweds were sneaking a kiss in front of the glorious view. Old sailors were comparing the quality of the rum punches. The light and joyful atmosphere meant everyone left their worries downhill.

I was dancing when Jay sauntered around the corner of the old stone building, heading towards the dance floor. When he saw me, his eyes lit up and he picked up pace.

'Regina!' he called out happily.

Lifting me up and twirling me around, he placed a firm kiss on my mouth. Laughter bubbled up in my throat as I noticed the surprised faces of the holiday makers around us. When my eyes fell upon the steel band players, I noticed a few of them had been watching us and were smiling. I laughed, embraced Jay and kissed him right back.

'Jay. Hi!' My eyes twinkled and I flirted seductively. 'Would you like to dance with me?'

'Yes, babes. Let's dance.' He held my face between his strong hands and kissed my lips once more before we started moving together.

We were dancing with new-found intimacy and connection. Slower, closer, more flirtatious. The lens of a film crew, here to capture footage for the Cricket World Cup, landed on us several times. I noticed but did not care, as I was filled with love and joy. I became aware that suddenly, my feelings had free reign, and acknowledged to myself that I was deeply in love with Jay. Surrendering completely, I enjoyed our closeness without restraint, allowing the electricity to flow freely between us.

Jay's perspiring body was pressed against mine for hours on end as we danced together. I loved his musky scent, the soft touch of his skin and was aroused by our sensual dance moves. He was irresistible and tonight I allowed myself to contemplate giving in to my attraction, not just emotionally but physically as well. At the end of the dance, as we were waiting for the musicians to pack up, Jay's eyes bored into mine and he murmured into my ear, 'Regina, would you like to stay at my place tonight?'

I was terrified and excited at the same time. Reason said no, but every fibre of my being resonated with a firm yes. I took a deep breath. 'Yes, Jay, I would like that,' I said, swallowing nervously. I locked eyes with him, my body tingling.

Surprised, I noticed that the clarity of this decision brought with it a sense of relief. Aware that my life was about to change course I took another deep breath. This was it. I was going home with Jay, and about to become more entangled with this man. I was going to have a love affair, while my partner in Australia remained oblivious. Another brief pang of guilt was swiftly wiped from my consciousness. Sven and I had made our agreement about potential flings, I quickly justified, although I never imagined that it would be me or that it would feel this intense. My life was about to get more complicated, and I accepted that there would be consequences to deal with. At some point in the future, but not right now.

I was buzzing with nervous energy all the way to All Saints. Busy with my sudden turmoil I did not engage in the light conversation and quietly sat next to Jay. He held my hand, gently stroking it with his thumb, noticing I had become withdrawn.

With a knowing smirk and a suggestive, 'Have a good night!' the lead singer of the band let us out, then drove off into the black night.

Jay gently held my hand and led me into his little home. As we entered, I left my conscience at the threshold. Jay embraced me with steadiness and strength until I was able to relax. He tenderly kissed my forehead, cupping my face with his strong hands, and I felt myself soften.

'Come, babes. Let's go to bed,' he whispered, offering me his hand.

I placed my palm in his. With a soft grip Jay gently guided me to the bedroom and I surrendered to his lead. The built-up current between us ignited with the first deepening kiss and our bodies connected with an unbridled hunger. My body responded with a need that surprised me and, unable to think or reason a moment longer, I let myself be swept up in our passion.

8

DECISION TIME

The morning after my big night out, I returned from All Saints on an early bus. Traipsing up the dock, trying to be inconspicuous, I nodded to the few yachties enjoying their early morning coffees on deck. Passing their boats, I felt their probing looks. There was, thankfully, no activity evident on *Zephyr,* as I urgently wanted to see Patrick first.

'Good morning, Patrick. Permission to step aboard?' I called out from the dock, happy to see and hear someone moving around on his boat. Patrick was already up. I was in luck.

He popped his head through the companionway and smiled. 'Sure. Hop on. Coffee?'

I sat at the table and sheepishly recounted my weekend shenanigans. Patrick patiently listened, his friendly and open face conveying a neutral expression. I took a deep breath, my mood noticeably turning a shade darker.

'Patrick, I need to tell you something.' He indicated for me to continue. 'Last night, you know…umm…Jay and I had intercourse and – I am really sorry to involve you in this – we had a condom accident.' My face flushed bright red and I felt jittery with nerves, ashamed of exposing my deeply personal situation and desperately hoping not to be judged. 'It broke.' Embarrassed by my confession, I looked down at the table.

'Oh dear, bella! You sure know how to get yourself into trouble!'

Despite my embarrassment I had to smile at Patrick's flamboyant charm and theatrical use of the Italian endearment. I had been right to confide in him.

'So, Reggie, what are you planning to do about it?' he quizzed.

'Patrick, I know I should get the morning-after pill, but part of me thinks that maybe this is it? Maybe I am supposed to do this? Maybe Jay and I could be together and raise our beautiful baby?'

For a moment I allowed myself to indulge this fantasy. I knew it was premature and unreasonable, but I was overcome with love and confusion.

'No. You cannot do that. You don't even know the guy. Reggie, you have to go into town this morning and take the pill. You are infatuated. I will go with you, if you like.'

I had never seen Patrick so determined.

'Bella, if this relationship with Jay does work out, you guys can have a baby later on. Now is not the right time.'

I listened to his reasoning and tuned in to my heart. Of course he was right. What was I thinking? I had never yearned for a child before. This romance had consumed me and thrown me off centre. I sighed.

'Okay, Patrick. You are right, of course. My apologies for, you know...' Shifting uncomfortably in my seat, I felt raw and ashamed. 'For dumping this on you. I will go into town and get myself sorted. I appreciate your offer to come with me, but I prefer to go on my own. It will give me time to think and digest.'

I felt lighter and more clear-headed, and with a small smile I added, 'I am grateful for your kindness and understanding, Patrick. It meant a lot, being able to approach you. Thank you.'

Patrick's arms enveloped me in a bear hug before he sent me on my way.

I quickly stepped aboard *Zephyr* and told Henry that I had something urgent to do that morning. My statement was met with silence and reproachful looks. Henry simply acknowledged my message with a curt nod, and without another word I climbed down the ladder into the cabin. Throwing on a new set of clothes, I grabbed my bag, clambered past Henry and Maude, and stepped off the yacht.

Finding the pharmacy was easy and getting the medication was a straightforward process. Outside I unceremoniously opened the pack and swallowed the tiny tablet with a big gulp of water. No second thoughts. No wavering emotions.

On the way home I thought about Jay and Sven and ruminated on how I had got myself into this position. I loved both men. One of them I knew inside out, the other was exotic and new. Suddenly I felt tired and worn out, both by my emotional rollercoaster and the challenges on the boat. Looking out the bus window as it rattled along, a tremendous loneliness crept up on me, like a mournful shadow on a late afternoon, and for the first time I failed to notice the scenery.

Decision Time

Stepping aboard, I was greeted by a frosty atmosphere. It was only midday Monday, and already it looked set to be an interesting week. I dropped my bag and quickly got to work. Henry wanted to show me how to properly splice a rope. He was avoiding my eyes, speaking in abrupt half sentences and at one point grumbled something barely audible.

'Excuse me?' I said.

'You weren't supposed to get involved with Jay!' he thundered, his words resounding across the peaceful morning bay.

'Henry, but you introduced me to Jay and told me he was okay,' I reminded him and went on, now rather upset myself. 'And besides, I did not plan for this. Life is unpredictable, and I have fallen in love with Jay. That's how it is and, like it or not, this is solely my concern and my situation to deal with.' I stood my ground, unwilling to let the grumpy old sod push me around.

'Okay. All right. You do whatever you have to do. But I *don't* want to hear about it,' he grumbled.

'Fair enough,' I replied, satisfied with the stalemate.

With a brief mutual nod, sealing our agreement, we continued our splicing project.

After lunch Yana and I started sanding the small wooden sections on deck. They needed to be varnished, but first we had to strip off the old paint. Sitting in the hot sun, we were soon caked in a mixture of sweat and fine brown dust. Yana and I got along well, and I enjoyed listening to her stories about her Eastern European upbringing and culture, and once more marvelled at the richness of human diversity.

After a while Yana haltingly asked about my situation and, glad to have another woman to confide in, I poured my heart out to her. Yana listened intently and acknowledged as I confessed guilt, doubts and confusion. She did not offer advice but was warm and compassionate. Her kind and motherly attention was a welcome change from the disapproving looks and snide comments of the yachties.

Andy and Clare didn't come to work on Monday and did not appear until halfway through the following afternoon, when they casually strolled up the dock towards our yacht. They looked relaxed and Henry stiffened at their appearance. The tension was palpable. Henry disappeared into the chandlery, muttering to himself. Maude started clanging and clattering in the galley. Andy and Clare asked me to take a break, so I followed them off *Zephyr* and onto Patrick's boat, where we all sat in the cockpit.

'We've been back and forth at the crewing agency and they've offered us a paid delivery to the US Virgin Islands.' Andy was too excited for subtlety and oblivious to my shocked reaction, he happily prattled on. 'We also inquired about a paid position on a charter yacht in the US Virgin Islands (USVI) for the season and it's looking hopeful. We can get a job as a skipper and cook/stewardess team.'

Clare smiled and looked happy for the first time since I'd met her.

'Wow,' I said. 'So, let me get this right. You have already accepted the delivery and the position in the USVI?'

For a moment their joyful expressions were overshadowed by guilt. They were aware that leaving *Zephyr* at this stage would most likely cause the trip to fall apart. We had already been delayed and the seasonal window to sail the Pacific passage was coming to an end. I exchanged a look with Patrick and was once more grateful for his quiet support and presence.

Decision Time

'Yes, we've accepted the delivery and we're waiting to hear back from the employer in the USVI. They need references and to organise a work permit for us both. But yes, we have decided to leave *Zephyr* and take this opportunity. Regina, we are sorry, but we've been working for over a month on this boat for free – long, full days as you well know – and Henry has been nothing but disrespectful and condescending. This is not how we want to spend our holiday.' Andy folded his arms across his chest.

Despite feeling sad that this was likely to mean the end of my dream, I understood their decision. Henry had been more tolerant and respectful towards me.

'Look, guys, I understand your choice,' I said, and Clare sighed with relief. 'This has been an unpleasant experience for you, and I am happy and excited for you!'

Clare spoke with an uncharacteristic intensity. 'Regina, you will have to think about what you are going to do. Henry won't find crew to replace us. You still have time to find another boat for yourself.' I could see the concern in her eyes.

'We asked at the crewing agency and they have other deliveries. Also, another private yacht is heading for the Pacific soon, you could check that out. You can't stay in Antigua, Regina.'

Hunched over in the cockpit, I suddenly wanted to cry. So much turmoil and so many emotions. I felt drained and wanted to curl up in my bunk and not crawl out until this was resolved. This was the end of the trip, my big dream, and I would have to say goodbye to Jay soon. I had avoided thinking about my upcoming departure from the island and this was a harsh wakeup call.

'I understand. Just give me a moment.' I sighed, resting my head in my hands.

Patrick consoled me, his hand on my back. 'You'll be fine, Bella. You'll find something else, I am sure of it.' He smiled warmly.

'I know I'll be all right, but...' Choked with emotion I continued haltingly, 'I was so looking forward to this great adventure. To sail across the Pacific, learning everything there is to know about handling a yacht, and exploring tropical islands. Then I fell in love with Jay. And now I have to leave ...' I felt tears welling up and took a couple of breaths to steady myself. No one spoke for a while.

I lifted my head. Taking another deep breath, I felt a new resolve take hold. 'Okay, I will go to the crewing agency today to look for other trips. I will be all right,' I said with more conviction than I felt. 'When are you leaving?'

'The delivery is in four days, but the visa has to be sorted out in the USVI first,' Andy said.

'Four days! Wow.' Things seemed to be shifting quickly. 'Right. When are you planning to tell Henry and Maude?' I asked.

'If it's okay with you, we can all go back to *Zephyr* and tell them now,' Clare said, and I understood that saying goodbye would be a huge relief for her.

I smiled and nodded in agreement. There was no reason to delay the news. I felt excitement stirring, knowing that I could adapt and would find a suitable alternative. This was only a bump along the way. I was not, however, looking forward to the conversation with our boat owners.

We found Yana and the couple sitting in the cockpit, quietly sipping their afternoon mugs of tea. Henry and Maude eyed us suspiciously. Once we were all settled in the confines of the small

Decision Time

cockpit, I asked Henry if we could have one of our 'deep and meaningful' chats. He looked almost amused and gestured for us to start.

Andy cleared his throat, took charge and spoke directly. 'Henry, Maude. Clare and I have taken on a delivery to the USVI and will then skipper a charter yacht there for the season. We are sorry to disrupt your trip. I am sure we are all aware of the personality clash here on board and Clare and I have decided to step off now, rather than halfway across the Pacific.'

'Okay, no worries.' Henry shrugged his shoulders and dismissively muttered, 'Is that it?'

'Yes, that's it,' Andy curtly replied and stood up. 'All the best to you then. Let's go, Clare… Regina, we'll see you around.'

Andy nodded at me, while Clare and I hugged tightly. They clambered off the bow onto the dock. I followed them to the front of the yacht, sad to see them go among such disharmony.

That was it. For a moment I sat at the bow and closed my eyes. I focused on my breathing to clear my mind.

Not wanting to discuss Andy and Clare's decision, I went below and asked Henry if I could finish up for the day.

'Sure,' he said, not looking up from his calculation on the chart table.

Yana looked at me inquisitively and I gestured to her to follow. She grabbed her purse and we quietly walked down the dock and boarded her son's vessel. Once we'd sat down, she asked what was going on and as gently as I could, I broke the unpleasant news. My heart went out to her. She had only arrived a week ago and was not flush with funds. I hoped her son would be able to help her.

Yana took the news gracefully and told me not to worry about her. We saw Sergey strolling down the dock and once he was on board, she told him about the three of us leaving.

'No problem,' he said. 'You can both sail with me. I am doing a transatlantic passage soon and have sixteen paying Russian customers on board.' The confident young skipper looked at me. 'Henry has said great things about your sailing skills. I am happy to take you as crew for the delivery to Europe.'

He would be captaining a retired racing yacht, which had famously won the Whitbread Round the World Race in the late 1980s. When Yana and I were invited on board, I saw that it was kitted out for speed, with huge grinding winches and a wide-open flush deck. Down below were simple hammock-like cots on either side of the hull, a basic toilet with a curtain for minimal privacy, a single burner gas stove and bucket showers.

I looked at the yacht and felt excitement bubbling up – what an incredible machine of a boat and amazing opportunity for me! This would be a massive kickstart to my yachting dream yet … there would be a crew of sixteen Russian men, plus the skipper. Yana and I would be the only female crew. Not my ideal scenario.

∿∿∿

With my little pack I was trudging along the road to English Harbour. I called Jay, told him the news and arranged to meet him later. The Antigua Classic Yacht Regatta, a race event for vintage wooden yachts, was starting. For weeks the graceful boats had been sailing in. Today was 'open home' day, where the public was granted limited access on some of the vessels. Curious, I decided to inspect the floating wooden treasures.

They were glorious vessels, each of them exuding timeless elegance. Their varnish gleamed in the warm light of the old brass lanterns, their heavy ropes were neatly coiled on the teak decks, and their interiors were immaculate. Tasteful cushions and vases filled with carefully arranged flowers completed the scene. I felt like I had entered an enchanting era from years long gone. In my mind I pictured what these stunning yachts would have seen and experienced in their time.

With a full heart I walked back to the marina buildings, just as Jay rounded the corner. He embraced me with his strong arms, making me feel safe and secure. We had a quick look at the boats together, then decided to return to his place. Once we got off the bus we hurried to his home, only for me to stop in my tracks when I saw his house. Barely days had passed since my last visit, but now the tiny building was glowing with a fresh, rich yellow coat of paint. Jay had promised to paint the house in my favourite colour and he'd already gone and done it! I was blown away by his sweet gesture and my heart swelled with love and appreciation.

Once we were inside, we sat on the bed and Jay asked about the implications of today's decisions. I said my visa would run out soon and that I needed to find another boat quickly. Feeling reassured by his supportive and understanding manner, I relinquished control. Unable to muster the will to leave, I fell asleep with his arms tightly wrapped around me, anchored by his presence.

The next morning, I felt a surge of new energy and resolve. I arose early and took the minibus back to the marina, by now familiar and at ease with this mode of transport. Boarding *Zephyr*, I saw Henry and Maude setting up breakfast in the cockpit. Their greeting was surprisingly friendly, and I asked if I could join them.

'Henry, yesterday's news was a big blow for me and I imagine for both of you, too. I would like to know what your thoughts are about our trip, considering all the changes,' I said.

'I don't know, Regina. It will be hard to find new crew and the weather window for a Pacific trip is closing soon. To be honest, I wasn't overly surprised by Andy and Clare's decision and have been anticipating it for a while now,' Henry replied. He turned his head, avoiding my gaze, and without remorse said, 'That's it, Regina. The trip's done for.'

His dispassionate response triggered a flash of anger in me. If he had anticipated their departure, why did he not change his attitude towards them in the first place? Or was this his way of subconsciously sabotaging our trip? He was old and his health was fragile. I was beginning to wonder if he was afraid of the long ocean passage. I questioned whether he held any concern at all for us, his crew. We had invested time and money to join his boat in the Caribbean and loyally worked for weeks, for free.

I sized up the man opposite me, taking in his deeply lined face, mouth unhappily dipping south, faded shirt and shorts with bony knees poking out. He was hunched over, as if weighed down by life. Examining his appearance, I felt a sudden compassion and a sadness for his closed heart, for his lost joy and for reaching the end of his dreams. Yes, I had lost a little time and money, but I always lived life to the fullest and with a positive attitude. That was my wealth. My anger dissolved and I smiled at him.

'All right. So, I need to know what I should do. Yesterday, Sergey, Yana's son, offered me a spot to do the transatlantic passage on his yacht … along with sixteen Russian male passengers.' A mental picture of being stuck with a competitive and testosterone-loaded crew in the middle of the ocean flashed before my eyes.

Decision Time

'Should I take his offer or look for another boat? I don't want to leave because of Jay, but my visa will expire soon. What would you advise me to do?'

'Regina, I can't tell you what to do. But yes, we will abandon our trip this year. As far as your options go, let me put it this way. The racer would be an exciting trip. However, you would be at sea for two weeks nonstop with a large group of men. Maybe look around and choose your best and safest option,' he counselled, quickly adding, 'But you can't stay in Antigua. There is no future in a relationship with Jay.'

'Right,' I said sarcastically, ignoring his last remark. But I listened to the first part of his advice and decided to go out and talk to yacht owners, check out flyers on notice boards, and chat to the crew agency. I wanted to find a satisfying solution.

I strode purposefully back to English Harbour and contacted the boat crew that Clare and Andy had recommended. They were indeed heading for the Pacific Ocean but were planning to cruise for longer than I could manage. I wandered up and down the finger docks but was suddenly shy and awkward, unsure how to approach people with my query. This was not as straightforward as I had imagined.

Later in the afternoon, not feeling confident to chat to more boat owners or crew, I felt disheartened by my lack of progress. As I passed a light post, I noticed a fresh flyer featuring a big heading: 'Crew Wanted'. I stopped and read the posting. It was for a transatlantic passage, unpaid, no sailing experience required and all food provided. Departure was set for next Monday. Perfect!

I dialled the number and the skipper, a man with a distinct Irish accent, answered. He gave a well-versed rundown of the trip. He wanted to meet me in person the following day and I excitedly agreed. With a new spring in my step, I returned to Falmouth feeling hopeful. I might be going on a sailing adventure after all.

Back on *Zephyr*, I told Henry and Maude about the prospective Atlantic crossing and my meeting with the boat's captain tomorrow. They looked relieved. In a legal sense they were responsible for me as long I was signed on *Zephyr*'s manifest. By entering a relationship with a local man, I had somewhat complicated matters for them. But aside from the legalities, I strongly felt that despite our occasional differences they genuinely cared for me and had not consciously set out for the trip to fail.

In that moment a deep love radiated from my heart, enveloping the weathered couple. I suddenly understood that we were thrown together for a reason, to learn from each other and our interconnected experiences. Unexpected changes and challenges were opening a portal to potential growth. Each chapter represented an exquisite pearl neatly lined up on my necklace of experience and wisdom.

That evening, elated from the day's events, I decided to check out one of the parties hosted by a sponsor of the Antigua Classic Yacht Regatta. The party was held at the end of the elegantly curved marina in Nelsons Dockyard. The surrounding historic buildings were bathed in glowing light and the yachts were decorated with banners and flags gently flapping in the cool evening breeze. As I approached, the music was blasting and the area was already buzzing with activity. Groups of sailors clutching large plastic cups, filled to the brim with alcoholic beverages, were loudly boasting about their racing escapades while others were dancing on the lawn in front of the stage.

Taking in the rowdy scene, I sashayed straight onto the grassy dance floor. Since starting to dance in Antigua, I had felt something in myself opening up. I closed my eyes, tuned into the rhythm and melodies, and let my body take command. Dancing helped me let go of lingering thoughts or worries and allowed joy and lightness to radiate from within. I also relished feeling feminine. Immersed in the moment, I smiled as I danced.

Occasionally men approached, in various stages of sobriety, and attempted brief staccato conversations over the top of the music. 'Which boat are you on?' was immediately followed by, 'Where are you heading?'

'The passage on the boat I was on got cancelled. I am looking for a boat to do a transatlantic passage,' was my usual reply, realising that communicating my query was much easier in this social environment. Unsurprisingly, before the night was over, I was offered a place on several yachts heading for Europe. But while some offers seemed genuine, others came seasoned with suggestive looks or sleazy remarks. I was not concerned. This was my night and I was having fun. Enjoying the light-hearted banter with these men, I felt unexpectedly flattered by their attention.

Then Jay strode onto the dance floor and sidled up to me. We had agreed to meet at the party but he was later than expected. My heart jumped at the sight of him. Noticing the attention from the surrounding males, he lowered his head and kissed me deeply, marking his territory. In response I leaned in, my body pressing against his. From that moment my focus was on us alone.

We danced with a new-found intensity, painfully aware that my departure was looming. When the party was over Jay did not need to ask if I wanted to go to his place. The end of the sailing dream on *Zephyr* had erased my loyalty to Henry and Maude, and I vowed to spend my precious remaining days with my new lover.

Next morning, I returned to the sailing community, eager to meet Aidan, the captain I had spoken to the previous day. Providing Aidan was a seasoned and reputable skipper, I wanted to be accepted as his crew for the passage, otherwise I would have to look for something else. I arrived early at the meeting point and was nervously shifting from one foot to the other. I scanned the sailors walking past, wondering if one of them was Aidan. Shortly after the agreed time, a guy in his late thirties, with a tanned face, wind-tousled short brown hair and the standard sailor's uniform of worn shorts, a torn shirt and a pair of non-slip sailing shoes, approached me.

'You are Regina?' he asked, his melodic Irish lilt diffusing his brusqueness.

'Yes. I assume that you are Aidan then.' I smiled and eagerly extended my hand. 'Nice to meet you.'

Aidan firmly grasped my hand and got down to business. 'All right. So, you want to join the trip back to Europe with my boat?' Lifting an eyebrow, he scanned my face.

'Yes, I would *love* to do that.' I said, hoping I didn't sound overly enthusiastic.

Aidan gave a quick rundown of the boat and the other crew. He was talking quickly and due to his accent, I had to focus intensely to absorb his information. The trip sounded professional and well organised. The other crew comprised an English woman and an Australian man, both in their early twenties. We would all move onto the boat the following Monday morning and immediately transfer the yacht to Jolly Harbour for provisioning.

Once that was done, the plan was to sail as soon as a good weather window opened and head for the Azores. This first part of the passage was projected to take two weeks and another week or so on to Ireland. I kept nodding as Aidan told me about the plans. He asked a few questions about me and my sailing experience and briefly checked that I could fund my onward travel upon arrival at the destination.

Once he finished talking, he looked at me and extended his hand. 'All right. See you Monday then.' He firmly gripped and shook my hand and was turning to leave.

'Hang on,' I called out. 'Is that it? You don't need to know any more? Does this mean I will be your crew?' This had happened so quickly and unexpectedly that I needed to make sure I understood correctly.

'Yes, Regina, you have the last spot on the boat. And no, I don't need to know any more. I am happy with what you've told me. Like I said, I am looking forward to seeing you on Monday at 10am on the boat. My yacht's name is *Orion* and we will be docked in Falmouth Marina. Easy.' He chuckled and I acknowledged the message with a nod. Giving a quick wave in my direction, he briskly walked off.

That was it! Once Aidan was out of sight, I could not contain my joy any longer and performed a happy dance on the spot. I had found a new boat and home and was finally about to embark on my much-anticipated adventure. I had a good feeling about Aidan. He was a straight-up kind of guy, seemed transparent and honest, plus he had ample experience. That was all I asked for.

9

ALL THINGS DELICIOUS

Glowing with happiness, I returned to Henry and Maude's yacht to announce my impending departure. The elderly couple were pleased, so next I looked for Yana. She had not moved onto *Zephyr*, preferring to stay with her son and I found them both aboard his boat.

Sergey was a serene and ambitious young man. His pensive eyes shone with a luminous intensity when he spoke of his goal of a career as a professional race skipper. Admiring his drive and sense of purpose, I felt sure that one day I would read about his success. When I told him about my decision to join the other yacht he looked mildly disappointed and said again that I was passing up a once in a lifetime opportunity. Yana said that she was doing the passage with her son back to Europe and she appeared content with her choice. We had each found a solution that was favourable for us.

Suddenly I realised I had only a handful of days left on the island. Hit with a sense of impending loss, I called Jay and we agreed to meet after he finished work. I went back on *Zephyr*, asked Henry for his laptop and, with a heavy heart, walked up to the bar to access the internet. I connected to Skype and punched in Sven's mobile number. He answered but the line was distorted and crackling as usual. Not that I minded, because the interference provided a suitable excuse to keep the conversation brief.

'Hey, Sven. How are you?' I asked, preferring to focus on his day-to-day life rather than talking about mine. He gave a quick run-down on the latest news of the wind farm, his colleagues and mentioned looking forward to his training in India and the subsequent holiday in Switzerland.

'And what are you up to, Reggie?' He sounded so untroubled and happy for me that my heart felt heavy. I relayed the boat dramas – Yana's arrival coinciding with Andy and Clare's departure, the cancelled trip, and finding the new boat. Again, I avoided mentioning Jay. I could not bring myself to do it. I would eventually have to tell Sven but had yet to decide the least hurtful way of doing so. Until I came upon a solution, my affair would remain my well-kept secret. I felt sad as we ended the call, realising that this was likely one of the last conversations that we would engage in as partners. I vowed to reflect during the upcoming passage and find the right solution on how to proceed, but for now I would enjoy my last days in Antigua.

I returned to *Zephyr*, handed Henry his notebook and packed my bags. I shouldered my duffel bag, filled with enough clothes for a few days, and climbed into the cockpit where Henry and Maude were relaxing with cups of tea.

'I'm going to stay with Jay until Monday. You have my phone number if you need to contact me. I left my backpack on the bunk downstairs and will pick it up around 9am Monday before moving to the other yacht.' I smiled non-committedly and without giving opportunity for comment, cheerfully added, 'All right, have a nice couple of days. See you later!' Then speedily clambered off the boat.

I called in at Patrick's and found him engrossed in a bilge, busy tackling one of the never-ending maintenance issues. Hearing my steps, he looked up, smiled and wiped his hands. Going to the stove, he prepared two steaming mugs of coffee. I loved watching him do simple routine tasks and realised that I had grown fond of his presence. He had a gentle nature, was warm, understanding and had a great sense of humour. He consistently made time to listen to me talking about our trials and tribulations on *Zephyr*. I was grateful for Patrick's friendship and support, especially in situations when others openly judged or criticised.

Once we were settled with our drinks, I updated him on my new venture. As I spoke, I saw the same relief I had witnessed with Henry and Maude light up his face. I expressed my gratitude to him for his friendship, the times we'd spent together, our conversations and the glasses of wine we had enjoyed on his yacht. Before I left, we embraced with a heartfelt hug. Walking out of the marina with my little duffel bag on my shoulder, it hit me that my time in Antigua was coming to a close.

I sat on the curb outside Jay's workshop, waiting for him to finish work. Hand in hand we strolled along the gravel path to his cute yellow home. Lying on the bed facing each other, our hands tightly intertwined, I told Jay about my upcoming trip. Until now I had never experienced two opposite emotions, tremendous excitement and profound sadness, simultaneously. I was looking forward to the sailing, but with a heavy heart. Jay scooped me into his arms and told me not to worry. I felt his lips gently and seductively kissing my neck. My hands found their way under his shirt and my fingers connected with his warm skin, slowly tracing his muscular torso. Jay shivered and with a sudden urgency lifted my dress over my head. Our beautifully contrasting bodies connected and with the touch of skin against skin I was overcome with all-consuming passion. Opening my eyes to meet Jay's intense gaze, I yielded unconditionally to his lead.

'I will miss you, Regina,' he whispered softly, as I fell asleep in his arms.

The next days passed in a blur. Jay took time off work so that we spend every moment together. During the days we explored beaches I had not visited before and playfully teased each other in the crystal-clear waters. In the afternoons we went for walks in the pastures near Jay's village and picked delicious ripe mangos and guavas from the local trees. We cooked basic stews at his home, eating the flavoursome food out of his handmade natural calabash bowls. Jay told me about his family, his upbringing and culture, and I shared stories about my background. Lying beneath the gently swaying mosquito net, we spent hours making love, consumed by our desire for one another.

During this time Jay introduced me to his brother who lived with his family in a bigger house on the same corner block. The two buildings shared an outside pit toilet as well as a rickety shower shack in the backyard. Whenever we wanted to have a rinse off, Jay and I undressed in his house, wrapped towels around our naked bodies and quickly traipsed across the not-so-private yard next to the gravel road. With no running water, showering meant picking up a bucket of cold water and splashing it over ourselves, in a bid to soap and rinse our bodies.

Walking through the little village I asked Jay if any white people lived in this community. Shaking his head, he smiled and said, 'No, Regina, no white people live here except for you.' His eyes twinkled mischievously.

In Switzerland I had grown up in a predominately white society at a time when there were hardly any people from outside Europe residing in my hometown. Certainly, none hailed from Africa or the Caribbean. For the first time in my life, I was in the minority. What stood out to me as we randomly bumped into Jay's friends and family, was how accepting and friendly everyone was towards me. I was disheartened to realise that Jay's experience would be different, should he spend time in my world.

Pushing those oppressive thoughts aside, I decided to embrace the novelty of my situation as I ventured far from my comfort zone. Life was much more basic than I was accustomed to, but the lack of comfort was not a concern. Instead, I was surprised by how safe I felt and how supremely content I was.

Monday morning came too quickly. We woke at dawn, entwined, and tenderly made love one last time. After a refreshing backyard bucket shower, I gathered my few belongings. We had agreed previously not to prolong the farewell, opting for a quick goodbye. I promised to keep Jay in the loop about my movements over the next few days and hopped onto the local bus. Back at the marina I wandered down the dock and onto *Zephyr*. Henry and Maude had returned to their usual grumpy selves, but nothing could dampen my spirits. I called out a friendly greeting and went to collect my backpack. After a last shared cup of tea in their cockpit I farewelled the couple with a hug and shouldered my bags.

My new home, the comfortable 50-foot cruising yacht *Orion*, was docked only a few boats down from *Zephyr*. Walking towards the boat with the navy-blue hull, I saw other bags piled on the dock and called out. Aidan's head popped up through the companionway.

'Ah, Regina! Good to see you,' he called. 'I didn't know if you'd turn up. Heard a rumour you'd shacked up with some local dude.' He lifted his eyebrows quizzically, eager for my reply.

Surprised by his blunt query I quickly gathered my thoughts and decided to give him a taste of his own frankness. 'Well, Aidan, let me put it this way. If I agree to something I stand by my word, whether or not I do shack up with a local guy.'

'Aye, no worries,' he said, throwing his head back in laughter at my candid response. 'Come on, then. Get yourself on board.'

'Here are your crew mates. This is Sasha,' he said, pointing towards a petite, young woman with big sparkling blue eyes and a wide smile.

'Hey, Regina. It's lovely to meet you!' she said.' I'm glad to have another chick on board.' Sasha buzzed with bubbly energy and I immediately liked her.

'Ken is in the stern cabin. Oy, Ken!' Aidan called out and a tall, athletic guy in his mid-twenties, sporting a big grin and tousled mop of auburn hair, squeezed through the narrow doorway of his cabin.

'Ken, this is Regina. She is the last of our crew. As soon as you guys have stowed all your bags away, we'll start our trip towards Jolly Harbour.' Aidan gave us all a nod and sat back at the navigation table.

Ken, Sasha and I helped each other pass the bags from the dock onto the deck, then down into the cabins. Aidan and Ken each had a cabin at the stern of the boat while Sasha and I were allocated the V-berth towards the bow, which housed a large V-shaped bed and numerous cupboards on either side. Smiling, I turned to Sasha and asked her if she was happy to share not only the cabin, but also the bed with me.

'No worries, chicky,' she giggled. 'I have no problem with that and during the passage we will be on rotating watches anyway.' Raising her eyebrows, making her eyes appear even larger, she asked, 'But are you okay with it?'

'Sure, I don't mind at all. I am looking forward to the trip and I'm basically happy that I don't have to share a cabin with a guy.' We exchanged a conspiratorial look and sniggered. Our bond was established and I looked forward to getting to know this spirited young woman in the coming weeks.

I was pleased with the captain and fellow crew on *Orion* and was excited about going to sea with them. Ken was a typically chilled-out Aussie dude, with a pleasant and fun personality. I knew I would get along well enough with Aidan, appreciating his straight-up attitude and professional manner.

Ken, Sasha and I quickly stowed our gear and Aidan started up the engine. Henry helped us to release the stern lines and as we slowly motored out, I waved goodbye to my old skipper, my friend Patrick and others I had met. As we passed by, I thought about this short, intense chapter in my life and wondered what would happen next.

Out of the bay, Aidan showed us how to hoist the main sail and the jib. I was surprised to find *Orion* much easier to handle than *Zephyr*. All the sheets led back into the cockpit and only a handful of self-tailing winches were placed within easy reach of the cockpit, the two main ones being powered. With the push of a button the sails rushed up the mast and all we had to do was trim the sails into the right position.

Once they were set to Aidan's satisfaction we relaxed in the cockpit. Aidan casually asked us about our respective travels and wanted to know what had brought each of us to Antigua. Ken had come to watch the Cricket World Cup and found himself with enough time left over for a sailing adventure, before returning to Melbourne. Sasha, as befitting her carefree and happy-go-lucky personality, had hopped on and off sailing yachts over the past year, and in this manner had managed to explore much of the Caribbean on a shoestring budget. She was ready to return home to England and commence her university studies.

The corners of Aidan's mouth curled upward as he turned to me. 'Now, Regina. What's the story with your local fella?' he asked, giving me little room to manoeuvre.

The other two perked up at the mention of a guy and eyed me with increased curiosity. I swallowed, chuckled and took a breath. I decided to be honest and upfront about my circumstances. The four of us were going to spend the next few weeks in close quarters and we were bound to get to know each other well. I had nothing to lose.

'Well,' I said, and smiled, 'my story might take a while. Are you sure you want to hear it?'

As the three heads eagerly bobbed in agreement, I began to recount my adventure. I related how I came to Antigua to crew for the sailing trip, explained how we got stranded on *Zephyr* and why the trip fell apart. I mentioned meeting Jay and confessed to a long-term relationship with Sven in Australia and my guilt in that regard. I described my deep feelings for Jay and my confusion about the whole situation. My new crew mates honoured my honesty and were empathetic as I shared my rollercoaster story. I finished by thanking Aidan for accepting me as crew and said I was looking forward to this trip. I expressed my gratitude for the coming time and space I'd have to reflect, while on a yacht in the middle of the immense Atlantic Ocean. I knew it would allow me to digest the recent events and gain insight and perspective.

After sharing my story, the conversation returned to more light-hearted topics. Ken, Sasha and Aidan were soon joking and teasing each other. I sat back, listening to their banter and enjoying the cheerful atmosphere.

Sailing to Jolly Harbour only took a couple of hours, with sandy beaches and palm-tree fringed coastline always in sight. By the time we were docked in the marina on the other side of Antigua, I was convinced I had found a fantastic boat and team with whom to cross the Atlantic. During dinner Aidan briefed us on the plan for the following day. He wanted us all to take care of the provisioning.

The skipper and Ken would purchase goods from the supermarket across the street and buy all the non-perishable supplies, ranging from toilet paper to tinned food, as well as the fresh meat. Sasha and I were paired up to visit the local fruit and vegetable market and instructed to return with plenty of fresh supplies. I had never stocked a boat with food for a passage and felt trepidation at this responsibility. The fresh goods had to last for the entire two weeks at sea, otherwise our dining experience would be considerably diminished. Sasha calmly reassured me. During her year of sailing she had gained plenty of experience provisioning a yacht. My mind at ease, I decided to relax and follow her lead.

After we had finished our evening meal, the other three went to the pub to savour a few last drinks before our dry passage to the Azores. I declined the offer to join them and called Jay instead.

'Babes, how are you?' He sounded happy.

'Jay, we have arrived in the Jolly Harbour marina. The trip across was smooth and the crew seem friendly. Tomorrow we are going to provision the boat and if we get it done by the afternoon, we will leave straightaway.' I felt heavy hearted, breaking the unexpected news.

'Okay.' I could hear the sadness in his voice.

'I'm sorry, Jay. I didn't know we were going to leave so soon. I will miss you.'

'I miss you already, Regina. Please, come back to Antigua.'

His simple and quiet statement tore at my heart and I promised to contact him as soon as we got to the Azores. It was heart-breaking to say goodbye over the phone. I wished I could sneak over to his place for the night but that would not have been the right thing to do by my new skipper. I hung up the phone, not feeling in the mood for the pub atmosphere, and instead settled in the cockpit with a hot cup of tea.

The next morning, I was woken by clattering from the galley. Aidan was up and busily making coffee while wolfing down his breakfast. As the rest of us crawled out of our cabins, he poured us each a cup and showed us where to find our own breakfast. As we sat and ate, he started counting out money on the table. He pushed a large pile of cash towards Sasha and me, with simple instructions.

'Here's the money allocated for the fresh goods. Spend it all, but make sure you use it wisely. Remember to buy lots of long-lasting vegetables and fruit. Take the bus there and get a taxi for the trip back.'

It sounded straightforward. Sasha took the money and I cleaned up the breakfast. Done with the morning chores, we set off in high spirits. We were having a good chuckle about our brief instruction and conspired to bargain hard and buy as much fresh produce as possible. We both loved a healthy diet and wanted to have a wide range of fresh ingredients available throughout the passage.

Shopping at the market was fun. Sasha and I rocked up to the busy hall and walked through the stalls assessing the produce. Having selected two or three stands with quality products, we started loading vegetables into large bags. They were bursting to the brim with pumpkins and potatoes, onions, garlic, carrots and eggplants. As the longest lasting vegetables, these would be our staples. We still had plenty of money left so we added tomatoes, zucchini, cucumbers and beans. For fruit we chose a few mangoes, passionfruit, some expensive imported apples and a couple of bunches of bananas. The banana was deemed an unlucky fruit to have aboard a boat due to an ancient and controversial fable, and we were glad our skipper was not of the superstitious kind. To top off our shopping spree we added a few luxuries like fresh herbs and lettuce for the first few days at sea.

We paid the market stallholders for the pile of goods, found a taxi and with the help of the market people, piled the bags into the boot. Once they were stowed, we took a seat, looked at each other and burst out laughing. What an experience! We had enjoyed the bartering, picking anything that caught our fancy as we pictured *Orion* stocked to the hilt with delicious fresh supplies. We had chosen vast amounts of perishables. Looking at the bags we wondered how Aidan would react, which promptly resulted in another giggling fit. It felt good, having female company.

The guys were still at the shop by the time we got back to the boat. One by one we started loading our bags onto a trolley, then carefully wheeled it down the dock. I passed the bags to Sasha, who had jumped onto the yacht. Just as we set down the last bag in the cockpit, we heard the metallic rattling of another trolley and saw the guys pushing not one, but two fully loaded carts. Sasha and I looked dumbfounded at the mass of groceries. We would not starve!

Aidan gave us a few hints on how best to stow the food after making clear that this would be our chore. The three of us looked at each other, a little overwhelmed, and had a good laugh while trying to come up with an efficient system. Eventually we followed Sasha's lead. She had the most experience and over the next hour we carefully stacked, packed and loaded little lockers, gaps and even some bilges with the goods.

Once we finished it was past lunchtime and the temperature was rising. Sitting in the cockpit we ate a quick sandwich washed down by a cold beer. Just as we were comfortably relaxing in the sun and digesting the food, Aidan asked for our attention.

'Guys, what do think, should we leave this afternoon? The weather is looking good and we are provisioned and ready. We could wait until tomorrow morning, but I would rather up and go today.'

I was taken aback at how casually he approached the departure for a transatlantic passage but remembered that he had completed more than a dozen ocean crossings. With that kind of experience this decision was not as big a deal to him as it was to me.

'I'm fine with that. Whatever you think is best,' I replied. I looked at Sasha and Ken, ignoring the pain in my heart. It was going to hurt, whether we left today or tomorrow.

They both nodded, although Ken looked the least keen. He had possibly been hoping for one last party night before our dry period at sea. Looking at us, Aidan nodded decisively and said that we would head off at 4pm. Seeing that we'd only be allowed a brief shower every second day while at sea, he suggested that we indulge ourselves at the amenities block while we could.

'Hello, Regina.' Surprised to hear Jay's beloved voice, I looked up and saw him standing on the dock. His cute stubby dreadlocks were tucked under a baggy Rastafarian beanie. Flashing the biggest smile, his eyes sparkled as he looked at me. And in his beautifully sculpted arms he was cradling a huge watermelon. Slightly behind Jay I spied his colleague, the driver of the delivery lorry, shyly maintaining his distance.

'Babes, I missed you and I wanted to say goodbye before you leave. I have a present for you and your friends for the trip,' he said.

Feeling both elated and bashful at his unexpected appearance and his affectionate declaration in the presence of my new crew, I jumped up and clambered off the boat. Jay handed me the heavy fruit and I passed it to Sasha, who flashed me a big grin and a cheeky, conspiratorial wink.

'Jay! What a beautiful surprise!' I could not hide my joy at his thoughtfulness and basked in his affection. 'Thank you for the watermelon and for making the time to come by.'

Self-conscious, we embraced awkwardly in front of our audience and exchanged a quick peck. Sensing our need for privacy, my surprisingly perceptive sailor mates disappeared below deck.

Grateful for their understanding I turned back to Jay, held his hands in mine and looked into his eyes. 'I miss you already. It will be hard to sail away from Antigua, but you know that I must go. I need to clear up my life and make decisions. I promise I will call you whenever I can.'

Seeing him here among the yachts, where I was about to depart and head back to my old world, brought home the difference between our lives and the unknown outcome of our separation. Would I see him again? As my emotions swelled, I gently tugged his hands.

'Come on. This is hard. I will walk with you back to the van.' My eyes were welling up with tears and I was trying hard to swallow my feelings.

When we reached the lorry, Jay's colleague kindly busied himself on the other side of the vehicle while I leaned against Jay's body. I lifted my head and our lips met for a tender and loving kiss, followed by a tight embrace. Sombrely Jay got in the passenger seat and after a last wave from the window, the two men in the lorry disappeared around the corner.

Needing a quiet moment, I sat down in the shade of a tree, closed my eyes and filled my lungs with deep breaths. During the past few weeks, I had grown to love this man and was astounded by the array of emotions I had experienced. I felt closely connected to Jay and couldn't imagine not seeing him again. Yet, I had to think about Sven and our relationship. I hoped to gain peace and clarity over the next two weeks at sea.

10

AQUAMARINE IMMERSION

Our skipper, Aidan, started the engine at 4pm sharp as the three of us stood on deck, thrilled and ready to start our Atlantic Ocean passage. With Aidan directing from the helm, we released all the lines, coiled them up and, together with the fenders, stowed them away. We would not use them again until our arrival in the Azores. Suddenly we were in the open ocean on our floating microcosmos. Our bow was pointed in a north-easterly direction and the sun was low on the horizon, casting the disappearing shores in a golden glow.

As soon as the sails and the course were set to Aidan's satisfaction, he described his favoured rotating twenty-four-hour watch system. Each of us would be rostered for a three-hour watch during the night. Throughout the day he planned three sets of four-hour shifts, leaving one of us without a watch during this twelve-hour period. Those occasions, Aidan said with a slight smirk, would be our 'mothering days' where we would be responsible for preparing lunch and dinner for all on board. I loved the idea of this rotation. It meant we would equally share all the watches and cooking chores, and I was looking forward to treating my new team with delicious home-cooked meals.

As we were pushed along by a steady breeze, Antigua's coastline eventually disappeared behind the horizon. We settled in for our on-deck shift routine and suddenly I was alone in the cockpit for my first watch. I closed my eyes for a moment, feeling the wind gently brushing across my face and hearing the soft swishing sound of our wake, as the yacht ploughed through the dark ocean. Keeping a lookout for other boats, I gazed in awe at the vastness of the ocean and the sky above me. I was struck by the insignificance of small *Orion* in this huge expanse. Yet, in this open space, I felt inexplicably safe and secure and sensed a deep calm settling within.

Over the next few days, the wind steadily increased and then turned against us. Aidan explained the seasonal prevailing winds were supposed to reach *Orion* roughly across her stern quarter. Instead, we were experiencing winds from an increasingly northward direction. This meant the yacht was uncomfortably beating into the oncoming wind and waves. In these deteriorating conditions I quickly learned that our captain, while well-seasoned, showed a tendency towards impatience and a rather short fuse.

'Aidan, how many days do you anticipate this passage will take to reach the Azores?' I wondered aloud as we were all sitting in the cockpit during the day, lapping up the sun.

'Hard to say in this breeze. Around fourteen days, maybe.' His face scrunched up and to my astonishment he fervently roared, 'I fucking hate these deliveries.'

'Oh, okay. Why's that?' I asked, curious as to what caused his immense frustration.

Aidan did not require any more prompting. Peppering his speech with profanities, he explained his dislike for ocean passages. To him they were boring, time-consuming, offered no challenge and to top it off, there was the ban on booze until the next port. His sole focus was to get to the Azores as quickly as possible. Being in a such hurry, he sailed the boat hard and in an uncompromising manner. In these conditions the consequence of his choice was that *Orion* kept leaning to one side at an extremely steep angle. The wind was pushing the yacht slowly up each massive oncoming wave, only to smash down into the next trough with a heavy, resounding shudder. I was astounded by the brutal force of these impacts and asked him about it.

'Nah, don't worry,' he said. 'The boat's built for this. It's a bit of wear and tear, that's all.' With that he turned back to the computer screen, checking for the latest weather report.

Sasha and I were finding the nights challenging. The sea grew rougher and our cabin at the bow, the front of the boat, was the most exposed to the violent movement of the yacht. Resting in our big V-shaped bed, we regularly found ourselves suspended mid-air, only to come crashing down onto the mattress and tumbling into each other as *Orion*'s bow fiercely ploughed back into the water. The sound of the sea crashing against the hull was ear-splitting, immediately followed by the tense shudder of the mast and rigging reverberating through the boat after the harsh slams down. Adding to the intense situation was the eerie sound of the breeze. With the force increasing, the wind blowing through the rigging rose to a squealing noise as gusts were pushing by. This made sleep near impossible. I had asked for an adventure and was dealt one.

I awoke one morning with a dull ache in my abdomen. During breakfast I mentioned it to Sasha and with a surprised look she confessed to feeling the same pain. Eventually we figured out that our bids to fix ourselves to the bed during sleep by clawing onto its cushions was causing an unusual muscle strain. Feeling a lack of sleep, I decided to make my bed in the saloon instead. The boat was heeling so much to one side that I was comfortably cradled between the back of the lounge and the seat.

Prior to the sailing trip I had devoured books on sailing, especially Southern Ocean racing tales that told of waves and swells the size of houses or even small office towers. Since I had not done any major sailing before, I naively assumed that these stories described normal or average sailing conditions.

One morning Aidan was airing his frustrations about our situation. 'I can't believe the bloody breeze. By now the trade winds should have kicked in and be reaching across the stern quarter. This is fucking insanity!' he growled, looking at yet another wind chart, desperately hoping for improvement.

'Isn't this normal?' I said cautiously. 'I mean a lot of ocean sailing books describe massive waves in the Southern Ocean?'

'You are positively insane, chick. The Southern Ocean is different to this. No, normally we would average 15–20 knots roughly coming from behind and pushing us nicely along. That's what we should get; not 30 to bloody 40 knots hitting us on the bow quarter. Unheard of,' he muttered, shaking his head.

Luckily, none of us suffered sea sickness and *Orion* was dutifully pushing towards the Azores. Apart from the apparent discomfort of the constant shaking, pounding and whistling, we were content with our progress.

Aidan was spending more time at the navigation table, musing over the weather charts. Rather than diminish, the winds increased and came almost directly from the direction that we needed to sail towards. To accommodate this change, we were forced to alter the course, which meant doing a detour and prolonging our journey. Aidan was not amused. We all suffered from lack of sleep due to the watch rotations and this, together with the constant movement and noise, meant that tempers would occasionally get the better of us. Luckily, any tensions seemed to cool off just as quickly.

For me, the weather was a welcome distraction from my emotions. Focused on my watches, cooking for the crew every few days, and sleeping when I could, took most of my energy. The conflicting feelings around Jay and Sven dimmed into the background and I slowly began to digest the situation. I missed Jay, but with no need to force a decision or solution, I focused on embracing the precious moments on board. The wild and wet weather failed to dampen my happiness at being immersed in this natural environment. Besides, this adventure was providing the time to evaluate my life.

One afternoon I was on deck starting my four-hour watch in stormy, wet conditions. The other three crew were hibernating in the warm, dry cabin. Carefully I opened the companionway hatch and chuckled at the cosy scene below.

'Hey, Aidan. I would like to take up your offer to hand steer the boat. Is that okay?' I asked with a big grin.

'Are you sure, Regina? It's blowing 30-plus knots sustained out there, gusting up to 40,' he cautioned, looking at me with new-found curiosity.

'Yes! I am certain. I really want to give it a shot. And while you are at the navigation table, would you mind putting Pink Floyd on for me at *full blast*?' By now I was laughing loudly, already envisioning my solitary watch party.

'Are you kidding? No, you're not. You are actually enjoying these conditions!' Shaking his head in disbelief, he said, 'Geez, you are one crazy lady!' He started chuckling at my blatant enthusiasm and demurred, 'Okay then. Go for it. Helm the boat. But be careful and make sure you maintain the course!'

Aidan changed the music to my request, and I closed the hatch, finding myself surrounded by a foaming grey ocean as I took the helm. The band's first epic song started booming out of the speakers. For the next four hours I stood behind the wheel, hurtling through the dark, confused ocean with Pink Floyd enhancing my stage. *Orion*, a sizeable yacht at 50-feet, seemed like a bobbing cork among the towering swells. The sea was approaching the vessel from all directions at once. Waves continually smashed into the bow, followed by a huge wall of water heavily crashing down over the entire length of the boat. Masses of white foam forcefully struck my face and body, drenching me from head to toe. At times, a wave would approach from the stern, colliding with the back of the yacht with a bang and violently spraying and flooding the cockpit and myself.

The ocean was majestic and mesmerizing. Huge rolling towers of grey swell topped with iridescent turquoise peaks moved towards, then disappeared under the yacht. Occasionally some of these massive waves broke, the white frothing mass contrasting with the dark ocean and the stunning aquamarine tips. Heavy, black clouds loomed low. I felt total respect for the natural force of the sea in those exhilarating, wild and untamed moments.

I steered the boat for hours, feeling the wind on my face and checking the compass every few seconds. My advantage over the autopilot was that I could anticipate the oncoming waves. Most likely we were sailing a less straight route, but a far more comfortable one for the yacht. *Orion* was behaving beautifully in these conditions, and I found her surprisingly easy to steer. The prevailing wind and swell came from slightly off the bow. As the big waves approached the boat, we slowly climbed to the top of the crest, where I adjusted the course, allowing *Orion* to gently tip her bow and surf down the other side. Rushing down the steep face of the waves, I noted the boat speed rapidly increasing from 8 to 10, and occasionally up to 13 knots. In the deep troughs the yacht abruptly slowed, in need of another course adjustment. Engulfed by mountains of waves and experiencing a momentary lull in the wind, *Orion* would gradually increase speed and arduously climb her way up the wall of the next oncoming wave.

Those few hours were among the most vivid and magnificent of my life. I loved my solitary time on deck, immersed in this raw and unpredictable environment with the intense music adding to the surreal quality of the experience. Soaked and labouring hard at the wheel, I did not feel cold or tired, even though winds were near gale force.

When my watch was over, I engaged the autopilot and clambered down the companionway wearing a huge smile. My fellow sailors looked up with bemusement. Aidan, up for the next watch and clearly dreading the conditions, was checking our progress on the chart.

'Man, you are one crazy chick to enjoy conditions like these. But I must admit that you helmed well. You hardly went off course. Good job.'

Aidan gave me a quick nod and I nearly jumped with joy. This was a rare compliment from the seasoned skipper, and I was stoked to receive his approval. I had assumed that with the waves and weather, my plotted course would have been messy. He showed me the line and it looked surprisingly straight indeed. As I went to change into dry clothes, I allowed myself the pleasure of basking in the praise and in my achievement. By now the excitement and physical labour were showing their effects and I was beginning to feel tired. I devoured my dinner with gusto and fell sound asleep almost before my head hit the pillow.

A few days later, just as the weather began to ease, we heard a mayday call on the high frequency radio. Another yacht motoring towards the Azores had been de-masted and its fuel was running short. Without propulsion by either sail or engine, a boat was at its most vulnerable, especially in disturbed seas. We were too far away to help but were relieved to hear soon after that a commercial vessel was offering assistance. This unusual weather pattern was taking a toll and it was sobering to realise how quickly a fun sail could turn into a harrowing experience.

The days and nights blended into a continuous rotation of watches, cooking and sleep. During the long and lonely night shifts I spent many hours contemplating my situation. Jay was prominent in my thoughts, and with longing I summoned up memories of our walks, electrifying dancing and romantic moments. Another part of me was still feeling ashamed and dreading the inevitable confession I owed Sven. Guided by the stillness of the night, with only the twinkling stars illuminating the darkness, I concluded that Sven and I had to part ways. It was time. We had contemplated a separation before but never had enough reason to follow through. Now, my feelings for Jay gave us a reason to separate.

Our ending would not be as neat and mindful as I'd imagined or hoped for, but I accepted this new understanding. I felt much lighter even though, after living in a sheltered relationship for thirteen years, the thought of facing the future alone was daunting.

During one of my few conversations with Sven, he had mentioned an upcoming holiday in Switzerland. I concluded that the best solution was to travel there and meet with him in person. Now I was faced with the impossible choice of how to communicate the devastating news. Should I tell him, sitting face to face in Switzerland, and dampen his holiday, or tell him by phone or email once I got to the Azores?

One night as I was sitting and contemplating these questions, I looked overboard. The moon was a tiny sliver and the vast black sky was sprinkled with millions of bright stars. The swell had calmed down over the past few days and was gently rolling under the yacht. When I stood up to scan the horizon for approaching ships, I noticed the bow wave shimmering and glowing in an unusual way. I took a moment to realise it was bioluminescence – I was seeing an unexpected treat from nature. I had heard about this phenomenon but had not witnessed it before. As I watched, fascinated, *Orion* became surrounded by magical sparkling water. Wherever the water surface was disturbed, the tiny cellular beings were stimulated and started to glow.

I had begun to relax when a big, illuminated ball began to quickly approach the boat from afar. Having no idea what it was, I froze in anticipation that this bright bullet-shaped body would hit us. The lit-up object had almost reached the boat, curiously aiming exactly for my position. Carefully leaning forward to investigate the mystery, I made out the shape of a dolphin, encapsulated by a cloud of light. I realised that the mammal was illuminated by the same bioluminescence I had seen only moments before. Relieved and overjoyed, I laughed, marvelling afresh at this incredible natural wonder. My eyes were transfixed by the glowing dolphin. Reaching the boat, near where I was standing, it changed direction and swam to the bow. It played in the sparkly bow wave for a while before turning away and disappearing in the distance.

I could never get enough of the ocean, the sky, and sailing. Before the passage I had often wondered if life on the water would become boring, suspended on the sea for days, or even weeks, at a time. But I had found that even though there was little stimulation beyond the boat, every day was novel and inspirational. The swell would meet *Orion* from a new angle. The colour of the water constantly changed. Some days we sailed among breaking waves and on others the water was calm and serene.

The same applied to the sky. With the ever-changing wind and sea state we were continually adjusting the sails and our course, trying to improve the boat's performance. Mile by mile we were nudging closer to our destination.

With the calmer weather, life became simpler. During the day we were socialising, cooking creative meals, napping, or enjoying our rationed showers. We ate our meals together in the cockpit, or below if the weather was wet. We played cards, told stories and shared more of ourselves. Soon we had bonded as a unit, like a family. There was honesty and openness in our communication. I wondered whether we had grown comfortable with each other more quickly due to our confined living space, or because we were too fatigued to bother with pretence. Whatever the reason, the close companionship was refreshing.

As we drew closer to the Azores the atmosphere on board changed. We felt motivated to move faster, so we would get there quicker. It was exciting to see the track of the boat on the computer chart slowly moving towards the archipelago, and we took bets on our arrival day and time. Then, as if tempted by some greater force, the wind dropped and we started to limp along. The sails flapped tiredly against the rigging and the ocean looked eerily flat. We were suspended in unusual stillness. The sky and sea merged in a silvery, grey continuum. Aidan's frustration soared and he complained profusely about the weather and our lack of progress. For the first time, I preferred to retreat into the cabin.

Luckily, our becalmed state lasted only a few days and soon land appeared on the horizon. After two weeks of seeing nothing but ocean and sky, this was a stimulating vision. We stood in awe on deck, watching the shapes of the mountains growing bigger and more defined. The island of Faial was lush, dipped in vivid green. As much as I was looking forward to stepping ashore and enjoying the luxuries the town of Horta and its main marina had to offer, I was also dreading the moment. Hitting land meant having to face my reality. I had to contact Sven and tell him about Jay and my choices. My heart was aching in anticipation and I was the only crew member not overjoyed when we docked the boat in the large and crowded marina.

Ken, Sasha and Aidan immediately walked off to the pub in search of a cold Guinness. I took a long, hot shower at the marina amenities, letting the soothing water run over my body. Dressed in fresh clothes I walked into the centre of Horta. Quaint stone buildings snugly lined the winding, narrow streets. People greeted each other and chatted in small groups, creating a friendly atmosphere. I found a small internet cafe and checked my email.

In my inbox I found a message from Sven telling me that he had left Australia and was enjoying his training in India. He mentioned finding the country interesting and controversial and feeling shocked by its profound poverty. He then described his plans for Switzerland and said he was looking forward to the holiday.

His brief but pleasant message reminded me what a wonderful man and friend he was to me. Loyal, honest and caring. For a while, my fingers lingered over the keyboard while searching for appropriate wording in my reply. Finally, after a big breath, I started typing.

My dear Sven,
This is possibly the hardest email I have had to compose and please excuse me if I am not expressing my emotions perfectly. I am writing with the best intentions only and hope you will understand in time.

We haven't had much contact since I left Australia and I would like to explain why. If we wanted to Skype, I had to borrow Henry's laptop, which was not always available, and the internet was not reliable. But the other reason, the one that is much harder to admit, was because I have been caught in an emotional conflict. For said reason it was easier for me not to be in touch often. I am truly sorry about that.

I did not expect this to happen, Sven, and there does not seem to be way to break the news gently. I have met a man in Antigua and I have fallen in love with him. You don't know how much it pains me to tell you in an email, but I didn't want to meet in Switzerland and drop this news on you unexpectedly.

As hard as it may be to face, I know in my heart it is time for us to move on in life in separate ways.

I have arrived in the Azores for a quick stop over. In a few days we will continue to sail the boat to Ireland. Afterwards I will fly to Switzerland, so we can meet and discuss our separation in person.

Sven, you have been the most important person in my life for a long time and you will continue to be an integral part of my life. Beyond being lovers and partners, I sincerely hope we can maintain our deep friendship in the future.

I am truly sorry to cause you pain.

Love,

Regina

I took a deep breath, swallowed my tears, and hit the send button. This was the end of a big chapter. Over the years Sven had become much more than my lover and partner. As a result of our extensive travels and life in three countries, we had neglected other friendships and, over time, had somewhat isolated ourselves. Sven had grounded, loved and supported me and had always had my back. I could not yet fully picture a life without him and my future suddenly seemed lonely and bleak. Finding a quiet spot on the rocky foreshore, I sat alone, allowing tears to flow. Adjusting to my new situation would take time. Once I had released some of my grief and felt calmer, I went to look for my crew mates. I found them tucked away in a little corner of the noisy sailor bar. Their table was littered with empty glasses and bottles, and they were well on their way to getting drunk. I felt overwhelmed by the noise and the atmosphere and went back to *Orion*.

As I walked along the dock, I studied the colourful view of the countless yachts that had either arrived safely from afar or were about to depart on a big passage. This was a stopover port, not a place where yachts lingered. Located far into the Atlantic, the Azores provided welcome shelter from bad weather. Here crews could stock up on fresh goods and water, and have repairs done to anything that had been broken during the previous passage. They also catered for the seasoned sailors with grotty and overflowing bars, where crews could commiserate and boast of scary oceans and damaging winds.

Although my fellow crew tried hard to entice me to join them at the pub, I was not tempted to drown my sorrows with alcohol. Instead I chose solitude and spent the stopover wandering the streets, doing yoga on the deck of the yacht and trying to find peace with my new situation and myself. Finding a phone booth, I gave Jay a short call to let him know where I was.

'I am glad to hear your voice, Regina.' In turn, hearing his warm voice was like balm for my wounded soul. 'I miss you. Please come back to Antigua.'

'I will try, Jay. But first I must go to Switzerland and meet Sven. I owe him that.'

Back in the internet cafe I nervously logged onto my email. Sven had replied. I clicked to open his email.

Dear Regina,
I cannot believe what you wrote to me. After thirteen years of relationship you are choosing to end it via email. I am disappointed and quite mad.
I agree to meet in Switzerland so we can talk this over. I will be there for the next three weeks, so please get in touch with me when you arrive.
Sven

His raw pain was embedded in the few sentences. Guilt emerged like an uncomfortable relative, and I typed a short reply. I hoped that the weeks before our meeting would give Sven time to adjust and accept our separation.

A few days after our arrival a de-masted boat limped into port. It was the same yacht that had issued the mayday call while we were at sea. The young Danes aboard celebrated their shock and subsequent successful recovery with an exuberant and boisterous gathering, an occasion that my crew mates could not pass up. The morning after, I offered them a hearty cooked breakfast and asked Aidan when he was planning to move on. I was feeling concerned as the days were blending into each other, punctuated by nightly parties and morning-after hangovers.

'Well, how about tomorrow?' Aidan perked up and suddenly seemed eager to depart.

'Okay, that's great. So, what's the plan?' I asked, to keep the momentum going.

'Well, we won't need to do much provisioning as we have a lot of stuff left. You and Sasha can buy some fresh goods and Ken and I will do the maintenance and fill up the water tanks.'

'Done!' I smiled and looked at Sasha. 'Are you with me?'

The passage from the Azores to Ireland was slow. Dreadfully so. For two long and patience-testing days, we hovered motionless mid-ocean, caught in a sea of dense mist and cloud. The water's surface resembled a mirror and the sails flapped listlessly against the rigging with the slightest movement of the yacht. We sat suspended in eerie silence.

Nothing is worse on a sailing boat than no wind, especially when everyone is keen to make progress. By now we were all making plans for what we'd each do after the passage, yet there we were, stuck on the water, observing the bleeping icon of our boat on the computer chart not logging a single mile of forward movement. Eventually, after repeatedly checking the weather forecast, Aidan switched on the engine. We motored for over a day until the breeze picked up and we were once again propelled by wind alone. Aidan set our final course for the southern shores of Ireland. With the increased speed our moods improved dramatically. Sasha and I found an empty glass bottle on board and began creating a message. After composing an elaborately decorated letter, we put it into the bottle, sealed it and catapulted it far overboard, hopeful of one day receiving a message in return.

The passage towards Ireland was expected to take roughly six days, but well over a week had passed when we sailed into Crosshaven. Being my first visit to Ireland, I was curious to see what the country had to offer. As the land appeared on the horizon, I kept my eyes peeled. Vivid green meadows topped dramatic cliffs like lush carpets and, as we edged closer, I noticed a quaint village huddled at the foot of sweeping hills covered in pastures and forests. I became aware of a fragrance and realised it was the scent of the land drifting across the water. I could smell the rich soil, fresh grass and the sweetness of blossoming flowers.

Once Aidan cleared us into the country, my crew mates disappeared into a medieval-looking pub. I took a walk through the sleepy village, past ancient buildings and along a cobblestoned road. I strolled for a while. It was a gentle kind of day. The sun was mellow and warm, and the bees were busy among the sea of blossoms. Ireland was presenting its most glorious side.

Later in the afternoon, Ken, Sasha and I sat in the local internet cafe, organising our onward travels. Sasha purchased a ferry ticket to her home in the south of England, Ken finalised his return to Australia, and I booked a flight to Switzerland. I was relieved that the passage was over. I had loved the sailing and adored the company but was ready to tackle my next move.

I emailed Sven with my details and called my mother to tell her about my surprise visit. She was happy that I would spend time in Switzerland but said that she and her husband were about to go on a holiday themselves. She offered me their home to stay in, which I gladly accepted. Relief washed over me, realising I would have space to myself as I dealt with the separation from Sven and figuring out my next step.

I sorely missed Jay and his warm, life-affirming presence. I longed to return to him but my savings were tied up with Sven's and I was unsure if my financial situation would allow me to go back to Antigua. While everything felt uncertain, I planned to return to Switzerland with an open heart and focus on a peaceful transition out of the relationship. After the separation I would have more clarity to reassess my future.

On the final day, I took a long walk along the top of the steep weathered cliffs, appreciating the views of the rich, undulating meadows and the infinite ocean beyond. My heart swelled in appreciation of my sailing voyage, for having journeyed safely, and all the experiences gained along the way. I took some deep breaths, grounding and mentally strengthening myself for the confrontation ahead. Everything was about to change.

Throughout our years together, Sven had been my anchor and our relationship had been my safe place. With him I had been at home, no matter where we were in the world. Adjusting to being alone and mastering self-responsibility would take time and effort. The change would leave me with no home, no job and little money in the bank. Bursts of anxiety bubbled up whenever the many uncertainties flashed in my mind.

On our last night, the crew went out to dinner together and, sitting with them at the table, a deep warmth and gratitude settled over me. I was glad I had met these three amazing people. Within a few weeks we had grown together as we learned to deal with each other's peculiarities and appreciate the positive qualities. We had shared a limited space, had cooked, laughed and occasionally quarrelled with one another. I counted myself lucky to have been with these people for my first crewing experience. We had a few drinks, jovially recounting our most fun and outrageous memories, and hours later tipsily stumbled back to the yacht. The following morning Sasha, Ken and I packed our bags. After a big round of goodbye hugs, we dispersed, leaving *Orion* and Aidan behind us.

11

A QUICK TURNAROUND

I arrived in my hometown quietly, feeling none of the joyous anticipation of previous visits. This time I felt alien and alone. Stepping off the train in Interlaken I took in the small two-platform station, the adjoining pharmacy and the big grocery store across the street. Horses harnessed into chariots stood as their drivers chatted and smoked while waiting for the arrival of the day's tourist trade. Eighteen months had passed since Sven and I had lived in Interlaken, before moving to New Zealand. Life here seemed unchanged. This consistency was in stark contrast with my travels and adventures, which had pressed change upon me.

Shouldering my bags, I walked to my mother's flat, found the key and let myself in. Closing the door behind me, I dropped my bags, sank onto the lounge and sighed deeply.

Silence. Space. I was grateful to be here and have access to this safe and secure home. Grabbing my handbag, I walked into the small town to buy a local SIM card for my phone. Sven had arrived about a week ago and had emailed me his local number, so there was nothing to stop me from contacting him as soon as possible.

'Sven speaking,' he said, sounding cheerful. My throat felt like it was closing.

'Sven? Hi. It's Regina. I am home,' I replied haltingly, unsure what reaction my call would prompt.

'Ah. Okay. Hi.' His voice had cooled a notch and he matter-of-factly continued, 'Where are you staying and when do you want to meet up?'

'I am staying at my mum's. They're on holiday, so I have the place to myself. Would tomorrow morning suit you? We can meet here, so we have time and privacy,' I nervously suggested.

'Yes, okay. That sounds fine. How about nine o'clock?' Sven responded formally.

We agreed on the time and ended the call. Suddenly I felt distant and separate from him. We were entering a new chapter and I desperately hoped that the love and respect we had nurtured and shared over the past thirteen years would transition into an enduring friendship. This became my mantra as I mentally prepared for our meeting.

The next day the doorbell rang precisely at 9am. When I opened the door, Sven stood there, jaw set square, unsmiling. Stepping aside I let him in and followed him into the living room where we both took a seat. Sven chose the single lounge chair and I perched myself on the edge of the sofa opposite him. For a moment we quietly looked at each other, each of us gauging the situation. When I could not stand the silence any longer, I cleared my throat and haltingly began to speak.

'It's really nice to see you, Sven. I am very sorry we're meeting under these circumstances,' I started. 'But there is never a good time for a breakup, is there?' My gingerly attempted joke was met with a glaring look.

'Well, no, actually. It shouldn't have been this way. Not after thirteen years together!' Sven's eyes were ablaze with anger and I recoiled in shock. This behaviour was in stark contrast with his usually gentle personality. 'We've shared so much! I don't understand how you can throw our relationship in the gutter like this, over another guy of all things. *And* you broke up with me via email.' His face was flushed. Shaking his head he threw a disapproving look my way. 'Honestly, Reggie. I really would have expected more loyalty and integrity from you.'

I was taken aback by the intensity of his anger and each of his words felt like a physical blow. I had experienced Sven's anger only a handful of times before. Today he was the most upset I had ever seen him. I understood his pain and anger and felt nauseous, knowing that I was the source of it. I had not envisaged our ending coming in this way and I, too, would have hoped for a more dignified and ethically appropriate separation. But this was life. Things are messy and change happens unexpectedly. I had not planned to fall in love, but I did. I silently mused that breakups were rarely convenient or well timed. For a moment I sat quietly, absorbing his message as I carefully formulated my reply.

'Look, Sven.' I focused intently on his eyes, allowing my heart to guide my words. 'I am truly sorry for causing you this pain. I can only imagine how much my email must have hurt you and I understand your anger about the breakup and the way I chose to communicate with you.' I could see his features soften somewhat and rushed on. 'Believe me, I didn't take this decision lightly. But for a moment, consider my perspective, please. I could have waited until we met here in Switzerland and dropped the bomb on you during your vacation. Or I could have called you on a distorted phone line from the Azores while you were in India and hoped for a conversation that wouldn't, in the heat of the moment, go pear-shaped. Instead, I took the option to carefully choose my words and send them to you in writing, giving you time to digest the painful message. I reasoned to myself that this way, at least, you would have time to absorb and consider the information. I didn't want to destroy your holiday and was aware that the news was going to hurt you, no matter how I told you. I chose email as the kindest and gentlest way to tell you. I am very, very sorry.'

I could feel tears welling up in my eyes. Taking a deep breath, I added, 'Sven, you must know that you are by far the most important person in my life, even now. And,' probing his eyes for clues, quietly concluded, 'I hope, from the bottom of my heart, that we can maintain our friendship. If not straightaway, then at some point in the future, at least.'

I lowered my eyes, feeling the full force of my guilt for being the source of Sven's confusion and pain. When I looked back up, I could see that he had registered some of my own struggle and hurt. He prompted me to tell him more about my Caribbean escapades. I gave him a brief recount of how the first sailing trip had started off and then fell apart, how I had met Jay and tried to resist the feelings I had toward him, and how I eventually gave in.

'Sven, you have to trust me that I never anticipated any of this happening and I most certainly did not go looking for it,' I pleaded.

'Yeah, well. But it has happened and now we are here. I am really sad and disappointed.' He still looked upset and I wondered how we would fare. I drew my last card.

'All right, Sven. I want to ask you a question then.' I looked at him and he raised one eyebrow quizzically. 'Do you remember when we took that walk on the beach in Australia, right before I headed off? You know, the day when we were discussing the possibility of either of us having an affair. Didn't we agree then that it would be okay, providing we didn't go chasing it?' I eyed Sven inquisitively, uncertain how this message would be received.

For a moment he looked stunned. He sat motionless, completely silent. I nervously hovered on the edge of my seat waiting for his reaction when, to my absolute surprise, Sven burst out laughing.

'Yes, *yes*, I do,' he agreed. 'Except back then I was convinced it was going to be *me* having the affair,' he said, and chuckled at the irony of his own statement.

We looked at each other and both started laughing at his confession. This marked the moment that transformed our energy and relationship. We became friends. Calmly we discussed our matters and reached an easy and mutually pleasing agreement. Pain lingered, but our strong bond ran deeper than this. This connection helped us to transcend any adversity and enabled us to look out for each other during this vulnerable time. I felt great respect and love for Sven.

'Sven, one last thing.'

He threw me a weary look.

'Our friends James and Susanne asked us over for dinner tomorrow. They don't yet know about our separation. Now, you can either go alone, or I can go alone, or we can go together. I'll leave it to you.'

Wanting to get everything out of the way I quickly added, 'I guess we will also have to consider how and what to say to our mutual friends. I hope we can find a way to relay the message honestly and clearly. I would like to reassure these people that we parted on good terms and that they can maintain a friendship with both of us. I was thinking maybe we could do a group email, a public statement of sorts. Please, consider this and let me know what you think.'

'Well, yes, I see what you mean and agree that it is probably best to send an email to avoid anyone feeling awkward. Regarding the dinner, I am happy to go with you to have dinner with our friends. We may as well step into our new future right away.'

I was at a loss for words, overcome by Sven's graciousness, generosity and presence. Just like that we transitioned from partners to friends. I looked into his gorgeous blue eyes and felt profoundly blessed for the many good years we had shared and for the friendship that would continue. This was true love indeed.

The next two weeks were busy, and I was bursting with ideas. To open the door to more potential sailing journeys, I applied for a special visa for the USA, which would allow entry to that country by vessel and give me the opportunity to work on a foreign flagged boat while in American territory. Haggling with the embassy over the phone, I managed to get a last-minute appointment with the ambassador. After a brief review he approved the valuable travel permit. I started searching the internet with a focus on Antiguan job websites, mainly within the tourism and hospitality sector. Maybe I could set myself up in Antigua for a while and see where that would lead. I felt like things were starting to fall into place.

I called Jay. He continued to dominate my thoughts and I missed him badly. I longed for his easy-going company, his infectious smile and for his strong arms to wrap around me. Many times a day I would flick through photos of our time together, recalling our magical moments and yearning to be close to him. I was hanging out to hear his voice and wanted to reassure myself about my budding plans.

'Regina. You called me! How are you?' Jay spoke excitedly. He sounded soulful as he continued, 'I miss you, babes.'

'Hey, Jay! It's so good to hear your voice.' I gave him a quick rundown of my past few days.

'Babes, when are you coming back to me?' The sexy combination of his velvety voice and the charming Antiguan accent made me weak at the knees. I could have listened to him all day long.

'I think I will come back soon. I am organising myself here and figuring out how I can manage. I won't have a lot of money, so I will need to work in Antigua and hope all goes well.'

Excitement radiated through Jay's voice as he reassured me that I would find work, and since I could move in with him, he reasoned, I would not have the expense of rent. After this conversation I felt exuberant and hopeful. Somehow, I would make this happen. Surely, a business would be willing to employ a hardworking, multilingual yoga teacher/dive instructor/admin person with a go-getter attitude.

My mother and my stepfather returned from their holiday just as I was preparing to depart. I could see the disappointment and hurt in my mother's eyes but could not resist my urge to move on. I had always admired my mother for her strength and independence and respected her unwavering belief in, and fearless defence of, social egalitarianism. My parents separated when I was nine years old, at a time when divorce was still frowned upon. After the failure of her marriage with my father, my mother took on the challenging role of a single mum. My friends described her as a fun, warm and caring person and I could see her display these qualities with them. However, I often felt exposed to her harsh comments, judgements and opinions. I don't think my mum was aware of how her criticism affected me.

Close to my final exam for my apprenticeship I had returned home from an outing and she'd looked at me with disapproval for taking time out for myself and declared, 'You'll fail anyway.' Another time, in my late teens, when I was socialising mainly with platonic male friends, she said I acted like a whore. I did not know if she meant her words, or if she envied my freedom and ability to have friendships. Whatever the reason, her comments stung. My parents' separation and subsequent divorce, and the interpersonal challenges between my mum and me, had a lasting impact.

Despite a predominantly happy childhood, I often felt sad, overwhelmed, lost and angry, and channelled my emotions into rebellious teen years. Driven by a fear of being further hurt or rejected, I became hesitant and emotionally withdrew from my mother. I knew the fractured connection caused us both pain, and yet we seemed unable to connect and resolve our disharmony.

My father was largely absent from most of my childhood. Early in my parents' marriage, he was absorbed in his work and studies. After the separation he rarely initiated contact and I eventually concluded that he was not all that interested in me. As a child I occasionally wondered if he would have loved me more, or spent more time with me, if I were a boy. I loved being with him and patiently listened to him talking about his passion: renewable energy. But mostly I was home with my mum, pining for the chance to spend some time with him.

My parents didn't separate on friendly terms and communication was minimal for a while. Regular visits to my father were forgotten among the chaos and not actively pursued by either parent. Mum took on a low-paying job at the hospital and suddenly I was left to my own devices. At ten years old I began to take long walks by myself, with a book tucked in a pouch. I learned to prepare a simple meal and as an only child, I often played alone. My mother and I lived in a unit block in modest circumstances. Without immediate family on my mother's side living nearby, my childhood revolved around my mum. She was my family, the focal point of my universe. But the older I got, the more we clashed, and I increasingly resisted yielding to her guidance or opinions. This led to an estrangement and I found it easier to have less contact and more distance between us.

Having just returned from Antigua and settled the separation with Sven, I was feeling deeply vulnerable. I was afraid of my mother judging me for my recent choices and decisions. Hesitantly I told her about my affair with Jay in Antigua and the subsequent separation from Sven. She was shocked and sad, but much to my surprise, she supported my decision to return to Antigua. I was relieved, but too raw to fully reveal my emotions. With minimal savings to support my plans, I reasoned that if I wanted to live in the Caribbean, I'd best start as soon as possible. I booked a flight a few days later and repacked my bags.

A Quick Turnaround

I met with Sven one more time and explained my plans. Disconcerted with my choice, he expressed hope that instead I would return to Australia and perhaps set up my own yoga studio. I understood it was painful for him to know that I was returning to the man who had effectively ended our relationship. Blaming the new man was easier than acknowledging that neither Sven nor I had found the courage or reason to move on earlier. However, our separation had long been in the making and Jay was merely the final breaking point.

Over a coffee, Sven said that once he was back in his job, he would decide whether to remain in Australia or move back to Switzerland. From the bottom of my heart, I wished him a safe return to Australia and a happy and fulfilled future. We hugged and parted ways. I was glad that we had been able to end our relationship in our hometown where we had lived for most of our lives. We had begun to create our store of memories here and it had always been the area where Sven felt the most grounded and connected with his roots. His eyes were sad, but I could see that he too was adjusting to this transition. Despite him being strong and stable, I was grateful that he would stay a little longer here, surrounded by close friends and family, before returning to Australia.

As quietly as I arrived, I departed. The train carried me past lakes and mountains and then further north towards Frankfurt. Throughout the almost six-hour journey, I sat by a window, barely glancing at the landscape sweeping by. Finally, the guilt, sadness and confusion I had felt over the past few weeks began sliding off my shoulders. With each kilometre the train covered I could breathe a little easier. I felt free, content with only a passport, a bank card and a backpack stuffed with my personal belongings.

Without keys to any home and no employment to go to, it was now solely up to me to forge my path.

Basking in the lightness of my new freedom, my gut unexpectedly clenched. A moment later, the magnitude of my current paradox washed over me. The consequence of absolute personal autonomy meant I had to assume full responsibility for my life. Indeed, I was free, but I was also alone and had only myself to hold accountable and to rely upon. Despite lingering anxiety about my immediate future, I was determined not to compromise my dreams. I was aware that I was at a significant crossroad in my life and hoped I had chosen the right path. I had always been spontaneous and gut-driven, but I had never ventured so far from my comfort zone. No matter what, I vowed to trust my choices and stay true to myself. Beyond the slight hesitation, a deep inner faith was relentlessly pushing me forward.

Before boarding the plane in Frankfurt, I called Jay and let him know I would soon arrive in Antigua. He sounded jubilant and promised to meet me at the airport. The plane took off, and for a moment I admired the lush fields and villages as they slipped away from my view. Then, exhausted from the weeks of emotional turmoil, I fell into a deep sleep.

12

NEW BEGINNINGS

I awoke as the plane began its descent into Antigua. Before my previous entry into this country, Henry had repeatedly cautioned me about the immigration officials at the airport, especially the formidable female officers who sat behind small wooden desks as though on thrones, their attitude resolute and unyielding. I walked into the arrival hall feeling anxious, even though my first experience had been positive.

Most countries grant entry automatically for the maximum visa-free period upon arrival, whereas the officers in Antigua requested proof of both residence and a return ticket and would stamp the passport with the precise number of days of the intended visit. Concerned I would be questioned about my first visit and sudden return, I chose to enter the country this time using my Swiss passport, hoping to avoid this issue. I had entered the country for my preceding stay on my Australian passport. Fortunately, Antiguan immigration had not yet transitioned to a digital procedure, so I hoped this would seem to be my first visit. Quietly revelling in my slight advantage, I filled out the form like any other holidaymaker on this flight and was unceremoniously stamped in for three weeks.

I collected my bags and nervously walked out of the terminal to the curb. Looking around, I scanned the crowd for Jay. There he was! Smiling widely, he rushed towards me. I dropped my bags and flew into his arms. Taking shelter in his embrace and inhaling his musky scent, I knew I had come home – to my new man, in a new country.

We took the bus to All Saints, bodies tightly pressed against each other despite the summer heat. Hands intertwined, I leaned my head against Jay's shoulders and absorbed that I was back in Antigua. I was marvelling at the animated chatter and the loud music blaring from the worn speakers. My body was tingling from connecting with Jay during the bumpy ride.

He carried my bag on his shoulders as we walked through the village hand in hand. Turning into his street, my new home came into view. The tiny yellow house sat on a corner block. Banana trees were growing on one side and the tiny verandah, barely wide enough to fit two chairs, faced the bumpy gravel road. A small kitchen was annexed to the other side of the house. Crooked windowpanes allowed the breeze to flow through cracks in the small dwelling. Jay's brother's children came running up as we walked through the gate, happily calling out my name.

We quickly settled into a routine. Jay usually got up at sunrise and boiled a pot of water, from which he prepared a sweet tea with herbs picked from his yard. He walked to work early while eating a piece of fruit and sipping the steaming liquid from an

New Beginnings

insulated cup. During the day, I focused on finding a job. I still had no laptop and was constantly looking for internet cafes with computers so I could trawl job sites, checking resort websites, tour companies, dive businesses, spas offering yoga, and anything else I could think of. I submitted applications hoping my mixed skillset would help get me a job.

For a week nothing much happened and I was conscious of precious days ticking by. I was receiving polite emails of rejection but no inquiries. To distract myself from the lack of progress I took the bus to English Harbour and was astounded by the emptiness. The marinas looked abandoned, with only a single boat here or there tied to a finger dock. Falmouth Harbour was equally quiet. A handful of moored vessels were sparsely spread across the wide bay, making it seem eerie and lonesome. The water, however, which had been murky and uninviting during the sailing season, was now crystal clear. A lovely surprise.

The absence of boats meant there was no yachting community to speak of and the marine related shops were either closed or running on skeleton staff. Only the shipyard appeared moderately busy, carrying out maintenance tasks on hauled-out vessels. Feeling dejected, I trudged through the empty streets and reflected on my situation. Sven had transferred a modest amount of money to me, as part of our mutually agreed settlement. These funds were intended to help me transition into my new life but would not sustain me for long. I needed to start earning money.

Not wanting to trigger my lingering anxiety I walked purposefully to the historic area of Nelsons Dockyard, which dated from colonial times. I treated myself to a proper coffee, a rarity since returning to Antigua. Sitting and savouring the pricey beverage, my eyes roamed over the worn, old stone buildings and the small cobblestoned square. The frangipani trees were in full bloom, their crisp blossoms adding colour, their sweet fragrance wafting past me. Despite the peaceful setting and the deliciously frothy cappuccino, a heaviness arose in my chest.

The lack of a laptop was complicating my job search. I had to pay for the use of a computer and internet every day, and it was difficult to maintain communication with anyone without my own device. I had a mobile phone with a local SIM card, but this was at a time when phones were primarily designed to make calls and not much else. To top it off, overseas phone calls were excruciatingly expensive.

I was lonely, isolated and overwhelmed with my choices. Briefly wallowing in self-pity, I suddenly recalled a similar situation and a chuckle bubbled within me. I had felt this same way when Sven and I had arrived in Australia on our permanent residency visa. Sven had considered our future well before we arrived, but I had focused on making plans to get there and not on the reality of what I would do in our new country. Only once we had arrived had the magnitude of our decision dawned on me, and I had been temporarily overcome until I adjusted to the change.

Sitting in the Caribbean with my treasured coffee, I realised there was an advantage in my spontaneous approach. My drive and curiosity propelled me and allowed me to manifest my dreams and adventures. I began to understand that this impulsive attitude provoked necessary moments of delayed surprise and realisation. I would need to create space to reflect, consider and absorb the changes before I could move on. Mulling over this personality trait, I mused that different people made different choices and created different journeys in life. And if this was mine, so be it. Smiling again, I paid for the coffee and returned home.

New Beginnings

Several days later I received a phone call from one of the island's big resorts with an invitation to attend an interview for a job as a yoga teacher at their spa. Many hours before the scheduled appointment I left All Saints on public transport, to ensure that I reached the resort on time. With confidence I walked up to the reception. An immaculately dressed man greeted me, extending his hand, and introduced himself as the chief executive officer of the successful franchise. I followed him into his office where he lounged back in a big leather chair and pointed to a seat on the other side of the large, solid timber desk.

'So, Regina. You are a certified yoga teacher?' he said once we were both seated. He asked about my training and teaching experience, and nodded in response to my replies.

'Well,' he said, lowering his voice and ogling me. 'You must be very flexible then?'

His brazen attitude made me uncomfortable and I immediately lost interest in the position. I was looking for a job, not an affair with the manager. On the bus ride home, my mood alternated between laughter about the strange interview and disappointment about its unsuccessful outcome.

Luck was on my side when another promising reply came in soon after. A local company offering day sailing tours, dinghy hire and instruction had a position for a customer representative/administration assistant. The job description was diverse with plenty of potential and I was keen to learn more.

The following day I met George, the owner of the business. Over cups of coffee, we discussed my qualifications and the job description. George was of Austrian descent and had moved to Antigua a few years earlier. He was short and compact in stature, and his exceptionally pale complexion was out of place in this tropical environment. He wore neat casual clothes and his lightly curled brown hair was trimmed short at the back. In contrast to his ordinary appearance, he turned out to be a captivating and charismatic speaker. I quickly became excited about the position.

George was running his sailing excursions and dinghy rental business out of two separate resorts. He planned to expand his company and needed an all-rounder to support him with the day-to-day running of the business. Most of the job would comprise administration-based tasks as his assistant, but I would also be welcoming and briefing new resort guests about the various services, creating sales, and stepping in when and where required. I loved the sound of the job's diversity and we concluded that I was the perfect fit for this position. The pay was minimal but enough to sustain myself in Antigua and, if I were careful with my spending, I could save a little each month. George promised to secure a work permit for me, which meant I could stay on the island. As we were discussing the finer details of my employment my heart was beating out of my chest. I had a job! I could stay!

'The only remaining problem we have is your lack of transport,' George said, just as I thought we had finished our negotiations.

'Well, I can take public transport to both the northern and southern resorts, that shouldn't be a problem. I will leave early and be on time.'

'No, that won't work,' George said. 'I want you to be flexible and mobile, so you can work from wherever and whenever I need you to. You need transport,' he said with finality.

As quickly as I had got excited, my hopes plummeted. Without the means to buy a car I saw my opportunity slip away.

'Can you ride a motorbike?' I nodded and felt a surge of hope.

I explained that I did hold an unrestricted licence and had owned two motorbikes in Switzerland. His face lit up.

'I saw these cheap bikes in a shop in town the other day. Let me find out the price for one of them and I will get back to you.' My concern must have been clear on my face, as he quickly reassured me. 'We will make this work, don't worry.'

We shook hands, then we both left the little coffee shop. I was excited and called Jay with the promising news. The prospect of spending my precious savings on transport was daunting but in the absence of another offer I hoped George's solution would be feasible.

My phone rang soon after our meeting. 'Regina, I have found a bike for you. It is a good deal and I think we should go ahead with it. Now, here's what I am proposing.'

George laid out a plan whereby his company would buy the bike, which was a cheap Chinese import, like a four-stroke Honda. He mentioned in passing that I would have to pay him US $1,500 as a deposit for the machine. This statement was quickly followed by the promise that I would get the amount refunded should I leave the job after a certain time, or that I would own the bike outright after prolonged employment. Neither of the timeframes was specified and, as I mulled over his comments, he continued talking. I was struggling to follow the complicated explanation. When I inquired about the actual purchase price of the bike, George skilfully circumvented my query in a vague manner.

I was left with the strong impression that I had to agree to this deal, or I would not have a job. The US $1,500 was a significant chunk out of my meagre savings and I was concerned about the haziness of this agreement. However, I also needed a job.

'All right,' I replied, suppressing my doubt. 'I can do that. How do we proceed from here?'

'Wonderful!' George happily continued, 'Can you meet me at the same place tomorrow at 10am with the cash? I will purchase the bike for you now and have them prepare it for you. Antigua Carnival starts this weekend and lasts for the next ten days, so I suggest you start work the Monday after the festival?'

Ignoring my underlying doubts, I felt jubilant. Securing employment took me a big step closer to my goal. I was living in the Caribbean with Jay, had a new job, and now was also the proud almost-owner of a motorbike. To top it off, I could enjoy the upcoming festivities without any worries. Life was looking bright.

To celebrate, I wanted to do something special for Jay and myself. Someone had mentioned an upmarket beach resort that offered a locals' breakfast buffet special. I could not think of a better way to mark the occasion than enjoying a delectable meal in a luxurious setting with my lover. Off we went on the new bike. My new mode of transport was a 250cc dirt bike with a four-stroke engine and an indecipherable brand name printed in Chinese characters on the bright blue fuel tank. Straddling the small machine, the two of us were a sight to behold. Perched in the front, I was the petite white woman tightly clutching the handlebars and trying to steady the bike, while Jay was the tall, dark man towering at the back. All Saints, where we resided, was located almost at the centre of Antigua and on this small island we could reach nearly any destination within a 20 to 30-minute ride. The motorbike opened new horizons for us, and I was looking forward to exploring in the weeks and months to come.

We parked outside the resort and entered the light, spacious lobby decorated with comfortable lounges and tropical plants. Rays of sun were filtering through large windows, framed by enormous marble pillars. Jay looked at me in awe and my heart jumped with joy. A waiter greeted us with a friendly smile and guided us to a small table by the window, overlooking the beach. We ordered coffees and the waiter disappeared. Jay looked at me, bewildered.

'Regina, tell me. How does this work here?' he quietly uttered under his breath and for the first time he did not seem his usual confident self.

'Okay. Can you see the buffet over there?' I discreetly pointed at the breakfast bar and explained, 'We walk over there and you can help yourself to anything you like. You can also go to the chef on the other side of the buffet and order a cooked breakfast from him. You can go back and get more, as often as you like.'

We walked towards the buffet and Jay made a beeline for the chef. They quickly struck up a conversation in the local dialect and Jay ordered an omelette with all the trimmings. I helped myself to a croissant and fresh fruit and yoghurt and we sat at the table. Jay looked at his plate and the cutlery that was laid out in front of him, not touching anything.

'Jay, have you used knife and fork before?' I gently asked, suddenly aware that we were always eating our meals out of natural calabash bowls and mainly used a spoon.

'No,' he said quietly, shoulders sagging. My heart went out to him.

'Jay. It is okay. You will learn quickly. See.' I smiled and explained how to use the cutlery.

He looked at me appreciatively. At first, he clumsily cut off the first bites, but quickly gained confidence as he improved this new skill. He smiled and my heart fluttered happily.

The waiters doted on us. I loved seeing Jay enjoying the food, the stunning environment and adored seeing him receiving top-class service. It brought to light to how privileged I was. I reflected on the many skills I had effortlessly acquired, the countless experiences I had been exposed to over time, and about which I had become blasé. I was deeply thankful to be with Jay who highlighted the preciousness of those simple moments.

The Carnival marked a first for me and I was eager for the festivities to begin. Jay had been talking about the upcoming parade and party events nonstop. He couldn't wait to show me this part of his culture. During the days before Carnival, we often heard people practising their instruments in various parts of All Saints, or saw people hurrying around, clutching parts of their elaborate and colourful costumes. One evening, while sitting on our little verandah, I heard a groovy drum beat in the distance. As the rhythmic clanging and banging approached, the sound grew in intensity and I caught myself tapping my feet to the beat. I was astounded to see a small group of teenage boys passing in front of our house, pounding together rusty car rims, steel tools, pan lids and other random bits and pieces, to create a captivating beat. An iron band, Jay explained. I was excited by its simplicity.

New Beginnings

Carnival was an unexpected feast for the senses. To kick it off, a day or two before the official start, Jay took me to a dusk-to-dawn concert. A single band was performing nonstop for the entire night. The concert took place in a dusty fenced-off yard with a small, basic stage tucked in one corner. The atmosphere was electric, and the energy of the band and the crowd was catching.

At some point during the concert, I noticed Jay animatedly talking with another guy. Not paying much attention I continued dancing, but when I looked at them again, their conversation and exaggerated hand gestures appeared to have escalated into a heated debate. Quietly I moved next to Jay. From the fragments I could pick out of the rapid conversation in the local dialect, I understood they were disagreeing about two rival local bands. Both men seemed adamant in their opinions about their favoured musicians. Their voices grew louder, and their hands were gesticulating and accentuating their words. First gently, but with increasing insistence, I pulled on Jay's shirt to diffuse the situation. Eventually, he reluctantly followed me. When we stood by ourselves, he asked why I'd pulled him away. When I said I was afraid that the other man might become violent, Jay started to laugh and planted a kiss on my forehead.

'I am not violent, babes, you know that. We were just having a chat about the two bands!' Of course, he was correct. I knew that he was not a violent person and for me this was a reminder that I was living in a different culture. What would have been labelled an impassioned argument at home was a simple discussion here. All was well, I just needed to chill out and go with the flow.

I loved the colourful parade at the start of Carnival. People were marching in big groups, everyone in each group was dressed in matching attire and make up. The handmade costumes featured vibrant colours, exotic patterns, feathered headdresses and sequined body-hugging pieces. Large floats competed by blasting out the current party anthems at ear-splitting level. Some floats carried full bands performing as they drove along.

My next favourite was the steel pan panorama. On a perfect, balmy summer night, we sat in a stadium facing a massive stage. The space quickly filled, as one immense steel band performed their signature tunes, followed by another. Some of the major contending groups took one hundred musicians to the stage. Their pieces were beautifully arranged, and I marvelled at the synchronicity among such a large group. I became almost entranced watching individual players pounding their pans at breakneck speed, each of them contributing to the magical creation.

There were a few music competitions, all entertaining. Performers of the Soca Monarch showcased their musicality and lyrical skill. The Party Monarch brought the younger generation to the stage and bands competed with catchy tunes, sexy costumes and sultry moves. I enjoyed listening to the different music styles, observing the crowd or immersing myself in the hustle and bustle of the dance floor with Jay. The dancing reached a new level during these celebrations. Occasionally my jaw dropped watching the provocative and raunchy playfulness between two dancers. The moves were breathtakingly seductive as couples engaged, their bodies glistening from the heat. I adored the free and uninhibited way Antiguan people moved and how they encouraged each other to showcase special movements or dance skills. It was sultry and stimulating but never sleazy. I had the impression that dancing happened by unspoken mutual consent and was viewed as a skill, rather than a courting or mating ritual.

New Beginnings

The carnival period was a relaxing time. Jay was on holiday, so we spent leisurely mornings at home sleeping in. We made love, snuggled, talked quietly, and got to know each other more. Jay took me to the picture-perfect beach of Long Bay. In the warm, turquoise water we kissed, flirted and floated around for hours. Each evening we ventured out, refreshed and ready for another fun and frivolous carnival experience. Before the shows we usually bought a variety of food from the many stalls outside the venues. Jay introduced me to the local *Ital* cuisine, explaining it was the local Rastafarian, vegetarian food. Their delicious legume stews, lasagnes and vegetable dishes were always fresh and flavoursome and quickly became my local favourite.

These early days in Antigua were fun. Without the worry of job hunting, Jay and I were inseparable, and I revelled in the joy of our blossoming love.

Once the Antigua Carnival came to an end, Jay returned to work and I settled into my new routine. Nervously I showed up on the first day at my new workplace. To give me an overview of the company, George took me to the sailing operations he was running at two resorts on either side of Antigua. As we drove along in the van, he mentioned his plans to expand his business to other Caribbean islands. He expected me to spend most of my workdays at his home office. It would become the hub for the business administration and for researching and brainstorming future projects. On days when I was rostered at one of the resorts, I was to report there in the morning, host the 'meet and greet' presentations, take bookings, allocate sailing instructors, and help with any logistics as needed. George mentioned that he had advertised more instructor positions for the dinghies, as two of his staff had resigned, and entrusted me with the preselection of the potential candidates.

George and I were facing each other across a large desk in his office when I gingerly brought up the subject of my visa. My tourist visa was about to expire and I was keen to start the process for my work permit.

'Just go and renew your tourist visa,' he said gruffly. 'We're too busy now and we can sort out the work permit later.'

The Immigration Department was a grim looking place. Located in the centre of town, it was housed in a worn-out building, behind a façade of bare concrete and dusty windows. As I didn't have a work permit, Jay had to come with me and act as my sponsor so I could qualify for a visa extension. When we arrived at the government department, the security guard at the entrance immediately turned us away. He pointed out a faded sign taped to the department's front door. No singlets allowed, nor any revealing tops. Shorts, skirts and dresses had to be at least knee length. I was wearing my best dress. While not a miniskirt, it did not comply with the over-the-knee policy. Jay tried to convince the doorman to let us in, but without success.

Disheartened we turned away, knowing we had missed the best time of the day to avoid the usually long and arduous queue. Rather than take the bus back to All Saints I asked Jay to take me to a retail store. I found a pair of jeans and a cheap, rather dull blouse. Fully compliant with the dress code we returned to the Immigration Department and were sent to the back of the line. We patiently queued for the next hour in a waiting room that was lit with flickering fluorescent tubes and sparsely furnished with grubby, old plastic chairs. The cramped cubicles for the immigration officers were uninviting and bleak and I imagined that it would be tiresome to work in this dreary environment. No one was smiling and the line moved slowly. The wait was nerve-racking, and I kept hoping it would all go smoothly.

When my turn came at the counter, I was asked to produce my passport and a return ticket that I had rebooked beforehand. Jay explained to the serious-looking officer that he would act as my sponsor so that I could extend my holiday. The officer eyed me sternly but to my surprise, she stamped a page in my passport and carefully noted the extension of my rescheduled flight. I was awash with relief. I didn't want to go through this procedure again and vowed to get onto George and start the application process for the work permit.

To celebrate the renewal of my visa, Jay and I went for a leisurely stroll along the cruise liner terminal, looking at the tourists and the large ships in the harbour as we each enjoyed an ice cream. This tourist visa extension afforded us the breathing space to get my working visa sorted. My life was on track.

13

EXPOSING TRUTH

I loved the independence and freedom of having my own motorbike. Before, we'd needed to beg friends for a ride to visit some of the more inaccessible places, but now Jay and I could hop on our two-wheeler to explore secluded beaches and remote locations. We bumped along pothole-riddled dirt tracks and climbed steep hills for unexpected vistas. We made for an amusing sight on the bike, but I didn't care about turning heads or getting surprised looks. I loved the feeling of Jay's body pressing against mine as we rode along, the fragrant hot breeze flowing over my arms and the sun peeking through my visor. I laughed and sang into my helmet, relishing in the joy and freedom of these moments.

    The weather was hot and the air was dense with humidity. A refreshing dip in the ocean was a welcome treat. On weekends, throngs of local people flocked to the beaches and large and exuberant gatherings took place in the sparse shade of the trees. The men set up the music and handed out cold beverages, while the women unpacked lavish picnics or barbecued on site. By now I was immersed in Jay's life and his social circle, and far removed from my previous life. I was enjoying the new sights, local foods and meeting Jay's friends and family.

One particularly hot day we went swimming at Pigeon Beach. It was a Sunday and the waterfront was abuzz with people and activity. The local beach bar cranked up their sound system and Caribbean party tunes drifted through the air. All around, people were joking and laughing, drinking, eating, or taking a refreshing dip in the water.

Arriving at the beach, we found a little empty hut, deposited our belongings and towels on a rustic bench, and went for a swim. When we returned, I rummaged through my bag.

'Do you remember where I put my sunglasses?' I asked Jay, frowning as I tried to remember where I had placed them, before heading into the water.

'No. Are they not here?' he asked, a concerned look on his face.

'No,' I replied, confused. 'I thought I put them on my towel.'

In our absence, another group had occupied the other half of the hut. Jay knew some of them and asked a friend if they had seen my sunglasses. Everyone shook their heads. No luck. Suddenly a young woman pointed a finger at a group of six young Antiguan boys riding their BMX-bikes around the area. Among them was a young local white boy. To my surprise the woman pointed her finger at him.

'It must have been the white boy!' the lady exclaimed, sounding sure.

I was perplexed. While the accused boy may have taken my sunglasses, I harboured doubts. The group of kids had been riding in the parking lot together for a while and they seemed preoccupied with practising and showing off their tricks.

What struck me as odd was that the lady had singled out the white boy. It made me wonder whether human conditioning caused people to default to accusing the 'other' – the outsider. Our neighbours called the boy over and he was sternly interrogated. Despite the intimidation of being questioned by several adults simultaneously, he steadfastly denied that he took my sunglasses. I asked the group to let him and his friends go. Jay was livid about my loss. He kept muttering to himself that such behaviour gave his people a bad name.

He could not let the incident go and a few days later he came home from work, saying that he had paid one of the men from the other group a visit. The guy confessed that, actually, my shades had been nicked by one of the women in their party. Go figure, I mused. I did not get my sunnies back but I learned a valuable lesson. Two actually. One, never to judge on stereotypes and two, to take greater care of my belongings.

At work I was rapidly learning that not all was turning out as promised. George was a driven man and had a clear vision of his goals. He had plenty of ideas but lacked focus during the execution phase of a project. To my annoyance he got into the habit of turning up late in the morning. Not only that, but when he did arrive, instead of allowing me to start on my own work, he wanted to sit and brainstorm for hours on end. George's wife did the payroll and accounting but was not overly interested in getting more involved in the business.

I got the impression that George was enjoying my company and the opportunity to exchange ideas with someone.

Consequently, he often asked me to join him as he ran small errands. Returning to the office by late afternoon, he would suddenly be filled with a sense of urgency and expect me to tackle my outstanding tasks. He ignored our agreed working hours and his arrogance frustrated me immensely. My days became longer and doubts began to surface. Yet, I was dependent on the employment, especially as I had put a chunk of my savings into the motorbike.

George was unquestioningly charismatic, a great conversationalist and a visionary. He could sell ice to an Eskimo. But I came to realise that I too had been lured by his convincing words and promises. I saw no physical evidence to back his plans. I regularly raised the topic of my work permit, as I was growing increasingly concerned about working illegally for a prolonged period. I was living in a tiny community and as the only white person in residence, I stood out. Whenever I raised the issue, George swept it aside. Alarm bells began ringing but rather than take much notice of them, I reasoned that it was best to work hard, make myself indispensable, and believe that everything would work out.

A new kind of everyday routine took shape in our beloved yellow shack in All Saints. I loved waking up and snuggling up to my man at sunrise. Now that I went to work as well, I got into the habit of preparing a simple porridge or muesli with instant milk and fresh fruit in our calabash bowls, while Jay boiled water and gathered fresh herbs for a sweet tea. Sitting on the little deck we ate breakfast in companionable silence, watching the village stir. Jay went to work before me, and I usually watched him saunter up the road before leaving home myself. In the evenings he was home early and would often cook a simple stew. We would sit on the verandah, recounting our day. After dinner we often went for a walk and explored the outer reaches of All Saints and the pastures beyond. Hand in hand, we strolled along, taking in the surrounding nature while contemplating our future. We sometimes lingered under an enormous mango tree and picked the fruit. Without electricity, we sat by the flickering light of an oil lantern, drinking a last cup of tea and enjoying the cooling night air. Bedtime usually came early.

By now even the near-naked trek across the yard for the nightly bucket shower had turned into a routine event. I was no longer bothered by the smelly pit toilet and did not miss electricity anymore. A few things had dramatically improved with the arrival of the motorbike. Previously I had done the shopping in town and hauled the heavy bags onto the bus, then from the bus stop to our house. Now I rode to the store, loaded my bike with the groceries and rode home. The most significant improvement, however, was our laundry. When I had first arrived, I'd had to wash our clothes by hand. Jay, I quickly learned, liked to change his clothes frequently. Sitting on the verandah, I would be hunched over a large water filled tub with an enormous pile of dirty clothing next to it. They all needed to be soaked, washed, kneaded, pounded, rinsed and drained. My knuckles often ended up raw and my fingers would be stiff and sore from resolutely rubbing the fabric to get it clean. When the bike became a part of our life, I rode to the nearby laundromat. For the first time I felt immense gratitude and joy while watching a washing machine do its job.

I was amazed to learn how intensely the Antiguan population worked. The Caribbean region is often portrayed as one of the most relaxed and easy-going parts of the world. Beneath the surface, however, were the many demands of the local lifestyle. The cost of living was expensive as most products had to be imported from overseas. A regular working week in Antigua was six days, leaving most people with only Sundays at their leisure. These days were mostly taken up with church visits, family gatherings, laundry and other unfinished chores. There was little time for relaxing.

One Sunday, Jay asked if I would like to meet his sister. I was curious about his favourite sibling, so we decided to surprise her. Arriving a short while later at her bustling family home, and feeling shy, I was humbled by how warmly everyone welcomed me. I could not help but wonder how my folks would react if I turned up unannounced with my beloved dark-skinned man.

Jay's sister was a voluptuous woman with a warm and loving personality. Her house was filled with youngsters, all of them excitedly bouncing around and curiously checking me out. One girl took a particular shine to me. She remained close to my side and kept touching my fine hair. After a while I asked her if she would like to brush it. Her face lit up and she quickly gathered some brushes and hair ties. Totally absorbed with my unusually thin long hair, she braided and combed, trying to style it in the local fashion. Eventually she gave up, and instead pulled it all back into a simple ponytail, then generously plastered it with a wax-like paste until every last hair stuck firmly against my skull. It took days to fully wash out.

Living with Jay and settling into his village posed some challenges. One that I had not anticipated was the steady stream of people who would turn up at our front door. I could not keep track of Jay's many cousins, aunties and uncles. Most of them came to borrow something. Sometimes it was money, but mostly they came for goods that I had brought home one or two days earlier. Jay, trusting and generous, kept handing out money for manicures here, a few notes to tide over to the next pay packet there, or his last cash to top up someone's SIM card. He readily donated lamp oil and groceries. Observing this behaviour for a while, I began to wonder how to address it. I was forever restocking our rapidly dwindling supplies. I had offered to pay for all household goods when I moved in, but now the cost was considerably more than I had budgeted for.

'Jay, where is the lamp oil I bought yesterday?' I was looking for the bottle, wanting to fill up our lamp before nightfall.

'My auntie came earlier, and needed some,' he replied calmly.

I took a deep breath, releasing my frustration. This was the third bottle I had bought in a week. I sat down beside Jay who was relaxing on the only piece of furniture in the little front room – a worn, single bed we had recently acquired.

'Jay, we need to talk about this. I don't think we can keep giving our things away. I am working hard for my money and you work hard, too.' I smiled at him and he listened patiently with his arms crossed behind his head. 'I have no problem helping your family out if they need food that they can't afford themselves. But aside from that we have to stop giving money and other things to them.'

'Yes, Regina, I understand. I don't want to give my money away, but it's hard to say no,' he said, looking uncomfortable.

We discussed the situation until we found a solution that we were both happy with. For the next weeks we politely kept declining the requests and to my relief, over time those uncomfortable visits became less frequent.

Around this time, I started to suspect that Jay had difficulty with reading and writing. I had slowly become suspicious, as he would not turn up at places at an agreed time, did not count his change when making a purchase, and replied in an uncharacteristically vague manner when I pointed out anything in writing. He was also working a lot of overtime. He complained about not getting paid more at the end of the week but, looking at his pay slip, I could tell he was not able to decipher the content.

Over the course of several conversations, Jay slowly started to tell me more about his past. He'd had an accident in his childhood, which had possibly resulted in a mild brain injury, and he did not return to school after the incident. He told the story in a fragmented way, but suddenly everything made sense to me. I was relieved to have an explanation for the strange little situations that I had wondered about.

Other than gaining insight about Jay's schooling, I did not need to know his full story. The fact remained that he was illiterate and I wanted to help him. Initially I was not concerned with his lack of education. It was his kind personality and his open heart that I was attracted to. Those were the qualities that mattered most. But I wondered if he was interested in catching up with his education. When I asked if he would like to learn to read and write, Jay nodded enthusiastically.

I promptly went into town on a new mission. Unfortunately, I could not source any literacy classes for adults, which I would have happily funded, so instead I purchased basic education supplies. When we went through the material later that night, I found that Jay could not tell the time, had no concept of numbers or basic calculations, and did not recognise any letters. Confronted with his immense educational limitations, I realised the learning task would be long and challenging for us both. We needed to start from the very beginning. We decided to start immediately by setting aside a little time each day for lessons.

Our attempt at home-schooling was successful for a week at the most. At first, I was frustrated and sad when Jay started to lose interest. I poked and prodded, hoping to achieve great things for him and us. After a while I realised that I needed to let go. I came to understand that Jay was intrinsically content with his life. He had managed to survive and sustain himself well without assistance from me or anyone else. Jay was happy within himself and if he chose not to learn then I had to accept, and be at peace with, his decision.

∿∿

Just as I came to terms with Jay's illiteracy, another upheaval occurred. One evening we were discussing events from our past. Jay was recalling his memories and began connecting events with certain years. But as I considered the information, I realised that the timelines did not add up. Having just learned about his lack of schooling, I began to question his stories and challenged some of his statements.

'Jay, you said you are twenty-eight years old. Are you sure about that?' I watched his face with interest, trying to gauge if he was indeed twenty-eight, or if he was possibly older.

'Maybe I'm thirty-two,' he replied.

I was stumped, realising that he had no idea. To him it was a number and twenty-eight must have been a believable figure that he'd used in the past, possibly for many years.

'But you said you were twenty-eight. Do you actually know your date of birth?' I stubbornly persisted.

'I was born on the 21st of December. That is my birthday. You think maybe I'm twenty-one?' Jay looked at me hopefully.

'No, you are definitely not twenty-one, you don't look that young!' I exclaimed, feeling a little anxious.

Suddenly, I realised that the number I was looking for held meaning for myself alone. Jay did not know, or care, how old or young he was. As far as he was concerned, he was healthy and happy. He could dance and work and I was by his side. To me his age did matter, especially to my precious ego. Did I have a young lover, or was I dating a man older than myself? I laughed and when Jay eyed me with uncertainty, I quickly reassured him.

'Don't worry. It's no problem at all. I am laughing because in my world we put a lot of emphasis on age. You have helped me to realise its insignificance. As long as we are healthy and happy, life is good. Anyway, I was wondering, do you have a birth certificate?'

Jay looked relieved, smiled and got up.

'Look, babes. I have some papers here.' He took out a thick, well-worn envelope and handed it to me as he sat back down on the bed.

I leafed through the papers. Most were meaningless old receipts among some family photographs, then finally, a certificate.

'Jay. You are *married*!' I exclaimed and looked at him in shock while waving the document frantically. This, I had not expected.

'No, Regina. I'm not married. I was married to an English woman before, but we are divorced now. Look, babes.'

He quickly pulled out another paper behind the one I was clutching in my hand. It was indeed a legal confirmation of their separation. I had been under the impression that Jay had been single. To stir matters more, I eventually found a birth certificate.

I was elated, but when I scanned it, and calculated the years, I looked at Jay in astonishment.

'Jay, it says here on your birth certificate,' I tapped my finger on the official paper and began to giggle uncontrollably, 'that you are forty-two years old.'

'Okay,' he said, confused by my laughter. 'Does that mean I am old?' he asked cautiously, and my heart missed a beat.

'No. You are still the same, Jay. I have just learned that age is irrelevant. Thank you for the lesson,' I said and leaned over to kiss him.

He genuinely did not know his age or what the numbers meant. Briefly I wondered what our societies would be like if we could all let go of attachment to the number of years spent in our human bodies and instead measure our existence by embracing each stage of life, by how we feel, or what we have achieved in a particular moment or day?

Jay continued to shed light on his marriage and divorce story while I sat and listened. Needless to say, I went to bed feeling bewildered and sombre. I understood why he withheld some of the information, but nonetheless I felt betrayed by the secrets. A voice in my mind persistently whispered: if I accidentally uncovered these, were there more?

I needed to digest these revelations. For the first time in the five months since meeting Jay, I felt a distance open between us.

It was late afternoon when I returned home from work. I noticed that none of Jay's brother's dogs had come running to greet me as usual, and shortly after, I spotted them listlessly limping around the yard. The puppy, especially, would often come for a pat and a play. But today it approached slowly, head and tail hanging low. Upon inspection I found some ugly wounds on its legs and torso. When Jay came home from work, I pointed out the injuries.

He looked at me sadly and shrugged his shoulders. 'Regina, many people here use their dogs for fighting. I think that's why they are hurt,' he said matter-of-factly.

My emotional outcry must have been resounding beyond my head, or maybe it was the disgusted look on my face that prompted him to speak again.

'Babes, I am sorry. I don't like when people fight their dogs, but I can't tell my brother what to do with his pets. My house stands on his property,' he added, subtly asking me to respect his predicament.

I could understand Jay's position. But arranged dog fights? For a moment I felt red-hot fury rising, closely followed by tremendous sorrow. Generally, I was a great trouble shooter, but this situation was beyond my control. I could not jeopardise Jay's living arrangement and saw no other solution than to suppress my displeasure and carry on.

Life at home and in my work was becoming complicated and I yearned for a chat with a friend, someone who knew me and would not judge my chaotic life. I was feeling lonely but calls from my mobile were outrageously expensive. Without a laptop, my desire to connect with an understanding friend remained unsatisfied.

Despite the turbulence, I enjoyed living in Antigua. I loved the ever-present music, the lively banter of the residents, the sunshine, beautiful beaches and ocean. The food was varied and tasty. Above all, I was proud that I had succeeded in establishing myself in a new country by my own efforts. During days of uncertainty or upheaval I kept reiterating these positives to myself like a cherished mantra.

My job situation was about to deteriorate. George announced that he and his wife would leave Antigua for a quick trip to St Lucia for a holiday, and scout for potential new resorts from which to base business operations. In their absence I was expected to handle everyday business and take care of their two rowdy dogs. I enjoyed the work challenge and particularly the freedom. Without George's constant interruptions, I felt empowered and productive.

Once they returned from their trip George was freshly enthused about his expansion dreams. But as far as I could tell, nothing tangible had evolved. He kept prattling on about his grand visions yet we were still in the process of selecting new staff for the Antigua bases.

One morning he directed me to communicate a new policy to the short-listed candidates. From now on, each new sailing instructor had to obtain a boat licence immediately upon starting the position, to align themselves with his future project requirements. George, or a close associate of his, would conduct this mandatory training. He expected the new staff to fund the course themselves, either with an upfront payment to his business, or paid in instalments deducted from their wages. I was feeling increasingly uncomfortable with this arrangement and his growing demands. The candidates, who lived abroad, had already started to prepare for an international relocation, which involved great cost and effort. Once again, I asked George about job contracts and work permits for the future staff and myself. I reminded him that my holiday permit would expire soon but, as usual, he avoided giving an answer.

A puzzling fact was that the US dollar amount George commanded from new staff to pay for the planned boat training amounted to precisely the same sum I'd had to pay as the deposit for my bike at the start of my employment. I began to suspect ill motives at play, and while working in one of the resort locations with Trevor, the longest standing staff member, I asked him about these training and bond schemes. Trevor, a weathered and lanky Brit who had travelled the world working in the sailing industry, shrugged his skinny shoulders in a resigned manner.

'You know, I've learned over time that George doesn't like paying wages. So, he usually finds a way of getting money back from his people,' he said. With a no-nonsense attitude, he continued rolling up the sails and stowing the dinghies for the day. 'It's another way to hold onto staff. They come and go easily enough here.'

'Trevor, what's the situation with the work permits? I still haven't got one. George is not taking any initiative to apply for mine, nor does he seem motivated to get them for the new staff,' I persisted, wanting to dig deeper.

'Regina, let me tell you one thing. Aside from me, no-one here has ever held a work permit.' He briefly looked up, eyeing me with a pitiful look. My heart sank as he continued, 'George doesn't like paying taxes either, and he believes that he's above the law. If people don't have a work permit, they don't pay local taxes. I am sorry to shatter your hopes, chick. Maybe you can find other work somewhere.'

After this short conversation, I felt as if a veil had been lifted from my eyes. Suddenly I saw that George had tricked me with his excellent ability to sell and project an exciting future, but on practicalities, he remained vague and elusive. He cleverly avoided any discussion about my work permit and I was starting to lose hope, yet I was trapped in this job.

One day, in George's home office, we were talking about the legal limitations regarding the business. I was outlining the required procedures when George interrupted with a flippant wave.

'Ah, Regina,' he said with a sly smile, and patronisingly carried on, 'let me tell you something. Around here you don't apply for permits. You buy them.'

I inhaled sharply, taken aback by his recklessness, but George continued undeterred. 'Look. I have a good friend high up in the police department. If I need something, the two of us have a beer. I slip him some cash and the problem is solved. Hell, if I murdered someone, I could put US $5,000 on the table and have the charge disappear.' With a self-assured sneer, George leaned back in his chair, folding his hands behind his head.

His arrogance shook me. Oblivious of the impact of his message, he swiftly moved onto meaningless chatter while I sat quietly, reeling. This exchange marked a turning point in my attitude. It was time to move on and the sooner the better, although I had no idea of what to do next. Repulsed by George's questionable business dealings, I knew that to remain in this situation would be morally unacceptable. This much I was sure of.

14
TURBULENCE AHEAD

Between work and Jay, my life was chaos. I needed to catch my breath and re-centre. During my free time, when Jay was at work, I often hopped on the bike and went exploring. I loved riding along, feeling the sun on my bare arms and legs, and inhaling wafts of blossoms, hot soil and the occasional home-cooked meal. After a few minutes, soothed by the humming engine and passing scenery, my racing thoughts would begin to slow and I would start to relax.

Antigua had spectacular landscapes. In parts, the island was almost desert-like, with hillsides covered in cacti and hardy shrubs. The low-lying areas comprised pastures dotted with goats or sheep, or vegetable plantations. One day I returned to the steep and exhilarating rainforest road – the one I had taken by bus during my very first explorations. The bike was labouring hard on the windy uphill climb. I sang jubilantly as I bounced around the tight bends. It was still hurricane season and although Antigua had not received much rain, the air was humid and fragrant wherever I went. In those moments I felt light and free.

Jay and I were still going strong, but I couldn't stop burrowing into his past, and doubts and insecurities started to trouble my thoughts. Deep in my heart I knew our love was genuine, but each time I asked Jay about past relationships and romances, he couldn't provide adequate responses. Either he was being deliberately vague, or he was unable to recall events accurately due to the suspected brain injury. I was giving him the benefit of the doubt, but a twinge of uncertainty remained. The yachties' early warnings would not leave me be, so one afternoon I cautiously approached Jay and voiced my concerns. I explained about sexually transmitted diseases and suggested we do an AIDS test together. To my relief, Jay agreed to take the test and a few days later we both received clear results.

I loved many things about Jay. His soulful eyes, soft lips, gentle and loving heart, and happy personality. I was attracted to his chiselled physique and adored his cute, stubbly dreadlocks that poked out in all directions from his head, like tiny antennas tuning into a joyful channel. When he showered or swam in the ocean, droplets of sparkling water clung to the stubbly protrusions, cascading like a shower of diamonds when he shook his head. To me they were a headful of bliss! Until one afternoon when Jay walked through the door. As I looked up from my book, my jaw dropped.

'Jay, you cut your hair off!' I exclaimed in shock. His dreadlocks were gone, replaced by a shaved scalp, with only a little curly fluff remaining. 'Why did you do that?' I asked, taken aback by this sudden and unannounced change.

'Regina, you always say how you love my locks. I wanted to see if you love me only because of them,' he said, while gauging my reaction.

I sat for a moment, digesting his message. A smile formed on my lips as uncontrollable laughter bubbled up from my belly. There was no way to argue his reasoning. 'Oh, Jay. That is hilarious! Man, I love you, with or without your locks. But they were such happy little things.' I giggled. 'Never mind, they will grow back. Come here and let me feel your head.'

His face lit up and as we snuggled on the bed, I let my hands roam across his newly shaven head and gently kissed his face. I could relate to his insecurity and appreciated the courage it took to lose his trademark hair.

At work on Monday morning, George announced that he was closing one of the resort operations, and we had to pack up and move all the office equipment and sailing dinghies out. This was the first time I had heard about this closure and was puzzled by the sudden downsizing. Since two sailing instructors had left the previous week and Trevor was occupied at the second resort, it was down to the two of us to remove all the equipment from the waterfront shack.

The summer day was oppressively hot and humid. First, we lugged the merchandise, computers, filing cabinets and chairs up the wobbly path to the van. After dropping them off at George's house we returned to move the sailing dinghies. One by one, we loaded each dinghy onto a little trailer. While easy to manoeuvre on flat terrain, pushing boat and trailer uphill to the parked van was heavy and awkward to direct. Once hooked to the van we towed the small boat to a storage shed, offloaded the craft and returned to pick up the next one. After several runs all the dinghies were securely stowed away. I was drenched in sweat and feeling nauseous. It was excruciating work and it wasn't long before my body ached from the unusual strain. Not usually one to avoid physical labour, I had reached my limit.

When I arrived home that afternoon, I immediately went and lay down on the bed. I was totally spent and my whole body felt stiff and sore. When I tried rolling over, an agonising pain pierced my abdomen, rendering me immobile. I was alone and couldn't move; even the smallest movement provoked searing pain.

Tears started to roll down my face. Something was terribly wrong with my body. I was distressed and unable to resolve the situation. Jay was still at work. I was stuck lying in the bed feeling very isolated. To make matters worse, I was acutely aware of my lack of medical insurance. I needed a break from my own thoughts and was in dire need of loving company. Clenching my teeth in a futile attempt to suppress the pain, I managed to grasp my phone.

'Jay, I hurt myself. Where are you?' I sobbed as soon as he answered the call.

'Regina! Babes, what's wrong with you?' Jay sounded alarmed, not having experienced my vulnerable side. 'We are just finishing off the round. I will be home soon.'

'Yes, please hurry. I need you. I am in a lot of pain.'

When I ended the call, I felt lonelier than ever. The weight of my decision to live in a country where I had no social network while juggling challenging circumstances at both home and work was wearing me down and the lack of contact with my friends and family made it worse. I longed for communication with my parents but felt unable to reach out. On top of my loneliness, this new physical pain broke me. I crumbled, weeping in despair.

Several hours later, Jay returned home. Though I'd called every hour, reinforcing that I needed him, in true Caribbean fashion he'd simply promised to return 'soon'. When he finally stepped through the bedroom door and saw me lying helpless, his shock was visible. My body had always been strong and healthy, but there I lay, moaning and motionless. I was defenceless and vulnerable as never before.

The next morning, I carefully rolled out of bed, groaning. The hopes I'd held of my pain dissolving overnight vanished. Instead, my abdomen throbbed and I struggled to hold myself upright. Kick-starting the motorbike was torture. Each time I punched down the bike's lever, pain shot through my torso. Eventually it started and I made my way to work. I could not see the point in staying home and figured that at work I could seek advice from Trevor or my boss on how to get help.

Hunched over, I hobbled into the sailing shack, hands protectively pressed onto my belly. Trevor looked at me in shock and called out, 'Reggie, what the hell's wrong with you?'

I could see the concern in his eyes. His empathy tugged at my heartstrings and I burst into tears.

Sobbing, I managed to groan, 'I must have hurt myself yesterday when George and I were moving the gear from the other resort. I am in so much pain.'

'Oh, sweetie. Where are you hurting?' Usually reserved, Trevor was being uncharacteristically tender.

Hunched over the bench, I described the pains I'd endured and confessed to not knowing where to go or what to do. Trevor took charge.

'Reggie, you can't work in this state. There is an excellent expat doctor on the island who does the aviation and dive medicals. I suggest you go and see him as soon as you can. If it's all right with you, I will call him now and arrange an appointment,' he said, turning towards the phone.

He managed to get me an appointment with the doctor early that afternoon. Meanwhile, he instructed me to buy some strong painkillers at the supermarket. As Trevor had to return to work, I called George and explained my situation. To my surprise he was understanding and supportive, urging me to take the day off and see the medic.

I managed to get my bike going and purchased extra strength Tylenol at the supermarket in Jolly Harbour. Usually, I would resist medication unless necessary. Today, I swallowed the maximum suggested dose without hesitation. I was desperate for a reprieve from the relentless pain.

Walking through a back street in St John's on my way to the doctor, I started feeling nauseous. On the verge of collapse, I entered a takeaway restaurant and ordered a Coke. I must have looked a sorry sight sitting at the table with my head resting on my arms. The staff rushed over in alarm to check if I was all right. I reassured them, asking for time to sit quietly in the hope that the soft drink might help me recover. Eventually the painkillers kicked in and I was grateful for the relief, however temporary.

While friendly, the doctor said there was little he could do other than recommend rest and pain medication for the next few days. However, since I was already there, he ran me through a general consult. He referred me to a gynaecologist for further examination and, as an added precaution, the specialist clinic for an ultrasound. I felt better already, knowing that I had a plan of action.

To my surprise, I was able to see the gynaecologist the same day and was ushered into his office immediately. After a few probing questions, he conducted a quick examination and confidently declared he could detect nothing amiss. Once I sat back at his desk, he swiftly changed the subject and started talking about the local music scene. Though puzzled by the turn of the conversation, I had grown accustomed to Antigua's surprises. He explained that he was the manager of a successful local band – one I had seen in concert over the carnival period – and he happily gave me one of their CDs. A very nice gesture, I thought, preparing to leave. Just when I assumed our consultation was over, the doctor somewhat proudly announced himself as the island's abortion specialist. As I was neither pregnant nor looking for an abortion, I was clueless as to where this conversation was leading. It became clear when he pointed at the phallic piece of equipment on the other side of the desk and offered me a free ultrasound. Suppressing an urge to laugh, I quickly and politely declined, and instead organised an ultrasound appointment at the specialist clinic for the following day.

I loved those painkillers. They allowed me to move around again without being constantly doubled over in pain. At home I tried to rest, giving my body a chance to heal. Lying on the old mattress beneath the gently billowing mosquito net, I had time to consider my predicament. I was removed from everyone and everything I knew. With loneliness creeping over me like a dark shadow, I reached out and sent my dad a short text message.

Hey Dad. I am still in Antigua and I am very much struggling at the moment. It would be nice to chat to you. Can you please give me a call soon?

It was morning in Switzerland, and I wanted to hear someone's voice from my 'old' life. After a few minutes I looked at the phone again and sent a message to Sven as well.

Hey Sven. I hope you are well. I am not doing well right now. Would you be able to call me by any chance? Please?

Worn out, I rested my head on the pillow, closed my eyes, and became immersed in my swirling emotions. I was afraid because I had no idea what was causing me such agony. I feared the medical bills I would potentially face. Waves of sadness and forlornness kept threatening to swamp me. I tried to acknowledge their presence and focused on my breath. I drew on my experience with meditation and my knowledge of the yoga tradition and Buddhist philosophy. This was a trying period and I was grateful to have tools to help me cope. I kept reminding myself that this was merely a temporary setback. I would get through this. It was just a matter of time.

Since the pain first appeared, I had been feeling increasingly concerned about my relationship with Jay. The injury had highlighted that I was shouldering most of the load within our partnership. During this profound experience with physical pain, Jay could comfort me emotionally, but could not assist in any other way. I realised that if we decided to make a life together – build a more substantial house and potentially have a child – I would need to fund and organise our life, and I would carry most of the responsibility.

Lying there on my back, I was faced with many uncomfortable questions. Did I want to pursue what appeared to be an energetically lopsided relationship? How would that affect my future, not to mention the future of any children Jay and

I might have? I was strong willed at best, and this personality trait would likely drive our relationship further into imbalance. I delved deeper. Was it enough for me to be with someone with a beautiful heart and soul, a kind and generous personality, but who could not fully support me emotionally, or intellectually? Or would I prefer an equal on my side? Someone with whom I could have stimulating conversations? Someone I could count on for moral support and who would challenge me on my path?

I became absorbed in these silent contemplations. Distractedly I noticed the afternoon sun filtering through the windowpanes and the mosquito net gently swaying in the breeze. The afternoon stillness abruptly ended. My phone was ringing. Sven!

'Hello?'

'Hey, Regina. I got your text and I am on a break at work. Tell me, what's going on?' He cut straight to the chase.

'Oh, Sven. Thank you for calling! I am in a real pickle here and need to talk to someone. You have made my day.' I babbled happily, for a moment forgetting my pain. I told him about my work injury and my subsequent struggle with the persistent pain. I mentioned the strange situation at work and touched on my doubts about my relationship. Sven patiently listened.

'Have you been in touch with your parents?' he probed softly.

'I sent Dad a text a little while ago. I haven't heard from him but that might take time. I haven't called Mum. I am not sure how she would react, and I can't deal with anything that's not supportive at the moment,' I added, knowing Sven would empathise with my familial hurdles.

'All right, I understand … but what will you do now?' His calm voice allowed me to relax as well.

I told him about my appointment for the ultrasound the following day. I could feel my tension easing as I chatted with him and was enormously grateful for the call.

Sven started telling me about his plans. Since we last spoke, he had decided to move back to Switzerland. He had given notice at his work in South Australia and had terminated the lease on the house we jointly rented. His move was taking shape. Somewhat coyly he confessed to meeting a Swiss lady online and I could tell from his voice that he was smitten. Besides being excited about moving back to his hometown, he was looking forward to meeting his new woman in person. I was happy for him. He had always longed for Switzerland, he was moving on emotionally, and I was delighted we were maintaining our deep friendship. When we ended the call, I felt content and satisfied with the conversation. My spirits had lifted and I felt ready to face the challenges at hand.

The next day I went to the clinic, but the ultrasound revealed little apart from a small hernia in my abdomen, which the doctor said could be the source of my pain. He said the pain would slowly subside over the next weeks and the hernia would either disappear naturally or settle down. Satisfied with the answers, I felt ready to resume my life.

15

CRASH AND BURN

The pain took some time to disappear. Jay was helping as much as he could with lifting tasks around the home. We started doing our shopping together and otherwise resumed our routine.

On Friday night I was looking forward to heading out with Jay for some much-needed diversion. This was the regular evening when many families set up a barbecue outside their houses, offering their homemade food for sale to the community. Enjoying a takeaway dinner from one of the many pop-up stalls had become a cherished habit of ours. Over the months we had tasted many different dishes but often ended up revisiting Jay's favourite: a plate of charcoal grilled chicken accompanied by a mix of rice and lentils, a spoonful of macaroni and cheese and a side of salad.

These mouth-watering home-cooked meals were handed over to us on plastic plates, straining under the hefty servings. My favourite drinks were the freshly pressed local fruit juices, especially the rich and naturally sweet pink guava juice. Often Jay and I roamed the streets of All Saints looking for a stall that had my special drink on offer that day. Aside from the culinary treats, these evenings were pleasant social occasions. As we stood and ate our food, small groups would gather and playful bantering would ensue.

Reluctantly I went back to work the following Monday. My enthusiasm for the job had waned since George had raised the issue of bribes. However, my injury had taken my focus away from a job search and I was aware that my holiday permit was due to expire in a few weeks. George rushed into the office in his usual manner and announced that he and his wife were going on another trip, shortly. Over the weekend they had booked last minute flights to Austria. They planned to stay for several weeks and were looking forward to a prolonged holiday in their home country while also scouting for potential investors. Once again, George ordered me to look after their two large hounds while they were away. Swallowing my frustration at his dictatorial manner and lack of thoughtfulness, I broached the subject of my illegal employment status.

'George, my holiday permit will run out while you are away. We have to start the process for my work permit immediately!' I said.

'Regina, I don't have time. Just go in with Jay and extend your holiday visa. We will get to it when we return to Antigua.' He waved dismissively, and I could feel the heat rise in my cheeks.

'George,' I insisted with a firmness that stopped him in his tracks. 'You must know that I am the only white person living in All Saints. The residents see me come and go, either with the bike or sometimes in the work van. It is apparent that I am working and Antigua is a small island. I need that work permit.'

'Look, Regina, these things take time and I can't do it before we leave,' he said, averting his eyes. 'There is too much other pressing stuff I need to get to.' I despised him for his condescending tone. 'Everything will be fine, I promise. Antigua is not as small as you make it out to be.'

George's negligent attitude and arrogance appalled me. I did not trust him but there was nothing I could say or do to change his mind.

'Okay. I don't like my chances but I suppose I have no other option than to try,' I said, with a heavy sense of foreboding.

'Atta girl.' George turned and walked off.

Several days later the couple departed. At least it was peaceful without George's annoying presence. I was upset by his lack of commitment to my employment status and felt betrayed by him. My nature was to trust people, but increasingly I felt I was being exploited and deceived. George cared for himself, first and foremost. Clearly, he did not intend to change my work status, as it was of no immediate benefit to him.

Grudgingly, I cared for his two unruly dogs. He had also left detailed instructions to resume the long and drawn-out recruitment process with the new candidates. I had to string some along with the hope of a potential job, but George had not committed to signing a contract with any of them. Having experienced his lack of integrity, I could see that future staff would end up in a similar predicament to mine. I felt for those hopeful young people and did not want them to spend a lot of money relocating in vain. This situation didn't seem fair and was certainly not honest business practice.

The pain in my abdomen, although more manageable, was persistent and I still took Tylenol regularly to help me get through my daily workload. With my work situation uncertain, I again became apprehensive about my future on the island. Jay and I were settled in our relationship, but doubts persisted about our future. We loved each other, but the longer I lived with him, the more I struggled to accept the shortfalls in our relationship. Jay lived in the moment and had completely lost any interest in his education.

I was saddened to observe the extent to which his illiteracy affected his life and decision-making. One morning, Jay was complaining about knee pain and shortly after returned with a can of WD40, intending to spray the liquid onto his joint for healing purposes. Another day, I found him swirling household bleach in his mouth, trying to brighten his teeth. I failed to relate with Jay's lack of education and struggled to accept his disinterest in learning and self-improvement. A part of me had sincerely hoped to help Jay empower himself but I was wondering now if that desire was more about me having a 'saviour complex'. While I could not understand Jay's lack of drive, I also struggled with my own inability to accept where he was at. I knew I had no right to make decisions for him. I loved him deeply, but could I fully embrace and accept him as he was? I was no longer sure.

With all the corner posts in my life now wobbly, I longed for the security of connection with home. Not wanting to overly rely on Sven, I reached out to my dad again. He had not yet responded to my first text message from a fortnight ago.

Hey Dad. I wonder if you got my text two weeks ago. I am having a bit of a rough time here in Antigua. Can you please call me? <3

The days came and went without a reply. Keeping busy, I tried to ignore my lingering sadness. Why was it so hard for my father to pick up the phone and call me? I was his only child. I was not expecting a long chat, or that he would rescue me. A quick conversation would have meant a lot. I did not understand.

At work, my days were quiet, other than one afternoon when I found the dogs secretly shredding my treasured flip flops. George was sending emails every few days with instructions, which I followed dutifully. My visa's rapidly approaching expiry was permanently on my mind, and I was anxious about its renewal.

On the day we visited the Immigration Department, everything started smoothly. Aware of the required dress code this time, Jay and I arrived in the appropriate attire and presented ourselves at the immigration headquarters early in the morning. My heart was pounding as we sat on the cheap plastic chairs in the waiting area. My face was hot and the palms of my hands were damp with sweat. Honesty was a cherished value that I lived by. Yet, I was in the impossible situation of applying for another holiday permit extension when I had been working for almost two months by now.

An officer called us to the counter and appraised us. 'Why do you want another extension?' she said abruptly, flicking through my passport pages.

'She loves me and wants to stay longer.' Jay was laughing, unaware of my nervousness.

The officer eyed me sternly. 'Is that so?'

'Well, yes, I would like to extend for another two months, please,' I stammered.

She flicked back and forth through my passport, the frown never leaving her face. Eventually she got up and started talking quietly to a colleague. Meanwhile, Jay recognising an employee in the back of the office, waved and called out to them. While my anxiety levels soared, he was carefree.

The officer returned to her cubicle and looked me straight in the eye. 'It's denied,' she announced. 'Please walk over to the door.'

A security officer came around into the waiting area. He told Jay to remain in the waiting room. He took my documents from the immigration official and instructed me to follow him. I felt all eyes on me. The sinking feeling in my stomach almost made me vomit. I was scared and had no idea what was about to happen.

The security officer led me into a small room, where two stern-looking officers sat behind a large desk waiting for me. They indicated for me to take a seat. Hunched over I sat down, feeling frightened and resigned. The door closed and they flicked through my Swiss passport, checked my plane ticket and when finished focused their attention back on me.

'Have you been working, Ms Meyer?'

The blunt question knocked the wind out of me. Inhaling deeply, I took a moment to evaluate my situation. I wanted to be honest and realised it was my only option, otherwise things might get worse. Fear choked my throat. I willed away the promise of tears. Tightly clenching my hands, I proceeded to explain.

'Yes, I have been working for nearly two months now. My boss has promised me over and over that he would apply for a work permit, but he hasn't started the process yet. He instructed me to come here and instead get my tourist visa renewed.' I lowered my eyes as I spoke, feeling ashamed that I had found myself in this predicament. I could feel disapproval radiating from the officers.

'Ms Meyer, we advise you that your visa extension has been denied. You have a plane ticket with Condor, and we will change your current reservation to a flight departing next Monday. You must take that flight. We inform you that should you not board this plane, we will come to your residence and take you away in handcuffs in preparation for deportation. Do you understand this statement?'

Their direct delivery came like a punch to my stomach and a fresh wave of nausea washed over me. The message was plain and while intellectually I understood it, I was in shock. Pain pierced my heart. That was it? In that instant, my dream to create a new life in Antigua was shattered.

I sat, trying to absorb the message. Refusing to accept the finality of the situation, I clung onto hope. Surely someone could salvage this? I pleaded desperately, 'I am sorry! I apologise. I trusted my boss that he would get me the work permit. He promised he would. I love Jay and I want to stay here with him. Please!'

Unable to suppress my tears any longer, they streamed down my face. My heart was breaking, and my dreams and hopes were imploding. While sitting in this barren room with my emotions in upheaval, time suddenly froze.

In that surreal moment I could see the situation from outside of myself, as if suspended above, like a scene in a movie. I saw myself as the distressed Caucasian woman hunched over in the immigration office facing two dark-skinned officers who were simply doing their job. In this strange time-lapse, I suddenly understood that this experience had a powerful underlying message. Like dense fog clearing before my eyes, I snapped to with sudden clarity and a deep sense of appreciation for the situation playing out in front of me. Deep in my soul I knew this was a profound and humbling gift whose meaning I had yet to fully grasp.

That's what it feels like to be on the receiving end of such rejection! The thought came booming out of nowhere and reverberated through my being. In that instant I felt deeply connected with all people who had endured a similarly traumatic rejection. Compassion arose for all those who had suffered through this before me and for those who would yet follow. I understood how profoundly privileged I was in comparison to many others, despite my momentary sorrow and distress. My tears were flowing freely now, not just for the pain of my personal situation, but for all people caught up in similar struggles.

After that, things moved quickly. The officers insisted that I change my flight immediately, but they failed to connect with the airline's reservation desk. I explained to the officers that I had no interest in disregarding their directive. I promised to rebook my ticket to the requested day and catch the flight as instructed. Reluctantly, the officers returned my plane ticket to me. When I reached for the passport, one of the officers swiftly moved the document out of my reach.

'You will get that at the airport,' she declared and escorted me out.

I cried into my bike helmet on the way home. Although I had doubts about the long-term future of our relationship, I was not yet ready to give it up altogether. The ultimatum only reaffirmed my intention to keep trying. The visa extension denial shook Jay deeply and on the way to the house he asked me to stop at his workshop. He started to discuss my rejected visa and threat of deportation with his colleagues and soon everyone was loudly voicing their opinions. At some point Jay's boss came out of the office to ask what the commotion was about, and Jay gave him a quick recount of the situation. I was relieved when we left the workshop, worn out from the emotional upheaval and longing to retreat to the safety of our little yellow sanctuary.

We crashed onto the bed, seeking solace in each other's embrace, staying quietly entwined until we felt strong enough to face the situation. Desperately we brainstormed, seeking an answer. It was Friday night but neither of us was feeling hungry and we were aware that it would be near impossible to resolve our problem over the weekend. The flight was only three days away. The officers had reiterated that I needed to catch the plane on Monday, and I had been cautioned not to return to Antigua anytime soon.

Jay's phone started ringing and he began to talk in the local dialect, which I still had some trouble following. I switched off, lost in my thoughts. I could not see a way to fix this situation. Usually I loved troubleshooting, but now my mind drew a blank. I felt drained and empty.

'Babes! Listen.' Rather abruptly I was jerked out of my thoughts. 'My boss is on the phone. He knows some people and he wants to talk to you. Here –' Jay smiled broadly and passed me his mobile.

'Hello?' I was taken aback and did not know what to make of this. Frankly, I did not want any more bad news.

'Hi, Regina. I'm Dwayne, Jay's boss. We were talking earlier and I made some enquiries on your behalf. I have a phone number for you, and it is important that you call this person and explain your situation. I hope it will help. Have you got a pen and paper?' he asked.

I was astounded that he had gone to such trouble for me. I had seen him around occasionally and we'd exchanged greetings but had never really spoken. 'Dwayne, thank you for going out of your way for me,' I stammered, reaching for a pen and paper. 'I very much appreciate your effort. Okay, yes, I am ready,' I said.

Dwayne spelt out the number and made sure I had it down correctly, then cautioned, 'Regina, now listen closely. This is the personal mobile number of the Prime Minister of Antigua. This number is only for this special occasion and *please* do not share it. Are you with me?'

I swallowed. Was this the grand gesture I had been hoping for? I could not believe what was happening. 'Oh, wow! Goodness, I don't know what to say. That's a surprise and a half,' I mindlessly babbled and then caught myself. 'Thank you! I will call him straight away and I will dispose of the number afterwards. No problem. Thank you very much for your trust and for helping me.'

As I hung up the phone, I laughed. I should have known in Antigua that anything was possible! Enjoying this little moment of hope, I picked up my mobile and nervously punched in the numbers to call the Prime Minister of Antigua and Barbuda. He answered immediately and politely prompted me to explain my situation. I related my story and after a short moment of consideration he calmly formulated his response.

'Regina, listen carefully. Monday morning you will return to the Immigration Department. I will make sure that you are granted an extension for a month, so you have enough time to sort out your work permit. But from here on, you are on your own. I wish you luck and take care.'

In that instant my fortune had changed again, and another door had opened. I was gifted with time to breathe and to consider my options for living in Antigua and the future.

Over the weekend I reflected on my situation. I concluded that I did not want to remain in employment with George and his business, under any circumstances. He had intentionally betrayed and lied to me. I could no longer tolerate his reckless ways and I did not want to be involved in his dealings. It was time to get out.

I realised too, that I did not have enough enthusiasm or energy to look for a new job. The past few months had taken a toll and I didn't want to end up in a similar situation in another month. I was drained and tired by the constant turmoil around employment. And finally, I analysed my doubts about a long-term future with Jay. Maybe it was time to move on? No, I decided. I loved Jay and was not willing to give up the relationship, though I wasn't quite sure if I felt this way because I still harboured hope for us, or because my choice had been taken from me at the immigration office.

The one thing that kicked me into gear was my rising fury with George. I despised him for giving me hope, then lying to me and crushing my dreams. I had invested so much energy and effort into my new life, only to have everything snatched away. I loathed his ways of deceiving the future staff with promises he did not intend to keep, and I was done with his manipulative tactics.

Engulfed by the heat of my anger I blamed George for everything that had gone wrong. Deep down I knew that he was not responsible for crushing my dreams, or for depriving me of a future in Antigua. But he had wronged me. I was angry and projected my rage onto him, refusing to take full responsibility for my decisions. Right then, I was unable to accept the slow decay of the relationship with my adored lover. Instead, I clung on for dear life and reacted to my circumstances.

On Monday morning, Jay and I reported to the immigration headquarters. Fear was running through me like a potent current. Unable to sit and relax, I was shifting from foot to foot with my hands tightly clenched. As we waited, I noticed several officers behind the glassed-off area eyeing me apprehensively. This time I did not have to wait for my turn in line and was ushered into the manager's office soon after our arrival.

I sat opposite the frowning supervisor. She did not hide her displeasure, and I understood why. The Prime Minister had starkly undermined her office's authority. Eyeing me coldly, she brusquely outlined the conditions.

'Ms Meyer, we are aware that you have been engaged in illegal employment in Antigua. You will be granted a one-off extension for a calendar month. During this period, you must organise a valid work permit. Otherwise, you will not be welcome here!' Her eyes bored into mine as she barked, 'Am I making myself clear?'

'Yes, I understand and accept the conditions. I appreciate your help.'

The officer took my passport from her file and swiftly filled in the new extension. She handed the passport back to me and with a curt nod, I was dismissed. I was escorted to the waiting area, where Jay was anxiously pacing back and forth. Once we were outside the building we stopped and Jay looked at me.

'All good, babes?' he asked.

'Yes, I think so. Look, the extension is here in the passport. They stamped me in for another month,' I said with a sigh of relief.

We wandered down to the pier. Despite the good news, my spirits were low. Jay and I needed to have a chat. I wanted to tell him about my plans for the immediate future. We found a little coffee shop and ordered some coffees. Once we had the steaming mugs in front of us, I took a deep breath.

'Jay, I want to tell you what I have decided to do next, okay?'

'Sure, Regina. You can get a new job, right? Then everything will be fine!'

'Umm … No, Jay. I am sorry, that's not what I plan to do. It is not easy to find a job here in Antigua at this time of the year and I would need proper employment with a company that is willing to immediately apply for a work permit. After the drama in recent weeks, I don't have the energy to do that. I am sorry.'

Taking another deep breath, I continued, 'I have decided to return to Switzerland. I need to see a doctor, find the cause of my pain and treat it. Then, I must figure out what to do next, Jay.'

His eyes turned dark and sad. He looked disheartened and I wished there was something I could do to ease his hurt.

'Are you coming back to me, Regina?' he asked quietly.

'I am not sure, Jay. There has been so much trouble here and I don't have much money left. I love you but I am not sure if we have a future together. First I need to leave and regain my sense of wellbeing.'

'Okay, babes. I understand. It will be good for you to spend time with your family. Say hi to your mum for me. And,' he said, flashing his signature megawatt smile, 'I know you will come back to Antigua.'

I smiled back and admired his unwavering positive outlook.

16

SAVOURING REVENGE

My mind was made up. I was going to end my employment immediately while George and his wife were still abroad. I did not wish to face either of them again. Over the weekend I had come up with a plan and on Tuesday morning I kicked into gear.

Just like any other workday, I arrived on time at George's home office. Nervously, and with a twinge of guilt, I reached for the company cheque book and issued a cheque to myself for the value of US $1,500 – the precise amount George had demanded from me as a deposit for the bike when I started my employment. Upon departing, I would leave the cleaned and locked-up motorbike at George's house, so in exchange, I reclaimed my deposit. To me that seemed a fair solution.

As casually as I could, I walked into the bank branch and joined the queue. During the past weeks I had made regular withdrawals to pay various bills, so the clerk knew me and my usual practice well. She barely glanced at the cheque and, without hesitation, stamped it and began counting the equivalent amount of US $1,500 in local currency. As usual, she asked me to double-check the money. Once I confirmed the amount was correct, I slipped the thick wad of cash into an envelope, wished her a good day, and sauntered out.

As I walked away from the bank, I sighed with relief and released my tension with a nervous giggle. Step one had been accomplished without a hitch. I was convinced that the money I had withdrawn belonged to me and that my reasons were valid. I was also aware that George would most likely have a different perspective.

The next step was sorting out the dogs. I had already found a kennel nearby and after an initial inspection, was happy that they would be well looked after until George and his wife returned. I loaded up the work van with the two canines and dropped them off at their temporary residence. Again I wrote a company cheque to cover the dogs' care until George's scheduled arrival in Antigua. With a final pat, I returned to the office and carried on with my list of tasks.

After returning the van to George's home, I refuelled the motorbike and gave it a good clean, restoring it to its original shine. I pushed it into George's driveway and locked it up with the big chain. Then I deposited the key and helmet on the dining table and locked the doors. Dropping the keys in the letterbox, I walked away from my job.

The following morning, I went to my favourite internet cafe. Finding a computer in a quiet corner, I perched on a chair and began drafting a long letter, outlining my situation in detail. I highlighted my illegal work status and explained that my boss had promised to obtain the work permit for me at the time of employment but had repeatedly refused to initiate the application process. I attached copies of my payslips. Besides providing proof of my employment, they also revealed that the business had not been paying the legally required taxes and government contributions. I noted that besides myself, the business had previously employed others in the same manner and that I had been instructed to recruit more personnel along the same lines.

George's casual conversation about bribery was vivid in my mind. I was determined to find a way to expose his illicit business practices. Knowing he would try to silence my accusations by resorting to bribery, I was intent on making law avoidance challenging, if not impossible, for him. I was appalled at his lack of integrity and the 'fuck-you-I-am-above-it-all' attitude. After thinking about this long and hard over the weekend I decided to send my letter to three recipients, simultaneously: the Immigration Department, the Internal Revenue Department and the Labour Department. On each letter I included the titles of all three recipients. This way, each of the government offices would be notified that two other ministries had received the same documentation. To cover up his misdemeanours, George would have to corrupt three departments at the same time. Rightly or wrongly, I took it upon myself to teach him a lesson. I was hurt and angry and determined that no one else would be affected by his reckless conduct.

Two of the letters I handed to staff at the departments' reception desks. The last, I saved for the Labour Department, the entity responsible for granting the work permits, having decided to deliver this letter personally. At the reception desk I asked to speak with the head of the department. After insisting multiple times, I was sent higher and higher up the building until eventually I was invited into a large office on the top floor, to take a seat opposite the director of the Labour Department.

I met the eyes of a beautiful and confident Antiguan businesswoman. Rather than feel intimidated, I openly met her formidable gaze, prepared to face whatever consequences flowed from my actions.

'Why are you here?' the manager asked, without betraying any emotion. I took this as a good sign.

'I am here to report that I have worked without a work permit,' I stated calmly and clearly, maintaining eye contact.

She raised one of her perfectly sculpted eyebrows. I had sparked her interest.

'Girl!' she sounded surprised, 'are you sure you want to be here?' She looked at me inquisitively and I nodded my head serenely.

'Yes, I made up my mind. I want to tell you my story, so hopefully this will not happen again in the future,' I replied with firm intent.

'All right. Go ahead, I am listening.' She leaned back in her chair and with an elegant hand gesture, motioned for me to continue.

I took a deep breath and proceeded to recount my story, from the beginning. Besides revealing my struggle regarding my job, I expanded on my relationship with Jay and my wish to have made a life in Antigua. I mentioned the hope and trust I had placed in George, and how I had been repeatedly and purposely deceived by his promises. To conclude, I mentioned the staff that George was currently recruiting and his 'above-the-law' mentality.

At times, as I relived my turbulent experiences, my eyes welled up with tears. Sadness, grief and loss threatened to overwhelm me, swiftly followed by contempt and a desire to expose this man's unscrupulous behaviour. My desire to prevent him from treating other people this way again overrode any fear of putting my own welfare on the line.

Throughout my monologue, the manager sat in her chair watching me with an impervious expression. She listened intently, without interrupting. When I finished, I felt an anxious tingling pulsating in my wrists. To steady myself I took a deep breath and closed my eyes for a moment. I waited, feeling unsure.

When I opened my eyes, I found her curiously and patiently scanning me.

'What will happen now? Will I be prosecuted?' I asked with a slight tremor in my voice.

Remaining silent, she leafed through the letter and evidence I had handed to her at the beginning of our meeting. 'Regina, tell me, what are your plans now?' she asked neutrally, still not revealing her position.

'I will leave the country. With all this chaos I cannot muster the energy to start again. I am devastated to be leaving Jay, but I have already changed my flight reservation to Monday next week. I am going home to Switzerland.'

'Okay, listen up,' she finally said. Leaning forward she spoke earnestly, 'No, you will not be prosecuted. You are safe, but I do ask you to take the flight you booked. I understand that your intention is to report the illegal business practices and that it wasn't your personal intention to work illegally. You can leave this with me.' Tapping her manicured index finger on my paperwork and fixing me with her eyes, she continued, 'I will take it from here. You are free to go now, Regina. I wish you all the best and take care.'

I rose, thanking her for her time and ran down the stairs. Only once I was outside did I stop and realise just how terrified I had been sitting in that office. While my intentions had been clear, the outcome of my confession could have gone either way. In the worst case, I could have been prosecuted and placed in prison. Relief washed over me, draining some of the built-up tension of recent weeks.

Feeling numb and exhausted, I walked to the docklands and sat on a concrete ledge overlooking the harbour. Gazing at the water lapping against the wall of the dock, I felt more at peace. The dice had fallen. I had made my choice and as much as it hurt, I was leaving Jay and Antigua in a few days. Watching the water shimmer and shine in the sunlight, I reminisced about my experiences; the joyful moments and the painful struggles. Reviewing my time on 'The Rock', as locals lovingly call Antigua, I knew that despite the adversities I had faced, I would not want to have changed a thing. The experiences had defined me; the positive moments as much as the tough times. With each encounter I had learned and evolved as a human being. There was a newfound resourcefulness and strength emanating from within me, along with a sense of trust in myself, knowing I was capable of navigating my way through the next chapter.

Still more tasks awaited. My next step was to meet with Trevor. We caught up over a drink in a quiet bar in English Harbour. I felt that I needed to explain what I had done, as my actions would likely affect the business and his life. He listened with surprising calm and assured me that he had been expecting something like this to happen one day. He had already put feelers out and was being considered for a promising position on another Caribbean island. He supported my actions and offered to drop me off at the airport. In the short time I had known him, Trevor had become a good friend. He was a man of few words with typically dry British humour. Plus, he had a heart of gold. I hugged the lanky man and we parted ways.

At home I sat down with Jay. He already knew that I was leaving on Monday, and now I brought him up to speed on everything else. I explained why and how I had reclaimed the motorbike deposit. I told him about writing and delivering the letters and my visit to the Labour Department. He nodded sombrely as I spoke, focusing his gaze on my face. Wrapping up, I reached into my handbag and pulled out the thick envelope of cash.

'Jay, I told you I took the money back from the motorbike, right?'

'Yes, Regina, I remember you said so,' he confirmed.

'All right. Here's the deal,' I said. 'The money is in this envelope. It is roughly EC $4,000. Jay, I want you to have the money.'

He sat motionless, eyes wide and mouth agape. I swiftly carried on. 'Look, the money doesn't feel good to me but I know it will help you. I'm giving this to you so you can buy your own small piece of land, like you have been talking about. You can use half the money for a down payment for the lease. With the remaining half you can build yourself a small house, buy a water tank and start your own little garden, so you are free and independent.'

I was excited that this money would give Jay a chance to fulfil his dreams and support a positive purpose. 'Maybe you can ask someone you trust – your sister? – to help you organise all of this. That way you will have something of your own in the future,' I said, gently nudging him with the envelope.

Jay hesitantly took the thick packet. He cleared his throat and started to speak. 'Babes, that is a lot of money. Are you really sure you want to give it to me?' he asked, looking at the envelope, then me.

Seeing my enthusiastic smile and nod, his face lit up. 'Wow, Regina. Thank you so much. I will send you a picture of my house on my piece of land!'

The words tumbled out in quick succession and Jay was smiling broadly. My heart lit up knowing the tainted cash would be redirected in a meaningful way. I was hopeful that it would mark a turn towards independence for Jay. That evening, despite the sadness about my impending departure, we went out for a celebratory dinner.

The last task that remained on my list was communicating with George and his wife. They were still in Austria and their planned return to Antigua was scheduled for the day after my departure. I prayed they would not move their flight forward. I was terrified of seeing them in person and feared their reactions. I had witnessed George's ruthless and unforgiving streak and was aware that my actions to seek retribution would anger him.

I kept my email to George short and concise. I explained that my holiday visa extension had been denied and I therefore resigned from my position with immediate effect. I outlined the steps I had taken regarding the motorbike. I explained how I reclaimed my deposit and that the bike was parked in immaculate condition at his residence. Lastly, I explained that the dogs could be collected from the kennel.

My hands shook as I hit the send button. I could visualise the couple's anger. Not just their pets, the dogs were rather like substitute children. George's wife especially would be furious. But

I'd had no other choice. Trevor, the only other caretaker option, had refused to look after them.

The next day I found two replies in my inbox filled with unfiltered, rampant rage. The couple's wrath jumped at me through the words. Trembling as I absorbed their messages, I hoped my plane would depart before theirs arrived. For the first time in my life, I felt threatened.

The day before my flight, I was packing my bags in the simple wooden shack that had become my home and sanctuary. As I gathered my clothes and loaded up my backpack, little by little, the place once again became Jay's solitary residence. I looked at the pictures that we had printed of ourselves and taped to the wall. Many happy snaps captured us on the beach, during picnics, and embracing each other in front of the little yellow house. Although deep down I knew our relationship had been built on a wobbly foundation, I could not let it go. Desperately, I focused on the things I loved about Jay. His carefree attitude, his loving and caring nature, his soulful eyes, glorious smile and strong arms that made me feel so safe.

The ring of my phone abruptly interrupted my thoughts. To my surprise it showed a Swiss number and I picked up eagerly.

'Regina, it's your dad. I got your message. How are you?' he asked. For a moment I was flabbergasted by his casual query.

'Dad!' I exclaimed, accusation seeping through my words, 'I contacted you a month ago!' My disappointment was palpable as I continued, 'I am okay now. I have sorted everything out and am returning to Switzerland tomorrow.'

I was not impressed with his delayed call and our conversation was brief. His offer to help seemed feeble at this point and I was not in the mood to explain myself. We agreed to meet in person once I returned home. I was glad that I had contacted my mother a few days earlier. During my call with her, I had explained everything that had been going on and that I was returning for a visit. Mum had been supportive and had invited me to stay with her and her husband. Knowing I had a temporary home was all that mattered for now.

The morning I was due to fly to Switzerland I woke early. I opened my eyes to see Jay pensively studying my face. For a while we quietly remained this way, gazing at each other. Moving closer, we started tenderly kissing and embracing. And with a sudden need we began to make love, the desperation of our renewed separation fuelling our hunger for each other. Passionately we explored each other's bodies, our fingers and lips memorizing each shape, curve, and line.

Fulfilled and relaxed we snuggled up, savouring these precious moments. Lazily we stirred and were harshly catapulted out of our blissful state by the sound of my phone's alarm. Trevor was scheduled to pick me up in little over an hour.

I was packed in time for his arrival. The three of us journeyed quietly to the airport where I checked in my backpack and received my boarding pass without complication. In the departure hall we sat at the bar and Trevor ordered a round of drinks. I was feeling tearful, thinking of my impending departure from Jay, and yet wanting to hurry to avoid seeing George. I was immensely grateful to Trevor for making the time to stay at the airport until my boarding time. Jay's and his presence gave me strength and helped me to feel calm. When my flight was called, I hugged each man tightly and passed through customs and onto the plane. I had lived in Antigua for nearly four months, which felt like a lifetime, and returning to Switzerland with no firm plans and very little savings made me anxious. Reaching my assigned seat, I took a deep breath, feeling like an alien in a plane filled with happy holidaymakers. Only when the captain announced that the doors had been locked, did I feel myself relax. I was safe.

17

EMBRACING UNCERTAINTY

For the second time this year, I found myself in Switzerland – a rare occurrence. Previously, I had only managed to fund a visit every other year. On my return, I took up the tiny spare room in my mother and stepfather's apartment. With my emotions in upheaval, I appreciated my mum's hospitality but felt nervous and apprehensive about sharing quarters with her. Raw and vulnerable after the chaos of the previous weeks, I dreaded telling her about my recent trials and tribulations, fearing she would be a harsh judge of my chaotic Caribbean escapades.

However, when we sat down to talk, Mum responded to my stories with unexpected kindness and understanding, and I was touched by her gentleness. She recognised my vulnerability and said she noticed a new softness within me. The small room I stayed in became my haven; a place I could retreat to, to contemplate and regroup. A specialist confirmed that my lingering abdominal pain was a hernia well on its way to recovery, and I was able to accept the dull ache as part of the healing process and release any remaining health concerns.

Handing the motorbike money to Jay had left me with few remaining funds. Considering my rapidly dwindling finances, I was aware that giving him US $1,500 was not the smartest decision. Despite believing that the money was mine and not George's, a part of me still felt ashamed of having reclaimed it without his consent. Knowing the money would serve a good purpose eased my conscience. Still, I needed to generate an income quickly.

A few days later I was walking up the hill on my way home from town when my auntie approached me on her bicycle. She was huffing and puffing and I grinned when I saw her assertively pushing down on the pedals, her bike loaded with bags brimming with groceries. When she saw me, she stopped.

'Regina, hi! I didn't know you were back home,' she said, smiling and looking surprised. I had not announced my visit to anyone but my parents. Gauging me curiously, she added, 'Tell me, did your dad give you the money?'

I looked at her. 'What are you talking about? What money?'

She frowned at my reply. She pointed her finger at me and with urgency, explained. 'Regina, when your grandfather passed away, he left each grandchild an equal amount as part of his inheritance. Your share was paid to your father in your absence. He had an obligation to pass the money on to you. You need to ask him about it, Regina, because you are entitled to your share.'

We had started to walk together and by now we had reached the crossroads. After making plans to gather for a family dinner at her home soon, we went our separate ways.

My aunt's news was unsettling. I knew my grandfather had died just after Sven and I had departed for New Zealand, but receiving an inheritance had never occurred to me. Here I was scraping by with barely enough money to make ends meet while my father had kept this a secret? I dialled his number.

'Hi, Dad. It's your daughter,' I said. 'How are you?'

'Hi, Regina. I am well. It appears you have made it to Switzerland safe and sound. What are you going to do now?' He sounded concerned and quickly fired off more questions. 'Are you going back to Australia to get a good job there? Or are you going to make a life here again?'

'Umm … I don't know. I only arrived a few days ago and will keep you posted. But, Dad, I have a question for you.' I paused, irritation stirring in the pit of my stomach. 'Is there anything you would like to tell me about the inheritance from my granddad?'

There was silence at the other end, then finally, 'How do you know?'

I could sense defence in his grudging question. 'Well, I ran into Aunty on the street, and she asked if I had received the money from my grandfather. Since I had no idea what she was talking about, she elaborated.'

I waited patiently for my father's response, allowing him to simmer in his own discomfort.

'Ah, well, Regina. Yes, I have your share of the inheritance. I kept it in my account because it was intended as an investment and not as spending money,' he said, his words dripping with judgement.

'All right,' I replied, barely containing my irritation. 'So you made the decision that I was not to be trusted with the money?' Annoyed with his condescending attitude, I aired my frustration.

'Dad. It is not for you to decide how and when I choose to spend my inheritance. This is my personal choice. The money was given to me by my grandfather free from obligation. When were you going to tell me about it?'

I could sense his unease and felt sorry for pushing the topic. But for all my adult years I had felt that my father had not understood me and had never tried to do so. I was aware that my life choices and values were in opposition to his and that he struggled to relate to my life, which he perceived as reckless and carefree. My decisions never seemed good enough for him and I often felt like a failure when speaking with him. Although I did not fully understand his life, his perspective and his decisions, I respected him. He was my father and I loved him and yearned for his moral support and approval. I hoped that one day he would accept me for myself, including my chaotic and imperfect life.

'Look, Regina, I apologise. You are right; it's not for me to decide. I will transfer the money to you immediately,' he said, aiming for a peaceful resolution.

'I would appreciate that, Dad. I am disappointed that you withheld the information from me, but I suggest we leave it behind us now.' Despite my feelings, I could relate to his position. He wanted the best for me. But it was 'the best' viewed from his perspective. Despite the awkwardness of the conversation, I was glad we had cleared the air and we agreed to meet up soon.

A few days later, the welcome monetary injection was credited to my account and the decision for my next chapter took shape. I would return to the Caribbean! I told my mum about my experience with Jay, how I adored him and felt drawn to return to Antigua. She admired Jay's deep sense of family connection and was grateful to him for urging me to stay in touch with her more frequently. She said that I was softer and more open, and attributed this welcome change to Jay.

Embracing Uncertainty

I had no home of my own and felt uprooted. Since my relocation to Australia I had only a few close friends living in Switzerland. As a result, I found myself sharing more than usual with my mother, including my doubts about the relationship and concerns about my future.

My new financial cushion would help me to return to the tropical island and the man who held my heart captive. Jay meant connection and love and Antigua had become a home. This time, however, my focus would not be on the relationship. Sailing season was about to start in the Caribbean and I remembered the sleek and luxurious yachts. Rather than wasting energy on finding another land-based job in Antigua, I planned to seek work aboard one of the elegant professional yachts.

With renewed spirit, I trawled the sailing websites. Eventually I singled out two boats looking for crew. After a few messages back and forth, I decided to join the smaller of them and booked a flight to the Spanish island of Gran Canaria, a popular European tourist destination in the Atlantic.

Before leaving, I went to visit my dad and his wife. He had recently sold the family business and accepted a management job in a different part of Switzerland. My father was enthusiastic about this opportunity late in his career and his wife was busy finalising the relocation arrangements. I was delighted that they were embarking on an exciting new chapter together. As we sipped wine and talked, my dad surprised me with a present – a laptop. Handing it to me, he said, 'You know, so we can keep in touch more easily.'

Not only had I been provided with funds to continue my onward journey, I now had the means to connect and interact with friends and family from wherever I was. I was touched by my father's generosity and kindness. This was one of the very few physical presents I'd received from him. Over the years he had dutifully contacted me on birthdays and Christmas and usually insisted on a cash gift. The laptop, an item I desperately needed, reflected his love, thought and consideration.

Sven also had arrived back in Switzerland, having divided and packed up our household in Australia, putting my belongings in storage and shipping his back home. He was renting a small flat and appeared content in his home environment.

We met for lunch and shared our stories. He had met his online friend in person and their romance was blossoming. Sven was radiant. I told him about my plans and he laughed, relieved at not having to match my pace of life anymore. I chuckled at his reaction. My life had picked up speed. Although I was now fully in charge of the choices, I was nevertheless surprised by my numerous adventures. I felt good chatting and laughing with Sven, to see him cheerful and to know that the decision to move on from our relationship had been right for both of us.

The end of November was near and I began piling my belongings into my backpack. Nine months after I had packed up in Australia, in anticipation of a three-month holiday, I would continue my travels with the same essentials I had started with. I loved the freedom and the absence of obligations and responsibilities to anyone other than myself. With each step, I was trusting more in my resilience and resourcefulness. Empowered by my aspirations to find work on a professional sailing yacht, I set off, and arrived at Gran Canaria airport ready for my next adventure.

'Hey! Are you taking part in the Atlantic Rally for Cruisers?' a male voice asked. I looked up from the baggage claim, where I was waiting for my trusty old backpack to appear. The pleasant voice belonged to a good-looking guy I had noticed at the departure gate in Zurich. He was tall and athletic, his blond hair short and neatly trimmed. He smiled and looked at me with crystal-clear blue eyes, waiting for my reply.

'Hi. Umm … Yes, I am. Are you crew, too?' I stopped staring and returned the smile.

'Yup. I was wondering if you know how to get to the marina?' he asked, looking a little lost and hopeful.

'Yes, I do. I was going to take a taxi. As far as I know it's the cheapest and quickest way. Would you like to share one, since we are going to the same destination?' I suggested, pleased to save money by sharing the trip. Plus, he was kind of cute.

'Yes, that would be great. By the way, what's your name? I'm Martin.' He beamed, extending his hand.

We retrieved our bags and got into a taxi. On the way to the marina we shared our sailing experience, and how we had each ended up crewing for this transatlantic rally.

'What boat are you on, Regina?' Martin asked.

'I'm on a 38-foot Beneteau First. Owned by an English couple. And you?'

'A 50-foot Moody. Two retired men own the boat together. They are British, too,' he said.

'Tell me, Martin, what's the name of the yacht you will crew on? Not *Phoenix* by any chance?'

'Yes, it is! But how do you know that?' He looked astounded. I could not blame him, as the coincidence was extraordinary.

'Well, I was looking at boats and singled out two. *Phoenix* was my second option. I've been emailing with Harvey, probably like you did.' I laughed and Martin joined in.

At the marina we shouldered our bags, promising to catch up soon. I walked off in search of my new floating home. I found the yacht, *Cleo*, tucked away at the far end of a finger dock. The owners, a British couple in their late forties, welcomed me aboard. I was shown to my small but comfortable cabin at the stern of the boat. The couple had been saving and planning for years to undertake this journey on *Cleo*. They were taking part in the World ARC Rally, an organised cruising yacht flotilla. They would circumnavigate the world with the added ease and safety of the organised tour. Jovial, easy going and dressed in the usual garb of worn shorts, dirt-stained shirts and unkempt hair, the skipper and his wife had the air of typical mariners.

The next morning, the skipper gave me a tour of *Cleo*, pointing out the preparations they had made for the ocean passage. He was distracted, as the rally authorities had scheduled an inspection of the boat later in the afternoon. Participating boats had to meet strict safety standards. In comparison with *Orion*, the yacht I had crewed on for my first Atlantic crossing, *Cleo* was a sturdy, small cruising yacht and looked well maintained. A few things concerned me, but I was hopeful the safety officers would address these. Below deck, the boat was a mess. The interior was filled with books, charts, food items in crates, and the lifeboat was tucked behind a bench. The owners seemed to have neglected the storage situation considering the imminent extended ocean passage.

That evening I strolled along the docks, admiring the large variety of yachts. Following his instructions, I found Martin on his boat. *Phoenix* looked gracious on the still water. I admired her dark blue hull, twinkling with the water's reflection. She was long and elegant with her teak deck and centre cockpit, and I felt a twinge of envy. I realised I had chosen the ugly duckling over the sexy beast. Bummer! But I'd made my decision assuming that on *Cleo* I would find like-minded company, the skipper and wife being a similar age to myself. In addition, the required financial contribution was less.

As I called out from the dock, Martin popped up from below *Phoenix*'s deck and invited me on. Barefooted, I stepped onboard and joined him in the cabin. The interior was bright and spacious, like a living room. I was impressed with the layout and expressed my admiration to the yacht's owners who were sitting around the table along with two additional crew members. I was quickly introduced and invited to join the group. We all marvelled at the coincidence of how I had considered joining *Phoenix* and subsequently met Martin at the airport. Harvey explained that he and Giles had jointly owned the boat for several years. Since purchasing *Phoenix,* they had mainly sailed her around the UK and in the Mediterranean Sea. Now, in their late sixties, the friends were fulfilling a lifelong dream to circumnavigate the world in their yacht with the rally. Upon return to the UK they were planning to sell the vessel, marking the end of an era for them. Harvey seemed a decent man and the ambiance on board was lighthearted. Walking back to my boat, I felt disappointed with my choice.

The next day my skipper said that we only had to amend a few minor items to meet the safety check and he and I started to work on those jobs. His wife went to do a first provisioning trip for the long passage ahead. Once the captain and I were on our own, I approached him about one of my concerns.

'Excuse me, I have a question. Why do you keep the lifeboat below deck?' I probed politely.

'Well, we put it below because the dinghy is on the foredeck. Our deck space is limited due to the yacht's size. The lifeboat's easily accessible where it is now,' the captain replied.

'Mm ... But the raft is wedged behind the bench and it's a rather heavy and awkward to carry. How would I manage to get it on deck in heavy seas if you or the other crew are immobilised?' I persisted, bringing up the worst-case scenario in which it would be most needed. Usually this emergency item was fastened onto the deck, granting easy access in a crisis.

'I won't be immobilised,' he said, dismissing the conversation.

I mulled over his comment as I returned to my task. The likelihood of needing a life raft was minimal. However, any situation requiring the use of emergency equipment was likely to be messy and disturbing. People could be injured. If the yacht were to sink, and the crew were unable to carry the lifeboat on deck, chances were the raft would be rendered useless. I could see no point in that.

In the early afternoon, the skipper's wife returned with the first round of provisions – dry goods and non-perishables. We formed a line and passed the tinned food and bags of dried legumes, rice and pasta on board. Once the groceries were transferred, bottle upon bottle of alcohol followed. Beer, wine, sherry, brandy. You name it, we stocked it. I was astonished at the amount of alcohol. In my limited boating experience and from many chats overheard among sailors, a consistent thread had emerged: under way, the best boat is a dry boat! No alcohol at sea seemed a sensible policy to me, yet here I was, on a boat drowning in booze.

As we began stowing the provisions below deck, the skipper's wife directed me to put the tins in plastic crates in the saloon. I assumed this was a temporary solution and eventually expected to transfer the solid food containers into cupboards, storage compartments under seats, or the bilges under the floor panels.

'Where would you like me to stow the tins?' I asked later in the afternoon, keen to make myself useful. 'Should I make space somewhere or do you have an assigned spot set aside for them?'

The skipper and his wife met my question with blank stares.

'No. All the storage is full,' she said. 'The tins will stay in the plastic crates for the passage. We will shove them under the table.' She smiled and the skipper nodded in agreement.

'But what if we hit rough seas? Each of those tins will turn into a solid projectile.' In fair weather the plastic crates would not be a problem, but they posed a serious threat in heavy conditions. During my last passage, tins stored in this manner would have created havoc.

'Look, we're sailing to the Caribbean. The wind will be behind us. Please, stop stressing. It will be fine!'

The skipper was not interested in discussing my concerns further. I knew I was on a sound boat, with a reasonably experienced skipper and aware that our chances of encountering severe weather during this passage were slim. However, I also knew enough about the misfortunes of sailing, an environment where emergencies rapidly escalated into catastrophic situations.

That evening, I wandered over to Martin's boat again and invited him to come for a beer with me. Once seated, drink in hand, I explained my safety concerns. Martin listened carefully and criticised my skipper's choices on the lifeboat location and stowage of tins.

'Look, Regina,' he said, 'you shouldn't go on an ocean passage if you don't feel satisfied with the safety on board. If you like, I can explain your situation to Harvey and Giles and ask if you can join our boat instead for the trip. What do you think?'

'Really? You would do that?' I felt hope rising and blurted out, 'Martin, I would love to do the passage on *Phoenix*! You guys are so organised, and I would feel safer with you. Plus,' I added with a big grin, 'she's a stunner of a yacht!'

'Leave it with me,' he replied with a confident smile.

The next morning, I was stowing more supplies below deck, when someone called my name. Martin was standing on the dock and was waving me to come over. As soon as I stood beside him, he spoke excitedly in a low voice.

'Hey. I had a chat to the owners and crew, and everyone is happy for you to join us for the trip!' Beaming, he continued, 'You would share the cabin with the two bunks with Harvey. If you join, we will have a crew of seven. All this manpower will make for a relaxed watch roster. See if you can visit us this morning.'

Martin looked pleased with the outcome of his negotiations and I was delighted. We decided to pay *Phoenix* a visit immediately.

The owners and crew on *Phoenix* welcomed me aboard their yacht with big smiles. With less than a week to the start of the rally, Martin urged me to move onto *Phoenix* promptly.

As soon as I was back on board *Cleo*, I explained my departure.

'I am disappointed that you are abandoning us this late,' the skipper grumbled. 'But fair enough. You have to do what feels right for you.'

The skipper gave a nod and his wife added, 'It's okay. There are other crew looking for boats. We will be fine, don't worry.'

I quickly stuffed my gear into the backpack and trekked over to my new home. On *Phoenix,* Harvey directed me to the small cabin with the two bunks. He was occupying the lower one himself, so I dumped my bags on the upper bunk and joined everyone on deck. Amanda was the only other female crew member. She was a hands-on woman in her late forties with a warm and welcoming attitude and a great sense of humour. I was grateful for her presence.

Harvey was tall, with a friendly face, neatly combed grey hair, and a shy demeanour. He walked with a slight limp and had the distinguished air of an English gentleman. His formal conduct was a welcome contrast to the casual atmosphere in the sailing community. I noticed him awkwardly pushing a loaded trolley towards *Phoenix*. It looked heavy and I jumped off the boat to help him guide the cart safely beside the yacht. As we offloaded boxes, handing them from person to person, we began joking and laughing. More trolleys arrived and soon the boat's large deck was covered in cardboard containers, each bursting with fruit and vegetables. After expressing surprise at the lavish selection of fresh produce, under Harvey's scrutiny, we began carefully stowing the goods in allocated lockers.

During the next few days of preparations, joint dinners and drinks at the busy sailors' bar, I became acquainted with the others. Giles, the second owner, a few years younger than Harvey, was lively and charismatic. His mischievous eyes outshone his receding hairline. Giles liked to tinker and was always laughing at something. Martin quietly confided that Amanda was Giles' long-standing mistress. I appreciated that they were agreeable people and good company for a long-distance sail.

The remaining two crew members were Franco and Drew. Franco was a stocky, middle-aged Spanish restaurant owner. He was quiet and his brown eyes often seemed mournful to me. Engaged in a conversation, preferably over a beer or glass of wine, he livened up and revealed a warm smile. A night owl, he often dragged us to the bar for far longer than I cared for. Drew, in contrast, was a tall, slim and suave Brit in his mid-fifties. He was jovial and confident, with a ready supply of exotic stories from his colourful expat lifestyle. Although a good-humoured guy, his overly smooth and self-assured attitude made me slightly uncomfortable.

Martin was closest to my age and his approachable manner impressed me. He was a competent sailor and eager to help, or explain a technical question. He had a radiant and infectious smile and deep ocean blue eyes. As well, he was a tall, well-proportioned and attractive man.

Before we left, I took my new laptop to the internet cafe and called Jay.

'I am in the Canary Islands. I am on a good boat and will leave for St Lucia tomorrow,' I said. 'Jay, the trip will take about three weeks. Then I will see if I can catch a ride with another yacht to Antigua. I hope to be with you on your birthday and if not, at least for Christmas.'

Jay finally managed to get a word in, 'Babes, that's great news. I hope you will be safe! Don't worry and don't rush, Regina. I am waiting for you.'

He was his usual relaxed self. No pressure, no expectations. I wholeheartedly admired this character trait. Regardless of my lingering doubts, I was looking forward to reconnecting with him. He had an unusual pull over me, I thought, as I walked back to the yacht. I loved him and wanted to be close again. At the same time, I was aware of our differences and my struggle to accept his lack of education. I wondered if he was my rebound relationship, the reason Sven and I needed to part ways. I had never experienced 'a rebound' but could see that my initial infatuation had diminished. Was I returning to Antigua to be with him, or because the country was now familiar? I felt an affinity with Jay but was uncomfortably aware of my current lack of social connection and support network. Arriving at the yacht, I pushed these thoughts aside.

For now, it did not matter why I was returning to Antigua and during the passage I would have ample time to think and reflect. I was eagerly awaiting the start of the rally when we would head out to sea on *Phoenix*. Ever since my first transatlantic crossing I had longed for the simplicity of ocean-going days. I looked forward to settling back into the passage; a routine dictated by watch times, sleep, shared mealtimes, and endless hours of contemplating the infinite seascape surrounding our yacht.

18

CHASING SUNSETS

On the day the Atlantic Rally for Cruisers was to start, we slowly eased *Phoenix* out of the dock. Carefully we manoeuvred her through the plethora of yachts into the open ocean. Sailing boats of all sizes and shapes were crisscrossing in front of the marina. This rally was primarily for cruising yachts, but also included a racing division, and all boats were timed for the passage. Several sleek and powerful racing yachts were gearing up for an exciting start, like eager racehorses edging and nudging for a win. Sails were hoisted, proudly bulging in the stiff November breeze. Our engine was switched off and we were discussing our tactics for the start. Not wanting to damage *Phoenix* at the beginning of its round-the-world adventure, Harvey and Giles opted for a conservative approach. I would have loved to be near the excitement of the start line but could not fault their reasoning.

The start cannon went off with a bang that resonated across the sea. We changed tack and watched the professional racers sail swiftly into the distance, closely followed by keen amateurs. We crossed the start line a little later, among a pack of cruising yachts, and set our heading for the beautiful island of St Lucia, about 2,800 nautical miles due west of our current position. On a sailing yacht, this distance could take anywhere between eight days and a month, depending on boat type, wind and weather conditions, and the course sailed.

With *Phoenix* on course, I let my hair fly in the cool wind. I laughed and rejoiced in the familiar feeling. There was no question about it, I loved being at sea. Strangely for someone raised in a landlocked country, on the ocean I felt liberated and at home. Every time I looked toward the horizon the view was different, mesmerising and surprising. Before nightfall, we hoisted the spinnaker. The enormous red sail bulged far beyond the bow, eagerly pulling us toward the Caribbean. I dropped my head back and looked up at the mast. Gently rocked by wind and waves, the sun twinkled through the gaps where the sails and boat structure converged. My heart opened, my mind relaxed and I took a deep breath. Warm and snug in many layers of clothes, I felt the cool breeze brush my face.

Harvey spent most of his time below deck, more restricted in his movements due to the yacht's rolling deck. What he lacked in sailing enthusiasm, he made up for with his cooking prowess. He delivered one tasty meal after the other, ranging from mouth-watering Italian pastas to spicy Indian curries. His meals quickly became a daily highlight.

Giles was a restless soul. He and Amanda often sat together sewing or fixing something or brainstorming plans and ideas to enhance the boat. Drew made for entertaining company. An engaging storyteller, he'd recount tales of the exotic places he and his family had visited and lived in. He was our crew's keenest fisherman. On the open ocean he installed a fishing rod at the back of *Phoenix*, hopeful of luring a tasty meal.

Franco, our Spanish crew member, was withdrawn early in the passage. If not on watch, he usually was resting in his bunk. A few days into our trip he showed us his trembling hands, admitting that he was experiencing alcohol withdrawal. As a restaurant owner he said he was obliged to entertain his customers and was paying dearly for it now. I credited him for his honesty and openness, and was grateful that all the crew vowed to support him during this challenging time.

On *Phoenix* we had a two-crew watch system. Martin was my main watch buddy and I was grateful for his company. During our night watches, when the two of us sat in the dark, we would talk deeply and candidly about our lives. The previous year Martin had lost his young wife to cancer and subsequently decided to take a sabbatical to help him deal with his grief and contemplate his future. He was open and unafraid to show his vulnerability, and I was honoured by his honesty and trust. Sitting beside each other night after night, looking out for commercial ships and small yachts, I developed a little crush on him. Martin was not only intelligent, but also in tune with his emotions and unafraid to communicate; he had a well-grounded and balanced personality and with his good looks he was appealing on many levels. Early in the passage he mentioned that he had recently started dating someone and was obviously in love. He was a decent and loyal man, and polite about my quiet adoration. His high moral standards only made him more endearing.

My conversations with Martin had forced me to revisit some concerns regarding my relationship with Jay. Our nightly conversations highlighted the qualities I sorely missed in my partnership with Jay and my doubts about our future resurfaced. On *Phoenix* with Martin, I enjoyed meaningful dialogue and stimulating and informed discussions. Our talks confirmed for me how much I was attracted to emotional and intellectual intelligence. Jay was caring, loving and mature, but he lacked the finesse in language to verbalise and understand his emotions fully. He had qualities worth praising but our relationship lacked intellectual depth. What if I could experience love and passion, as well an emotional and intellectual connection with someone in a partnership?

These thoughts remained while I perched in the tiny pulpit seat at the very front of the yacht. I listened to music as the boat gently bobbed up and down on the long, mellow swell and evaluated myself, my life and my future. After this trip, I was heading back to Antigua, but with less enthusiasm and energy for the relationship. Yet, of one thing I was certain. Once back in Antigua I would secure employment on a yacht. I loved the life of a sea gypsy and to be paid for the privilege of living and working on a yacht would make it perfect.

A few days into the journey, the weather shifted and we started to experience more squalls. The rain usually showed up as dark cloud clusters looming on the horizon. As we approached, the mini systems provoked the wind to change direction and increase with sudden force. These localised weather patterns caused havoc on deck. Sails urgently needed to be reduced or changed until we safely passed under the saturated clouds.

On one occasion we didn't notice the weather change until it was too late. Suddenly, a spinnaker shackle let go and the enormous sail was flapping violently.

'*All hands on deck!*' came Giles' resounding call.

Immediately, we scrambled to our spots. Adrenaline pumping, we grasped for the wild sail and hurriedly lowered it to the deck. In its place we unfurled a small portion of the headsail. Luckily, the spinnaker had remained intact, surprising considering the force it had been exposed to. Deciding that we had experienced enough action for the time being, we stowed it away.

We were on a sailing route commonly known as the 'Rhumb Run', heading from east to west to the Caribbean. Usually, boats left Europe in late autumn, in search of warmer climes. Driven by steady seasonal trade winds, this was known as a long but pleasant and comfortable passage. Surprised when the weather steadily deteriorated, we were pummelled by rapidly approaching gusts. We were on guard, watching the radar for nearby squalls and continually trimming the sails.

During one of the daily roll calls organised by the rally officials on the high frequency radio, we were informed of a sad and sobering incident. A skipper on another yacht had been knocked unconscious by the boom as the mainsail swept across the yacht due to an uncontrolled gybe. The captain was picked up by a cruise liner a day after the accident, but sadly died. Struck by the news, our crew sat in front of the radio in solemn silence. We eventually shared our thoughts about the fragility and preciousness of life, and vowed to take extra care.

A few days later, in calmer weather, we were in steady but still uncomfortable conditions. We began trialling the 'twizzle rig', which was a sail configuration I had not encountered prior to this passage. Harvey and Giles were proud of their unique arrangement and happily educated me. It was a double headsail, each of the sails poled out on either side of the yacht, rendering this configuration perfect for dead downwind sailing. Among the seven of us, the twizzle rig created some controversy and was the cause of many debates. The upside: it was simple to set up and the boat sailed easily downwind, involving none of the attention that a spinnaker required. The downside: all the sail area was on the very front of the yacht. Having so much sail area forward pulled the bow downward, and without a mainsail, the boat was unbalanced and unstable. This unpredictable rolling motion along with the inconsistent tinkling and clanging sounds were challenging. Being flung from one side of the bunk to the other, and first my head and then my toes pressing uncomfortably up against the cabin walls was not my idea of a good night's sleep.

Personally, I did not enjoy the quirky sail configuration. I found it awkward, turning the gorgeous yacht into a clumsy duckling. But Giles and Harvey were in charge, and they loved it. Without much other distraction, the debates on the 'twizzle' kept us entertained.

As everyone adjusted to the 'watch-sleep-eat' routine, we began to spend more time chatting and getting to know each other. Franco, to our relief, resurfaced after his unexpected detox. He became more social and jovial as the days passed. I could see his caring personality shine through and enjoyed listening to his quirky hospitality tales. Martin continued to send expensive daily messages via satellite phone to his beloved in Switzerland, while Harvey cooked and wrote eloquent stories for the rally blog. Giles and Amanda kept to themselves and seemed content in each other's company.

As we sailed on, the weather improved. We were still experiencing an occasional squall, but nothing overly dangerous or stressful. Other yachts were not as lucky. Although all yachts had departed from the Canary Islands at the same time, due to the varying sizes and builds, the fleet was now scattered across hundreds of miles. While enjoying these pleasant conditions, we were rendered speechless upon hearing a high frequency radio broadcast mid-afternoon.

'*Mayday, Mayday, Mayday!*'

All heads shot up in unison and my heart thumped at the sound of the most dreaded of marine emergency broadcasts. Everyone focused intently on the distressing transmission.

'This is yacht *Somersby* and we are taking on water. Our position is …'

Martin frantically scrambled for pen and paper and scribbled down the vessel's coordinates. Sombrely, we listened to the end of the broadcast. The boat's hull had a hole that the crew were unable to plug. The pump was working hard but the water was entering the hull at a faster rate. Their yacht was slowly sinking.

We compared our positions and noticed that we were within thirty nautical miles of the yacht in distress. *Somersby* was located behind us, meaning we would have to take the twizzle rig down and retrace our course for five to six hours, until we reached the floundering yacht to rescue the crew.

Martin and I looked at each other and simultaneously declared, 'We have to go back and help!'

Harvey and Giles remained silent for a moment, looking at each other and then at the chart. Harvey eventually murmured, 'It would mean motoring a long way back. Surely, someone else is closer and can get there quicker …'

Silence filled the cabin. Martin and I looked at each other in disbelief.

'But, Harvey, Giles!' Martin insisted. 'It is an unwritten marine law that while at sea one *must* help a vessel in distress. We *must* go back. Their boat is sinking!' He spoke with an urgency and ferocity I had not heard before, and I nodded in agreement.

Just then the radio crackled again, and we listened in. 'Yacht *Somersby*, Yacht *Somersby*, Yacht *Somersby*, this is Yacht *Dream Chaser*. We are within twenty nautical miles of you and have changed our course to assist you. We will be with you within three to four hours; please change to VHF Channel 16 and keep advising your position there. *Dream Chaser*. Out.'

The collective relief was tangible; we had been gracefully let off the hook. I was thrilled that another vessel was closer and already on the way to assist the sailors. Over the following hours, our thoughts were with the people on the damaged yacht. What were they doing? How were they feeling out there, surrounded by nothing but the sea? Was the water rising slowly or were they sinking fast?

We desperately hoped that they were safe and that the rescuing yacht would arrive in time. I remembered my hesitation and guilt about changing boats before this passage and was glad I had followed my gut instinct. The sinking vessel was not the yacht I'd initially planned to crew on, but my concern that disasters do happen at sea had been validated. I was grateful to be on a boat that was safe and sound.

The hours dragged. Finally, during the scheduled radio roll call in the evening, we were notified that *Dream Chaser* had reached the sinking boat and *Somersby*'s crew members were safe aboard the rescuing vessel. Unfortunately, *Somersby* was semi-submerged in the ocean and had to be abandoned. We were given the yacht's last known coordinates, in the hope of preventing collisions with the remaining fleet.

As we sailed closer to the Caribbean, the temperatures increased while the wind decreased, markedly slowing our progress. After *Somersby*'s tragic experience, no one complained about the easing conditions and we made the most of the balmy weather. There was hardly any swell, only a slow and gentle rise and fall; a movement so subtle it felt like the breath of the ocean. We peeled off layers of clothing in the warmer weather, and caught up on much-needed sleep. Feeling rested and revitalised, we began to socialise more.

Somewhere around the halfway point between Gran Canaria and St Lucia on the large chart of the Atlantic Ocean, I celebrated my birthday. I could not have wished for a better way to spend this day. The sky was clear and the ocean extended like an infinite shimmering navy carpet. I was in my element, surrounded by endless sea and sky. My sailing companions celebrated my birthday with a surprise gathering. Harvey opened a bottle of wine for the occasion and raising our glasses we sat in the streamer-adorned cockpit, wearing paper hats and sharing a cake topped with a candle. I was touched by the crew's thoughtfulness and felt grateful and blessed for my wonderful experiences. Life was good.

We had been at sea for more than two weeks now and were moving ever closer to St Lucia. Harvey and Martin were diligently marking our location on an enormous paper chart every twelve hours. I loved watching our progress on the oceanic map. The massive blue expanse was crisscrossed with latitude and longitude lines and showed only minimal landmass on either side of the page. Harvey explained that he had chosen the paper chart as a backup, in case of complete electronic failure.

As we started to approach our destination, Harvey and Giles took more interest in our speed and progress. Spotting an identical yacht participating in the rally, they realised we were inadvertently engaged in a match race. In recent weeks we had slowly gained ground on the other boat. Motivated by sighting it, Giles and Harvey steadily increased our lead.

With our arrival imminent, everyone began talking about their plans ashore. Martin was flying back to Switzerland and looking forward to being reunited with his lady. Franco had enjoyed the sobriety aboard and voiced mixed feelings about returning to his old environment. Harvey, Amanda and Giles were looking forward to exploring the Caribbean before sailing *Phoenix* into the Pacific. I was hoping to catch a ride on a boat to Antigua.

Anticipating our arrival in the Caribbean, excitement rose as St Lucia finally appeared on the horizon. Slowly the Pitons, two tall and distinct peaks, emerged. The bay was buzzing with vessels. The committee boat honked its horn as we crossed the finish line and many little yachts and dinghies cheered us on. Caught up in a surge of exuberance, we punched the air with our fists, high-fived and embraced each other, expressing our gratitude about our enjoyable and safe passage. My second transatlantic crossing had been significantly different to my first one, more social and comfortable, but both had been memorable and enjoyable trips. The crews on both journeys had been genuine and respectful individuals and I counted myself fortunate to have had such positive experiences.

We celebrated our arrival with a crew dinner at the marina restaurant. The food was divine, the wine palatable and plentiful, and the company vibrant and joyful. Later, intoxication transformed merriness into rowdy bragging. Not drinking much myself, I felt sobered by the loud proclamations and exaggerated tales. Sailors, I thought, and with an exasperated sigh I quietly went outside for a short walk. It felt odd, being on solid ground again. If I stood still, I noticed myself gently swaying in the memory of the ocean. After the long period on the water, I filled my lungs with the island's fresh, scented air and embraced the night's silence. Tomorrow I would have to scout for another boat and prepare for the transition ahead.

On my way back to *Phoenix,* I saw Franco staggering out of a bar. He waved at me and was slurring incomprehensibly. I walked up to him to see what he was trying to say. He was very drunk and indicated that he wanted to return to the boat. His coordination was faltering, so I put my arm around his waist and guided him along the wobbly floating dock to the boat. Once we reached the yacht I pushed and shoved, determined to get Franco safely on board. He landed on the deck on his hands and knees. I put a cushion on the cockpit bench and Franco immediately curled up and fell asleep on it. Tired, I prepared myself for bed and went to my bunk. Harvey was quietly snoring in the bottom bunk and the cabin felt hot and stuffy. After a while, unable to sleep, I decided to get up and rest on the second cockpit bench in the fresh air. Traipsing through the main cabin I noticed Franco curled up in foetal position, stark naked and sound asleep on the galley floor. Perplexed by the unusual sight, I considered my options and decided I could not leave him there for other crew members to discover.

'Franco! Wake up!' I nudged him and when he did not stir, I called out louder and prodded more decisively.

'Whaaaat?' Groggily he opened his eyes.

'Franco, you must go to bed now!' I stared at him sternly, channelling my inner mother. Much to my surprise the approach worked. Without another word he got up and awkwardly clambered across to his bunk.

'Regina, you want to come into bed with me?' he asked, looking at me with puppy eyes. I suppressed a laugh.

'No, dude. Not going to happen. You need to rest.' I pulled the cover over him and he promptly returned to sleep.

Chuckling to myself, I went up to the cockpit. Sitting on my own and enjoying the cool air and the peace, I began to relax again. Just then, Drew turned up from his night out. Seeing I was awake, he sat next to me.

'Hey, girl. You look tired. Would you like a shoulder massage?' he asked and though taken aback by his offer, I nodded, accepting the kind gesture.

Skilfully he started rubbing the tight muscles in my neck and shoulders and I felt myself relax. The massage stopped and Drew's hands rested on my shoulders.

'Hey, sweetie.' I felt his breath on my ear as he whispered, 'You have a beautiful body. I would love to explore it. Will you let me?'

Pardon me? I quickly shuffled sideways to create some distance between us. I turned to look at Drew, attempting to gauge his intent. It was possible the married man was joking, but seeing his facial expression, I knew he was serious.

Before I could formulate a reply, he continued, 'Regina, I want to make love to you before we go. Please, sweetie.'

I was stunned by his frank request. What a strange night this was turning out to be.

'Drew, no, let me be clear. We will not have sex. It's a definite "no". Please, leave me alone and go to bed now.' I must have made myself clear, as he stood up and, without further comment, disappeared into his cabin. I sighed with relief and sat up a little longer, absorbing the night's bewildering events. After a while, fell into a restless sleep.

Unsurprisingly, the next morning was slow to start, with several members of the crew nursing hangovers. I decided to go scouting for a lift back to Antigua. Psyching myself up for the dreaded task, I felt relieved when my initial clumsy attempts were met with friendly smiles and pleasant responses. After a few positive experiences, I started to relax into the process and soon was directed towards a boat with *Ventura Racing* boldly displayed on its hull. This was no ordinary cruising vessel, and I was curiously checking it out, thinking that a trip on this fast-looking yacht would be thrilling. I saw a guy working on deck and approached him.

'Hi,' I called out and he looked up.

'Hey there,' came the friendly reply. He waved and put down his tools.

'Umm …' I cleared my throat nervously. 'I am looking for a spot on a yacht to get to Antigua and the crew over there have pointed me in your direction.' I smiled shyly.

'Yes, that's right. I'll be heading there the day after tomorrow. Do you just want to sail to Antigua?' he asked. His demeanour was calm and friendly; he had a pleasant smile and a regular sailor's bleached and untamed mop of hair.

'Yes, I have been to Antigua before and I want to base myself there so I can look for work on a superyacht. I'm hoping with the season just starting, luck will be on my side.' I rambled on nervously, my heart beating.

He wiped his calloused hands on a washed-out work shirt and extended one hand to me. 'I'm Sam. Nice to meet you.' He smiled again, and we shook hands while I introduced myself. Sam continued, 'Regina, you're welcome to join me. As I said I will leave in two days, so how about you move on board tomorrow, if that suits you?'

I had to pinch myself to believe my luck. I was going to sail to Antigua on a racing yacht. Overjoyed I returned to *Phoenix*, smiling all the way. I was amazed by how everything was working out with ease. All it took was a little initiative and a gutful of trust.

That evening, as we sat around the dinner table, I looked at our group. Harvey, Giles, Amanda, Franco, Drew and Martin were all eating and talking amicably. Once again, I was reminded how quickly friendships were forged on a boat. When I mentioned my plans, the crew members expressed their happiness at my continued adventure.

The next day, all of them lined up on the dock and I put my bags down so I could farewell them properly. I was sent off with big smiles and hearty hugs. At the end of the line Franco quickly pulled me aside and I felt him slip something into the palm of my hand. Money. Surprised, I looked at him.

'I know you don't have much, Regina. You will be able to put this to good use. Take care and please, look after yourself,' he said with a warm and genuine smile. He nodded, insisting I keep his gift. My heart warmed at his goodwill and sweet gesture.

19

MANIFESTING AMBITIONS

Sam was on deck, busy with maintenance chores, when I walked along the dock.

'Regina. Welcome!' he called as I handed him my bags and stepped aboard. 'You're the first one here. Two more crew will be joining us. You get first pick of the bunks.'

I went below deck to check out the sleeping arrangements: four simple bunks in an open-plan cabin. I sat down to figure out which would be best for me. The prevailing wind direction would cause the boat to heel to port, so sleeping would be easier on the left side bunks. I deposited my bags and went back up. Sam looked at me and smiled.

'Which bunk did you go for?'

'Top port,' I said, and explained my theory.

'Good choice!' He nodded approvingly and asked me to help him with some easy maintenance tasks.

We got busy preparing the boat for our early departure the next day. One by one, the remaining crew arrived; both friendly, easy-going guys in their mid-twenties. One was Spanish, the other came from Denmark. Over our quick and simple pasta dinner, Sam briefed us on the short trip ahead. The boat had enough provisions for the twenty-four-hour sail, so all we needed to do in the morning was get up early and set off.

The trip was quick, fun and social. The breeze pushed us along at a steady pace. Sitting in the cockpit we shared stories of our respective passages across the Atlantic. The Spaniard mentioned he had done his crossing on a 50-foot Moody and I nearly splattered my mouthful of tea over the cockpit. That was the sister yacht of *Phoenix*, the one we had been secretly match racing all the way! When I told him, he looked at me in disbelief and began to laugh.

'That's hilarious because we certainly did not race!' he said. 'The owner of my yacht was a wealthy Spanish dude and I crewed on his boat because he paid me well to do the trip. We left Gran Canaria, put up the sails, and never touched them again until we reached St Lucia. All he cared about was that I served him wine and cooked good food. Lots of food,' he added, rolling his eyes.

I hooted with laughter. Back on *Phoenix*, Harvey and Giles had repeatedly boasted about our performance and expressed pride about our victory over the sister yacht. Little did they know that we had been racing a lazy glutton.

The next morning, Antigua became visible on the horizon. I watched with both joy and trepidation as we approached the land. Nudging ever closer to my island home, I was wondering how this stay would work out for me. I could not, and did not want to, keep leaving and returning. I knew this visit would be the deciding chapter for Jay and me.

Sam interrupted my thoughts to announce that we were heading into Falmouth Harbour. This was where Henry and Maude had been docked and where my initial holiday on Antigua had begun. I tried not to look surprised or worried at the information and hoped that Sam would not face problems signing me in.

After we swiftly docked in the marina, Sam collected our passports. This time I handed in my Australian document, which I had used during my initial visit. I was hoping that my nationality swap once again would provide a smooth re-entry into Antigua.

Sam returned an hour later and returned our passports. Checking the pages, I looked for the familiar mark. I was stamped in for two weeks. It was narrow window in which to find a job, but I had been allowed in, and that's what mattered most.

Once we'd finished a quick clean up, Sam released us and we dispersed. I had called Jay as soon as we'd docked, and he said he had left the door open for me. Trying to keep a low profile, I left the marina quietly. It felt strange bumping along in the tired old minibus, taking in the familiar sights. Although I had left Antigua less than two months earlier, it seemed a lifetime ago.

I made my way to the little yellow house and let myself in. Everything looked the same: smelly shoes airing on the verandah, the worn daybed in the front room, and the tiny adjoining kitchen. The bedroom was unchanged too, its queen bed covered by the mosquito net and Jay's gigantic pile of clothes in the corner. I dropped my bags and lay down. I was here.

For a moment, I closed my eyes, allowing my soul to arrive. My return journey had been eventful and enjoyable. Now that I was here, I was struggling to feel enthusiastic. With fresh eyes I took in the haphazard build and the frugal furnishings of Jay's home. Could I live like this, not just for a few months, but permanently?

It was only a few days before Christmas, and I was aware that the clock was ticking. My priority was to find employment. I decided to cast aside my doubts and worries about the relationship for now and instead focus my energy on finding work. The goal was to get a job on a superyacht, to avoid repeating the work permit fiasco – crew employed on superyachts were subject to the laws of the yacht's country of registration. I was lying down, visualising my new and exciting job on a stunning vessel with lovely colleagues, when Jay bounced into the little house. The shack's recycled timber floor and wall panels trembled under his quick footsteps.

'Babes! You're back!' he called out, beaming. He gave me a fierce hug and planted a kiss on my lips. At his joy, my hesitation evaporated and my spirits lifted.

'Happy belated birthday,' I said, followed by a teasing kiss as I snuggled into his strong arms. Inhaling his familiar scent, I sighed. 'It's good to be home!'

Christmas was a quiet day for us. Waking up late, we sat on the verandah, drinking the fragrant herbal tea I had come to enjoy so much. Curious about his situation, I asked Jay about the money I had given to him before I left.

'I gave the money to my sister, and we took half of it and went to the government department to register a piece of land in my name,' Jay said.

Hearing this, I became excited, until he continued. 'We had to sign many papers and pay the officer in cash.' He stopped suddenly, gaze downcast. He took a breath before continuing, 'Then nothing happened. When we went back, the man wasn't there anymore, and we asked someone else. They couldn't find any proof of my registration or the down payment. The new officer said that the man I dealt with had cheated many people and recently fled the country with the money he stole.'

I was gobsmacked. Half the money I had given to Jay was lost. For a moment I sat quietly, absorbing the news. This was yet another aspect to life in Antigua, I realised with sadness. I was devastated that Jay had been unable to proceed with the purchase of the land.

'Okay, don't worry about it, Jay. It's not your fault. But that is only half of the money. What happened to the rest? I mean, you can go in again and put less money down for the land and still go ahead with your plans, right?'

'My sister has the money and my auntie borrowed some for something she needed to buy. I'll get it back and get the land then.' By now, Jay was avoiding my eyes and his voice fell into an inaudible mumble. My stomach sank.

All the money, my savings, which I had put into the motorcycle and then uncomfortably retrieved, seemed tainted. By gifting it to Jay, I had hoped it would serve a good purpose. Yet the money was slowly sifting away, like sand through our fingers.

Maybe it was just as well. Jay was comfortable in his situation. Perhaps I needed to take a step back and allow him to live his life the way it suited him. My intentions had been good, but with the money gone, I finally and fully accepted Jay's reality. I had no right to expect a result from my gift, nor was it my responsibility to improve Jay's life according to my values. He was content with himself, whereas I was restless and in constant search for my own contentment and equilibrium. Jay had never asked me to change him, instead I had insisted and volunteered. The time had come for me to accept him for who he was, and back off from attempts to rescue and improve him or his situation.

Having shared the uncomfortable news, Jay looked more at ease. I smiled and gave him a kiss. I too felt lighter and relieved. Interesting, I thought, how everything had a way of taking care of itself.

Effortlessly, we slipped back into our familiar routine. A few days after Christmas I started feeling sluggish and sore. My joints began to ache, followed by a croaky and inflamed throat. I had come down with the flu.

I spent a few days bound at home; sleeping, sweating and aching. Jay brought me some rum and prepared a 'healing remedy' of rum, lime, brown sugar and boiling water. After swallowing the steaming sweet concoction, I promptly fell into a restless sleep, filled with vivid dreams. By New Year's Eve I was able to venture out cautiously. We chose to celebrate the turn of the year in All Saints, eating local food and attending a concert held on the football field in the middle of the village.

With my health improved, I began to feel anxious about the precious days I had lost while bedridden. There was less than a week of my holiday permit remaining, and I urgently needed employment. I showered, cleaned myself up and made my way to English Harbour. Purposefully, I approached the first dock and sauntered up to a lady who was working aboard a stunning little wooden yacht.

'Hi!' I called out and she looked up and smiled. A good start.

'Ciao,' she replied with a distinct Italian accent. 'Can I help you?'

'Yes. I'm Regina. I'm looking for work on one of the sailing yachts. I was wondering if you know who may be hiring?' I shot her a hopeful look along with an endearing smile. I needed all the help I could get today.

'Oh, okay. Let me think.' Frowning, she tilted her head pensively, tucking a stray curl behind her ear.

'Yes, I remember,' she said excitedly. She pointed towards a yacht. 'Try *PuraVida* over there. I think they are looking for a stewardess.' Her face lit up with a big smile and I felt drawn to her warm-hearted decency.

'Thank you. I really appreciate your help.' I said. 'I will go there now and try my luck!'

She waved and returned to work. I threw my shoulders back, made sure my hair was neat and tidy, and headed towards *PuraVida*. The stunning 100-foot vessel was elegant and modern, and from a sailor's perspective, very sexy. Her topsides were sparkling, stainless steel gleamed in the sunlight, everything looked immaculate. I was impressed.

I gathered up my courage and called out. A guy with shoulder-length brown hair tucked behind his ears and a friendly face, popped up from below deck. As he climbed up, I saw that he was of solid build. His warm smile gave him the air of a gentle giant.

'Hello,' he said, exposing a perfect set of teeth.

'Hi. I have been talking to the lady on the vessel over there and she mentioned that you may be looking for a stewardess?' I asked nervously. 'I'm looking for work and I would love to work on a beautiful yacht like yours. I am a hard worker and very motivated. If you are interested, I have my resume with me…'

'Yes, that's right,' he said, and gestured for me to step aboard. 'I am Enzo, the first mate.' His eyes twinkled as he smiled and extended his hand. Another Italian and clearly a charmer. I smiled back and shook his hand.

We sat in the cockpit as Enzo took a quick look over my resume and asked a few questions. He asked if I would mind coming back in an hour to meet the captain.

I was thrilled with the opportunity and promised to be back on time. This was looking positive and I was feeling hopeful. We shook hands again and I felt like skipping down the dock.

Rather than just sit around and wait for an hour to pass, I decided to look up the second crew agency in town. I had heard rumours about this agency's owner. Her reputation as a tough and uncompromising woman preceded her and though some found that intimidating, I respected that she successfully ran a tight business. Still, I approached her office with apprehension. I was conscious of being far beyond the average age of superyacht crew – the majority being in their early to mid-twenties. Also, as I didn't have someone who could vouch for my professional experience in the industry, I wasn't sure how she would receive me.

When she invited me into her office, I had to suppress a chuckle. Like a queen on a throne, she sat in an enormous wicker chair, its oval-shaped back enveloping her small stature. She had immaculately coiffed hair, a pale complexion and was wearing a conservative designer outfit. Her manicured hands rested gracefully on the large desk in front of her.

I refused to be daunted by her regal appearance, the surroundings or her reputation.

'Hi, there. How can I help you?' she asked with no smile, a raised eyebrow and a stiff stare. I smiled cautiously.

'Hello. I am looking for a job!' I chose to be direct, not wanting to waste time. 'I have sailed the Atlantic twice but have no professional experience on a superyacht. However, I have plenty of customer service experience, speak several languages and have a great work ethic. I work hard and always give my best,' I said, meeting her unflinching gaze.

'What kind of job are you looking for?' she asked calmly.

Taking this as a good sign, I explained. 'I would love to be a deckhand. I want to learn everything I can about sailing and sailboat maintenance. I know I am a small person,' I said, jumping out of my chair, '*but ...*' I flexed my biceps.

Her eyebrows rose in astonishment.

I continued, 'I am strong, determined, and I can do it!' I finished with a hearty laugh, satisfied with my performance. Right at this moment I did not care about her thoughts or judgements. I had presented a taste of 'me'. To my surprise she started to laugh, and I relaxed.

'Well,' she said with a smile, 'getting you a deckhand position is difficult because you have no qualifications and no experience. I don't doubt your strength, but I think a stewardess position would be easier to find. Would you consider that?'

'Yes. I realise that my chances for a deckhand position are slim. But I still had to try, right?' I added, 'At this stage I want a job on a superyacht, so I can learn as much as possible about the industry. I am excited and motivated. This I can guarantee.'

The agent nodded. 'I have something in mind for you. It's a stewardess/cook position on a large superyacht with a crew of three. The job just came in and you would be in the right age group. I think you would be a great match. If you are interested, I will put your application forward,' she said.

This was turning out to be an incredible day. She sent me off, promising to be in touch shortly.

I treated myself to a fresh juice and digested the morning's events. I was buzzing and found it hard to contain myself. I felt like jumping for joy and shouting how lucky and excited I was. Instead, I quietly sipped my juice and basked in the glow.

When I approached *PuraVida* I could see Enzo and another man on deck. He was short and slender, with wispy blond hair. He had a confident stance and there was no doubt he was the man in charge. I called out and they both turned to look at me.

'You're Regina? Please, come aboard.' The skipper waved and invited me on deck, with a smile.

'EZ, as in "easy", my nickname for Enzo, has mentioned that you are looking for a job. Let's sit down for a moment,' he said, gesturing towards the cockpit table. We both took a seat, while Enzo disappeared below deck.

'Now, Regina. My name's Simon. I am the captain.' He shook my hand. 'I took a quick look at your resume. You haven't any industry experience, so what makes you suddenly look for a job on a sailing vessel?'

I described my love for sailing and what I had done so far. I told Simon I wanted to learn everything I could about sailing and the industry. The captain nodded and went on to explain more about the position.

As he described it, my job would be to keep the interior of the yacht immaculate, as well as to cook for owners, guests and crew. Simon outlined that the cooking was not expected to be to restaurant standard, as the owner preferred simple cuisine. I would work a five-day week while the yacht was in port and nonstop when the owner or guests were on board. He quoted a salary, indicating that it would increase with experience, and asked if I had any questions.

'Yes. I have one, actually. I have heard of wild parties and drugs on boats. I do not want to be involved with a boat that is in favour of such behaviour. I want to make that clear.'

Simon looked surprised at my frank statement, but quickly agreed that this was a fair comment. He assured me that drugs and wild parties would not be a concern on his yacht.

'Well, Regina, I must be honest. I was planning to employ someone in a few weeks, upon my return from a business trip to South Africa. *PuraVida* is a new yacht and we have just completed her maiden voyage. I need to leave the boat and visit the shipyard to discuss some modifications.' Simon looked thoughtful as he continued, 'However, I like what I see in you, and I believe you will fit in well with EZ and me, so I would like to offer you the job now. When can you start?'

For a moment I was stunned. I could not believe that I had managed to secure a job in one day. 'Mm … tomorrow, if you like?'

'All right, good. We have a deal.' Simon grinned and stood up. 'You can move your belongings on board tomorrow morning, and we will take it from there. Welcome to *PuraVida*!'

When I told Jay about my new job, he lifted me up and twirled me around, happy for me. He knew this meant I would soon leave the island, but he understood that I needed an income. As I left his little home with my luggage in hand, I felt both sad and relieved. Sad about the chapter with Jay nearing its end, and relief for being free and secure.

20

CLEANING, COOKING, RACING

Calling out, I dropped my heavy bag onto the dock with a thud. Quick as a flash, a beaming Enzo popped up from the stern locker and rushed over.

'Welcome, Regina! It's nice to have you on board.' he smiled. A true Italian gentleman, he grabbed my backpack and carried it across the narrow gangway. He walked down the stairway and I followed him below deck.

'This cabin on the right is mine, and this one on the left is yours,' he said.

He dropped my bag on the floor of my cabin as I quickly assessed my new home. It was a sizeable space, containing two bunk beds and plenty of storage lockers. A hatch in the ceiling allowed natural light to filter in and brighten my cosy nest. I was thrilled to have the luxury of privacy.

'For now, just unpack your bags. We will all go for lunch together today and in the afternoon, Simon will explain your chores and daily routine.' He gave a little wave and another cheerful smile and left me to my own devices. I unpacked my belongings, for the umpteenth time, and happily made myself at home. When everything was in place, I sat on the bottom bunk, appreciating my surroundings.

Within a day I had moved from Jay's basic wooden shack onto this brand-new multi-million-dollar superyacht. The contrast was mind-boggling.

Lunch with Simon and Enzo was a laidback affair. They were both good-humoured and friendly, trying their best to make me feel at home. Afterwards, Simon got down to business. Walking through the yacht, he outlined his expectations of me. As well as the daily cooking and cleaning duties, my first assignment was to create a comprehensive inventory of all internal storage spaces. On a 100-foot yacht, this would be a time-consuming mission. A plethora of cupboards, cubicles, bilge spaces and hidden crevices were filled with non-perishable foods, alcohol, household items, sailing accessories and tools.

My workdays were mostly spent down on my knees, bottom up, unpacking and repacking each storage space while compiling the detailed inventory. I also polished all the toilets and bathrooms until they sparkled, and painstakingly wiped down the interior woodwork to maintain its immaculate condition. I made beds, delivered laundry and prepared meals for the three of us. The job was not as glorious as it appeared from the outside looking in. After a week, a thick layer of protective skin developed on my knees, from the continuous cleaning and crawling around tight spaces, and my upper body grew more muscular from all the scrubbing and buffing.

Simon, I quickly learned, hosted a steady stream of male friends on board each afternoon. Without fail, those men arrived with an unquenchable thirst for cold beer. *PuraVida's* owner not only provided complimentary food for the crew, but also free alcohol, on the condition that it was consumed on board. As I was in charge of provisions, I found myself hauling beer crates to the yacht each day.

A little over a week into my job, Simon reminded me that he was soon leaving for South Africa, and that Enzo would depart shortly after, to obtain his Yachtmaster licence in Miami. Suddenly, I found myself boat-sitting a new luxury yacht, worth 15 million US dollars! Diligently I did my chores, often reflecting on my situation while scrubbing and cleaning. The move from Jay's modest little house onto the luxury of *PuraVida* had been a giant leap. There were moments when I was confronted by the incredible divide and struggled with the opulence of the superyacht industry. Jay was working hard and earning around US $100 a week, while I was working in an industry where bigger was considered better. A crew member of another superyacht mentioned their owner handing out cash gifts of US $20,000 to each guest as 'spending money', and it was not unusual to have exclusive items flown in for a demanding or eccentric owner.

As a break from life on board, I'd discovered a gorgeous little hiking trail and often walked it after work. The trailhead started from Pigeon Beach and was partially overgrown, making it hard to spot. The narrow path wove uphill through a shrubby forest, then meandered along the exposed cliffs overlooking the ocean on one side and dry rocky landscape on the other. I frequently encountered wild goats up on the higher section of the path, before the trail led down a steep slope terminating in Nelsons Dockyard. The walk filled my soul with peace and gave me time to reflect on my relationship with Jay. I called him frequently for a quick chat and some afternoons he would visit me after work. Occasionally, we walked to Pigeon Beach or followed the coastal trail to a lookout point, where we caught up on our day and stole a few kisses. I tried to keep my life as private as possible on the dock, not wanting to be the focus of community gossip.

Jay and I were together most weekends, usually concluding with the Sunday night party at Shirley Heights. I still danced with abandon to the familiar tunes and loved connecting with the local visitors, performers and staff, who I had come to know well. Weekends became a time to reconnect with 'my Antigua', far removed from my yachting reality.

Antigua had become my home. Everyone was friendly and welcoming. Much to my astonishment, I realised that for the first time in my life, I felt a true sense of belonging. At first this surprised me but upon reflection I realised that I had always felt unconditionally accepted in Antigua, even as a white woman immersed in a predominately black population. Jay's family and friends, people I had met, and the community at large, had all welcomed me. I felt content and at home among the local people and was awash with gratitude for their kindness, openness and for accepting me in their midst.

Enzo returned from his trip in an exuberant mood. He had successfully completed the course and was now the proud bearer of a Yachtmaster certification. He was close friends with the all-Italian crew on the neighbouring vessel, and in honour of his return and to celebrate his accomplishment, we were invited for dinner on their yacht. The chef cooked up a storm. We were served several courses of scrumptious Italian food and, courtesy of the owner, the finest red wines to accompany our meal.

The evening was delightful and companionable. Surrounded by Italians, I did not try to follow the conversation. Instead, soaking up the merry atmosphere and company of Enzo's friends, I realised that I had missed the company of my own people. Sharing a meal and engaging in meaningful conversation with close friends felt like nourishment for my body and soul and was one of my favourite pastimes. With a sense of nostalgia, I wondered when I would reconnect with my tribe in Australia again.

Simon, our captain, returned from South Africa and resumed his work on board. Soon after, I noticed Enzo had lost his usual sparkle and was keeping to himself more. While Simon was onshore with an errand, I took him aside.

'What's up, Enzo? Have I done something wrong?' My concern must have been written on my face, as Enzo quickly reassured me.

'*No!* No, Reggie, nothing's wrong with you. It's Simon. He treats me like crap and it's really hard to work with him.' His shoulders sagged and he looked deflated.

I was surprised. I had thought that everything was hunky dory. I made us both a cup of coffee and we sat down for a chat.

'You know, Reggie. It's like my work is never good enough for him. He is so pleasant with his friends and everyone else on the dock. But with me, it's a different story. It's almost as if he's waiting for me to do something wrong, so he can criticise me.' His eyes filled with a brooding look. 'You also need to know that Simon has a reputation with female crew. He considers himself a bit of a stallion and doesn't seem impressed that you and I get along well.'

I swallowed this piece of information like a piece of dry bread. Here we go, I thought, finally the friction and interpersonal subcurrents of *PuraVida* were being revealed. I chuckled at the complexity of human relationships, especially on boats. Considering that we were all strangers, shacked up together in a limited space, I was not surprised to encounter tension. We would just have to negotiate a way to coexist.

After his revelations, Enzo relaxed somewhat. I was glad he had shared his concerns with me and took a mental note of Simon's womanising habits. Even though he had never acted inappropriately toward me, I stayed alert and vowed to keep our connection strictly professional.

We began preparations to get *PuraVida* shipshape for the upcoming Heineken Regatta in St Maarten. Simon spent most of his workday sitting in his little computer cubicle on board. He was making countless phone calls and sending emails, trying to coordinate flights and accommodation for the race crew. Many of these sailors were his friends flying in from Australia. Last minute adjustments to the equipment kept Enzo busy while I began organising the catering. After a few weeks of *PuraVida* sitting stationary on the dock, I was looking forward to setting sail and racing her. Still, I felt trepidation towards hosting twenty or more men aboard during the regatta.

Sonny, one of Simon's friends, was one of the first to join us. He was a happy-go-lucky, raggedy looking man; a serious drinker and a renowned party animal with a cute smile and a good heart. Taking note of my limited industry exposure, he took it upon himself to brief me about the days ahead.

'Reggie, you need to know that this week will be a rough and ready time, okay?' he said. When he saw my questioning look, he continued, 'There will be roaring parties, packed with rowdy drunken sailors.' A sheepish look passed over his face. He and I both knew he would be at the centre of this crowd.

'Look, I don't know how to say this, Reggie, but it ain't pretty. There will be girls; some paid, some not. They will shag around and be pretty much fair game.' By now, he avoided my gaze completely and I remained silent, trying to absorb the disturbing message.

'You won't be able to escape the talk. So just toughen up and try to grin and bear it, all right?' he said.

I knew he was trying to help me, but this was troubling information.

'Another thing, Reggie. If you don't want to engage in those kinds of frivolities, you will have to establish your boundaries. Am I clear?' Finally, Sonny looked straight into my eyes and I nodded. His words made me feel sick to the stomach, but I was also immensely grateful for the advance notice and steeled myself for a tumultuous time ahead.

PuraVida was a dream to sail. She glided gracefully through the water, piercing it neatly with her sleek bow. We were making speed without any effort. Simon, Enzo and I relaxed on deck, enjoying a few quiet hours at sea before the craziness set in. As we waited for the drawbridge to rise, so we could enter the marina in St Maarten, I was stunned at how low the planes thundered over the boat. I was certain their wheels would catch on our mast during their landing approach. We docked in the marina and hooked up the power and water. Simon and Enzo immediately went off to the nearest watering hole and I took a walk to soak up the atmosphere. Colourful banners and flags were dancing in the breeze, adorning the gleaming and glorious yachts. People were calling out to each other as they recognised friends from way back. The air was buzzing with excitement. The boats were polished to perfection, the hulls sparkling in the warm sunlight.

During the regatta, I was relieved from my regular cooking duties. Instead, I was required to cater for all the race crew with simple wraps for breakfast and sandwiches for lunch. Simon organised a young woman to help me to feed this large group. I made sure I was well prepared and went to bed early.

The next morning, the crew started to arrive. Some of the Aussies took a cabin on board, others were staying in accommodation ashore. Most of the guys were in their forties and fifties, congenial, passionate about sailing and ready to let loose. Our racing crew included a dozen experienced sailors, plus a weather expert and a seasoned tactician. The day of the first training sail, I finally met my employers. The owner of *PuraVida* was in his mid-forties, of average build, shy and seeming like your typical gawky IT millionaire. He and his attractive blonde wife stepped aboard, and I was pleasantly surprised by their unassuming and easy-going personalities.

On the morning of the first sea trial, I was in the galley preparing sandwiches for the crowds later in the day. Rick was a cocky, confident Aussie with a party-hard-or-go-home attitude. He flashed me a megawatt smile, walked up behind me and, in passing, suggestively grabbed my butt. I froze, realising it was high time to stake my boundaries to this joker and all the other guys that were hanging around.

'Rick! What the hell do you think you are doing? Don't you dare touch me again like that!' I flew around, eyes ablaze and determined to stand my ground.

'Ah, Reggie! Come on, don't be like that!' He sneered, 'I was only joking!'

'Right, Rick. Let me clarify for you: I do not share your sense of humour. Hands off! I will not tolerate any such behaviour again.'

I turned, scanning every man present in the crowded cabin. 'That goes for *all* of you guys. Am I making myself clear?'

To my surprise, like a bunch of reprimanded little boys, all heads dutifully bobbed in agreement. Inwardly, I released a huge sigh of relief. It had worked. From that moment, I earned their respect and was able to enjoy their company without further harassment.

During the sailing we hosted around twenty-five people on board. The majority of the crew was made up of sailors that Simon had recruited from far and wide, as well as the owner of *PuraVida* and his wife, a few of their friends and several young women. Some of these young ladies were reputable friends of the captain or crew. Others were, as predicted, invited along as sailors' prey.

One of these women was assisting me with the catering. A bubbly blonde, confident and sassy, she was working her charm and got plenty of attention. One morning, I could not help but overhear the guys crudely comparing their exploits with her, while others boasted about other conquests and predatory experiences over the previous days. Having never been exposed to a male dominated environment like this before, I was horrified by their vulgar and disrespectful attitude to women, and grateful to have firmly put my boundaries in place early on. Most of the men now treated me as a motherly addition to the crew, rather than a female worth pursuing.

Racing the Heineken Regatta was thrilling, if occasionally a little frightening, and the yacht was abuzz with activity. Each sailor had a set position on deck and a specific role. Simon was calling the shots relating to sail or direction changes, but the tactician advised Simon precisely when to perform them. Rick was our primary helmsman, focused on maintaining a perfect course. These multi-million-dollar vessels were competitively aiming for the best start positions. Bows were crossing each other with only inches to spare. Our bowman was standing at the very tip of the yacht, pointing out other yachts and calling out race rules. Meanwhile, the rest of the crew was working like a well-oiled machine to place us into a prime starting position. The cannon sounded and *PuraVida* charged across the start line only seconds later. My pulse was racing, and I was caught up in the excitement of the moment. Simon stationed me at a winch in the cockpit, which was less frantic than a position on deck and allowed me to enjoy the sights of the regatta.

As we crossed the start line and sailed along the race course, I noticed the other yachts from our group disappearing into the distance. After our lengthy preparations, intense practice sails, and the many discussions about tactics, I had anticipated we would perform better. Clearly, our standard was not up to par with our competitors' and unfortunately, our ranking did not improve over the course of the race week. I was astonished that *PuraVida*'s owner seemed unconcerned about this.

When I asked Simon about the overall cost of this project, he casually mentioned that the event came with a staggering US $200,000 price tag for the week. I found the costs mind-boggling but was fascinated by the owner's composure, considering our mediocre performance and his substantial expenditure. I wondered if, for him, this was purely a week of fun with his new toy.

Throughout the race, tensions began to simmer then rise, especially once it became obvious that *PuraVida* was falling behind the rest of the fleet. As more mistakes happened, tempers flared, and I witnessed the dark side of my captain. Simon regularly lost his temper, verbally lashing out at anyone who caused his wrath. He seemed under pressure and was highly strung. The smallest incident set him off. So far, I had avoided being in his line of fire but was worried that it would only be a matter of time before I found myself on the receiving end of one of his tantrums. I went to Rick and pulled him aside.

'Rick, tell me, is Simon normally like this?' I asked.

'Ah, Reggie.' He sighed. 'I wish I could say otherwise, but yes, that's very much him. I don't know why. He's got a charmed life. A great, well-paying job. An easy-going owner of the yacht. A devoted girl in South Africa,' he said. 'Look, Simon is a good bloke and he's been my mate for many years. I love him dearly, but I am also aware that he's by no means perfect. When he's in one of his highly strung moods, it is best to lie low and hope it will pass quickly. I know he respects you, Reggie. You should be fine.'

Once the regatta was over, the owners departed on their private jet and most of the enlisted sailors returned to their homes. *PuraVida*, thankfully, grew quieter again. Rick and a few of Simon's close friends stayed on board for another week and together we departed for St Barthelemy. The passage to the neighbouring island only took a few hours and was relaxing, especially after the tumultuous time in St Maarten. I was glad to leave it and the affiliated craziness in our wake, heading for calmer shores. I'd had enough of guys running amok each night, turning up hungover and reeking of booze the next morning. Not to mention their endless bragging.

St Barths was a small, exclusive island with an evident French influence. From afar, it looked dry and sparsely populated. We dropped anchor in a crystal-clear bay, a little distance out from the main township, a quaint little village that hugged the bottom of a rugged hill.

Once secured, we lowered the dinghy into the ocean. Simon tersely instructed us all, ordering me to handle the power winch. Confidently, I pushed the button and promptly heard a whirring noise. The winch was feeding the rope into my hands, but oddly, the tender remained on deck. Confused, I briefly took my finger off the button and pushed down again. Suddenly the dinghy jerked upward and began wildly swaying about and I could see the guys struggling to tame the bucking boat. Seeing the havoc, I quickly released the button but the sudden stop only seemed to worsen the dinghy's jolting.

'*You moron!*' I looked up to see Simon's furious gaze locked on me. 'Stop fucking pushing and releasing the winch button, you idiot!' he yelled. 'Such a stupid little task. I can't rely on anyone to do anything,' he bellowed.

At his hurtful remarks, I felt a jab of pain sear my heart. I swallowed. No, I am not going to cry, I resolved, taking a breath. I looked at the boys who quietly stood, eyes uncomfortably downcast, holding the now stable tender.

'I'm sorry, Simon. I have never done this before!' I said quietly.

Rick smiled and Sonny sent me a conspiratorial wink and quickly reassured me, 'Don't worry, Reggie, we got it under

Cleaning, Cooking, Racing

control. Because of the size of the boat, the dimensions of the ropes are bigger. This means that they stretch a bit more before they start to pull. Plus, the tender is heavy. That's all,' he simply said. I was grateful for this explanation. It made sense. 'We need to lift the dinghy about half a metre higher and then we will lower it outside the hull.'

Simon gave a curt nod and we managed to launch the little boat safely into the water without further incident.

Our stay in St Barths was quiet and lazy. The guys enjoyed their last days on board, swimming and sunbathing. After finishing my chores, I went for long walks, exploring the area surrounding the little bay, charmed by the combination of Caribbean and French cultures; reggae sounds mingled with smells of fresh baguettes. Beautiful boutiques in picturesque stone buildings sat alongside wooden beach shacks, each glowing in various shades of the rainbow. Confident and attractive Caribbean labourers crossed paths with chic French ladies. The contrasts were delightful and gifted this island with a unique, fresh air.

Each night, all of the *PuraVida* crew and guests were invited for lavish dinners. On this exclusive island, many high-end restaurants catered to the world's rich and famous. Among them was a revered Japanese establishment in which I enjoyed sushi that was presented like artwork, and a breathtaking beachside restaurant that served flawless French cuisine while stunning models showcased the latest swimwear between courses. These splendid affairs were generously covered by the boat's credit card. After my initial uneasiness with the opulent dining events,

I resolved to embrace and enjoy these special experiences rather than resist them. This was an opportunity to, quite literally, taste a different way of life.

After dinner, Enzo usually dropped me off at the yacht while the boys went out. I enjoyed having the boat and the stillness of the anchorage to myself for a few hours. Listening to the gentle sound of the water, I witnessed an array of colours at dusk. Each sunset transformed the sky into an ever-changing, glorious canvas. The harmonic reflections softly shimmered across the water's surface. I could sit for hours appreciating the quiet sounds and sights, sipping a cup of tea, or reading a book. These moments were my slice of heaven.

21

FUN AND FRIVOLITIES

Once we were docked back in Antigua, Simon, Enzo and I resumed our daily routine. The air aboard remained tense. Simon's temper kept erupting like a moody volcano and Enzo cocooned himself with his deflated attitude. To avoid the stress, I hightailed it to All Saints and retreated to Jay's house for the weekend. We had been apart for two weeks and had barely spoken. Jay's warm smile and big enveloping hug felt like my salvation from the mayhem on *PuraVida*.

We went for long walks through the pastures behind the village. We picked ripe mangoes and ate them immediately, savouring the sweet, juicy flesh. Immersed in nature, I felt grounded and content. The glamorous professional superyacht lifestyle had lost some of its gloss and I was glad to connect to the earth beneath my bare feet. In recent weeks, I had started to feel more unsettled and unsure about my future. The hurricane season was not far away and soon all the yachts would leave the Caribbean.

'Jay, the sailing season is almost over. *PuraVida* is heading for the Mediterranean and I need to decide whether to go with them or not. I can't stay in Antigua without a work permit again. I need to figure out the best next step for me.'

'Babes, follow your heart. Maybe you can go home and spend time with your family,' he suggested.

I loved the way he graciously accepted and surrendered to my unfolding future.

'I don't know about that. I don't really want to live and work in Switzerland.' My voice trailed off, as I pictured a life in my home country. I promptly dismissed this vision. I was not ready to make a life there. With more resolve I said, 'I am not happy on *PuraVida* anymore. Simon has changed since we left for the regatta. He is angry all the time and there is a lot of tension between him and Enzo. I should probably look for another boat, one that might be going to the Mediterranean or North America. Who knows?' I chuckled and bit into my sweet, juicy mango.

'Are you happy, Jay?' I asked after a little while, wondering if he ever felt as torn as I did.

'Me? I'm happy, babes. I've got my little house, my work and Carnival is soon.' He beamed, exuding contentment.

I admired that he was satisfied with his life and his meagre belongings. He never wanted for anything and accepted his life for what it was. Carnival was still months away, but that did not matter to him. It would arrive when the time was ready. For Jay, as I experienced by his side, life was an effortless stream of memorable events: soon Carnival, soon birthday, Christmas, sailing season events, soon Carnival … A part of me envied the way he could ignore the state of the world, its game-playing politics and the rise and fall of economies. There were no terror threats in Jay's reality. No marketing temptations. Instead, there were mangos on a tree. Work and shelter. Dance. And love.

I reclined on the grass and sighed. Part of me wished I could adopt his way of embracing and surrendering to a simple life. But deep down, I knew that this was not my path. Should I choose it anyway, I was certain that in time I would grow restless. I needed stimulation and yearned to continually grow and evolve as a person. I knew I had to move forward if I wanted to succeed and improve myself.

My time in Antigua was coming to an end. I had left and returned. I had given my heart to this man and experienced deep love and joy, revelations, disappointments, and heartache. Here I had learned to stand on my own two feet and fend for myself.

The Rock had become my home. I knew this country would forever hold a special place in my heart, but the time had come to move on. I was filled with love and gratitude for Jay, for all we had shared and experienced together. I reminisced, honouring the countless lessons, each a unique learning opportunity, that I had experienced during this period. It would take time to absorb everything that had happened. I knew I would savour and treasure those moments in years to come.

I took a deep breath, opened my eyes, and turned to Jay.

'You are aware that once I leave Antigua this time, I will not come back to you, Jay?' I spoke softly, from the heart and with all my love.

'Okay, Regina. I understand,' he replied quietly. His eyes looked sad, but he nodded. 'You need to do what you need to do.'

'It is hard for me to leave, Jay, but we can't have the future I pictured for us. I know I wouldn't be happy here long-term. But I am immensely grateful to have met you, for your love and for the wonderful time and experiences we shared.'

'Will you go soon?'

'I don't know. I need to leave *PuraVida* and find another boat. I will be here for a little while still.'

Jay rolled onto his side, facing me. His eyes twinkled mischievously.

'In that case, babes, let's enjoy the time we have.'

I returned to work, determined to do my job and stay out of my colleagues' way as much as possible. Simon, Enzo and I went through our days like satellites, each orbiting around the yacht, minding our own business. One day over lunch, while Enzo was out on an errand, Simon confessed that he'd had enough of the boating life and wanted to settle in South Africa with his girlfriend. But after decades in this industry, he had grown accustomed to the generous tax-free salary, the many perks that came with a yachting job and was struggling to leave the lifestyle. He was hoping to receive a job offer from the shipyard he often collaborated with, but so far nothing had emerged. I wondered if his temper tantrums were due to his unhappiness with the current situation.

I could see how a transition to a land-based life would be confronting, as maintaining this high living standard with a 'real' job would be near impossible. In the past two months I had met numerous disillusioned and unhappy sailors. Most of them were in my age group or older, and had lived and worked in the industry for many years. These people mentioned huge savings and sizeable assets ashore, but their eyes often looked sad. Witnessing their conundrums, I vowed not to be trapped by the superyacht lifestyle. I would do this job while it was fun and leave the industry as soon as it grew stale. Yachting was an enjoyable, temporary solution – not my future career.

Of course, I also came across happy ocean-going professionals. The happiest people I encountered were couples employed to run a yacht as a team. Usually, their boat owners only visited occasionally, allowing them plenty of privacy and spare time on their own. As well, there were rare vessels where an entire crew worked together harmoniously for several years. The common ingredients of a 'good boat' were generally a personable and fair captain, an equally respectful and just owner, and mature-minded crew. Too much pressure or personality from any one direction promptly tipped the delicate balance out of kilter.

On a visit to Falmouth Harbour, I called in to see Henry and Maude, with whom my boating adventure had begun. They welcomed me on board and over a cup of tea I recounted my story. Henry was pleased about my employment on *PuraVida* and encouraged me to follow the superyachts on their seasonal migrations to Europe or North America.

After the visit, I wandered up and down the dock, checking out the new yachts in the marina. I ended up in conversation with a young couple. As we talked, they were full of smiles. Spontaneously, they invited me on board, and for the first time, I felt like I had entered a boat with the ambiance of a home.

During our chat, the couple mentioned the annual Wobbly Race. Henry and Maude had told me about this event, and this year, I was determined to be a part of the boisterous boat-building extravaganza. I went to the marina office to sign up, hoping to be paired with a fun group in need of an additional member. By chance, I was teamed up with the same professional couple I had just met. Right from the start, this promised to be a hilarious and playful day. Each team had to build their own boat in less than three hours, using only sheets of plywood, glue, tape and whatever material could be pirated. The only rule: Anything goes but no engines allowed! After a rambunctious skippers' meeting, the sound of a cannon initiated a manic construction period with each group trying to build a boat that would float successfully for the duration of the race.

Our team agreed to build a rectangular paddle board, which would involve minimal construction work. Quietly, we boarded my team-mates' vessel, returning with armfuls of empty plastic bottles. After we had nailed and taped the bottom board to the sides, we filled the empty space with the drink containers for extra flotation and adhered the top sheet. With a little time to spare before the deadline, we left our paddle board and went to spy on our competitors' efforts.

The atmosphere was joyful and music was blasting out of huge speakers from the marina bar. The crews were laughing and talking among themselves and jokingly discrediting other teams' efforts. Mischievous looks were exchanged as mystery objects were slyly incorporated into elaborate constructions.

I realised that I had been missing playfulness and laughter, and soaked in the merry atmosphere like a pig in fresh mud. The Antiguan boat builder team had vanished at the beginning, plywood sheets and all, and reappeared shortly before the deadline with a perfectly constructed miniature sailing boat. One group was particularly secretive about their creation and revealed later that, against all rules but in good humour, they had attached a scuba scooter to their craft. Some boats looked perilously haphazard, and I was curious to see which would stay afloat.

Fun and Frivolities

Once the three-hour time limit was up, the contenders proudly displayed their models. Our paddle board was among the clunkiest of the crafts, but it felt and looked sturdy and I was confident of our work. We carried the vessels to a little beach and one member of each team was selected to conduct the race. My team-mates honoured my unbridled enthusiasm by offering me the captaincy.

At the sound of the cannon, a mad frenzy ensued and vessels were hurriedly launched and mounted. Immediately, collisions and capsizes occurred. Some teams were scrambling to recover while others sabotaged with sly attacks. Among the chaos, we found a gap. I hopped onto the board and gripped the paddles. Once secure in my kneeling position, I began paddling with ferocious determination. I was soon overtaken by the little scooter boat. I laughed as it motored by effortlessly, its captain sending me a cheeky wink in passing. The next team to pass me was helmed by a pair of toned Antiguans guys. Sitting in a charming little boat, they rowed by in perfect harmony. That they had managed to build a boat strong enough to sustain two grown men was impressive. I hollered as they overtook me.

As we were approaching the end of the marina, I could see and hear the crowd on the dock cheering. My arms were starting to tire but motivated by their support, I carried on paddling with determination. Our board floated well, and I was pleased with our construction. As I was nearing the finish line I caught up to a man who was feverishly paddling. As I moved closer, I noticed his craft was submerged almost to the water's surface. The guy was sitting waist-deep in water. I burst out laughing at the sight of him ploughing through the sea connected to an invisible vessel.

'Hey, dude, I love your submarine! Great idea!' I taunted, as I reached his side.

He grinned, paddled harder and we crossed the finish line together, and by the time I reached the dock, I was in stitches. Scanning the happy crowd, I relished the fact that it did not take much to turn an ordinary day into an extraordinary one. A few sheets of plywood and a group of motivated, positive people were enough.

A few days later, I experienced my first full lunar eclipse. Preferring the company of the yachties in the smaller, less pretentious marina, I joined my new-found friends in Falmouth for the event. People were sitting on picnic blankets and deck chairs on the dock, chatting and enjoying a sociable drink. I took a seat with my team-mates from the Wobbly Race and observed the scene. The night was clear, with only a few puffy clouds highlighting the dark sky. The full moon illuminated the hills in the background, and the gentle breeze created sparkling ripples across the bay. Beneath the dock, the water was softly gurgling, while music drifted through the happy, relaxed gathering. I felt grateful to witness another exceptional occasion on this island, wistfully aware of my approaching departure.

The moon disappeared behind a cloud but reappeared in time for the eclipse. Mesmerised by the transformation, we sat until we were immersed in complete blackness, with only a delicate ring of light visible. Slowly, the moon emerged on the other side. In celebration, we cheered and hugged, before settling back in our seats. Fuelled by the grand natural display, debates soon raged on humanity, the environment and the current state of the world.

The evening reaffirmed my appreciation for deep intellectual conversation. Until now, I had not felt able to end my relationship with Jay, but the decision to separate had required time to ripen and today I finally came to accept it as unavoidable. I remembered a yoga teacher, an accomplished woman in her sixties, sitting cross-legged in front of our class. Radiating health and contentment, she looked poised as she stated, 'There is always a beginning of the beginning, a middle of the beginning and the end of the beginning. The same goes for the middle part. So of course, there also must be a beginning of the end, a middle of the end and the end of the end.'

The simple message profoundly resonated with me. Each stage of a cycle held a distinct purpose. As this memory revisited me, I recalled the conversation that I'd had with Jay a few days earlier, acknowledging that we had arrived at the 'end of the end' of our time. Together, we had experienced a beautiful, relational cycle. During the course of a year and a quarter, we had shared inspirational, thought-provoking, heart-warming and heart-breaking moments. But soon, both of us would transition to our next chapter.

'How are you, Jay?' I decided to call him mid-week to see if we could meet up. 'I am going to walk the goat trail from Nelsons Dockyard to Pigeon Beach. Would you like to join me? If you catch a bus now, I will prepare a picnic dinner for us.'

I loved hiking the rugged trail. Walking helped to clear my mind from the day, especially if the tension between Simon and Enzo had surfaced.

Jay met me at the petrol station and we set off. Climbing the trail, Jay told me about his work. They were busy and he had been doing long hours of overtime but, as in the past, his boss refused to compensate him for it. Jay had approached him several times over the matter, without any success. I assumed his boss was aware of Jay's lack of education and was taking advantage of the situation. Having tried before to help him, this time I simply listened to him, neither wanting nor needing to fix his problem. I let him vent his frustrations but left him in charge of his life. Even with all the complaining about his work, I knew he loved the job, enjoyed its social side and got along well with his colleagues. Once he'd vented, Jay immediately returned to his jovial self, nicking the new sunglasses off my head. He was fooling around, checking out the polarised lenses and teasing me playfully. To my surprise, he had never walked the trail before, and admired the sweeping view over his country and the vast ocean surrounding it.

'Meh lub Anteeega, babes!' he drawled in his thickest dialect, promptly exploding with laughter.

On the way down, we stopped at the lookout and I set up our picnic dinner. Overlooking the bay, with the sun slowly setting behind the mountains, we savoured the meal. Toasting plastic cups filled with exquisite wine, we smiled in appreciation of our feast for two. As we ate, we told stories of the times we'd experienced together. Carnival, our evenings at Shirley Heights, exploring beaches together, family gatherings, the bumpy motorbike excursions, our foraging walks through the fruit orchards, Friday barbecue dinners and sailing parties.

Something had shifted between us, and we both noticed the change. Ever so slightly we had moved apart and had re-acquainted ourselves with people outside our relationship. I was glad Jay had a solid support network and I knew that he would be safe and well when I left. In recent weeks, I had met some warm and wholesome people. Along with my friends scattered around the globe, I knew I was also well supported and connected. Life would continue to be good for both of us.

The day I decided to leave *PuraVida* began without fanfare. Enzo had left the boat for a few days to sort out a visa at the US Embassy in Barbados. It was a Friday, our wind-down day. On Fridays, Enzo's chore was to hose and scrub the hull and the teak deck, and finish by polishing all the stainless-steel fixtures. I had my usual chores but had made it a habit to help him with his duties once I had finished mine.

While Simon sat in his computer cubicle reading the newspaper, I made sure all the cabins and bathrooms were gleaming. Then I wiped down the wooden cupboards inside with a soft, damp cloth. Once the interior looked satisfactory, I was not sure what to do next. Simon had been chatting on the phone to his girlfriend for some time, and eventually I indicated that I had a question. With a slight frown he lowered the phone, motioning me to speak.

'Excuse me, Simon. I've finished inside. What is your plan regarding the deck and hull? Do you want me to wash the topsides and deck, or do I just polish the stainless steel on deck today?' I asked.

'Fucking hell! Just do what you guys always do. Wash the topsides and deck. Then polish the fucking stainless after,' he exploded. Shocked, I stepped backwards. Pressing the phone against his ear he continued ranting, 'Seriously, I can't believe the stupid questions! I am sick and tired of these fucking brainless idiots. I have to spell out everything!'

Even though he was not talking to me directly, I knew he wanted me to hear his outrage and tears welled in my eyes.

I flew up the ladder, seeking refuge on deck. Once the sting of his careless exclamations abated, I was hit with ferocious anger. How dare he address me like that! I never did anything to disrespect him and was diligent and focused on my work. I asked questions to avoid misunderstandings and gain clarity, but never twice, and certainly not in jest. In my anger, I hosed the hull and scrubbed it vigorously until my muscles started to ache. Several crew, passing along the dock, commented jokingly on the intensity I was bringing to the chore. Curious, some of them asked me why, as a stewardess, I was washing down the large yacht on my own. I rolled my eyes, and with my emotions reinflamed, attacked the deck with renewed ferocity.

What a complete prick, I decided, hot rage fuelling my thoughts. There he was, sitting comfortably in his navigation corner, reading the paper, or chatting to his lady and behaving like a bloody five-year-old.

Having had enough of this treatment, I resolved to look for another boat this weekend. Pushing the soft brush back and forth, scrubbing every inch of the deck until it was clean, I successfully channelled my rage into the work. Flushed from the exertion and emotions, when I finally rinsed the yacht, I pointed the hose at myself, welcoming its cooling soak, clothes and all. Out of the corner of my eye, I noticed several crew laughing at my erratic behaviour, but I did not care. Simon had snuck out while I was polishing the yacht's stainless steel. After hours of labouring hard on deck, *PuraVida* looked her best and most of my anger had disappeared. Even so, I was determined to make Simon face his lack of team spirit. Other captains would have stepped in and helped, whereas he had bailed out and gone for a drink in the middle of the day.

I showered, changed into clean, dry clothes and marched to the bar. There he was, looking relaxed, slouching comfortably among his favourite drinking buddies. Sonny, already glowing with alcohol-infused happiness, looked up and waved me over.

'Reggie, glad you could make it!' he sang out, unaware of my simmering frustration.

I briskly walked up to the table and looked down at Simon. 'You!' I proclaimed, pointing my index finger at him. My voice was firmer and louder than I had planned, and I realised I had claimed the attention of the entire table, if not the bar. I continued undeterred, 'You'd better go and buy me a decent drink right now, buddy, for making me work like a bloody Trojan!'

Dumbfounded, Simon looked up at me, nodded his head and immediately jumped out of his chair. Without a word he pointed at his chair, indicating for me to sit down, and rushed off in the direction of the bar. I had half expected another outburst from him and was surprised and satisfied that I had managed to render him speechless. He returned shortly after, with an enormous gin and tonic. He put the drink down in front of me, with an apologetic smile.

I could not help myself and burst out laughing. Gripping the massive tumbler, I raised it. 'Thank you, Simon. Apology accepted,' I chuckled as I took a sip. 'But next time, you better offer your help, man.'

Simon smiled in a noncommittal way and after a few sips of the potent drink, I relaxed. I assessed the unruly bunch of guys around the table. They were Simon's closest mates and had become a part of my life on *PuraVida*. Though they had different outlooks and values from mine, they nonetheless treated me with respect and kindness. Sonny and another slightly older guy that showed up on *PuraVida* almost on a daily basis, were especially supportive. My time on *PuraVida* had been an eye-opening introduction to the yachting world, the racing scene and life on board a professional yacht. I was grateful that Simon had given me a chance and I was able to gain valuable industry experience, but I was ready to move on. At least now I knew what to look out for.

22

JUMPING SHIP

The next morning, I set out to find another boat. Though my anger had abated, Simon's escapades had motivated me to act. With the Caribbean hurricane season looming, the weather was becoming hotter and more humid, and most of the yachts were in preparation for an ocean passage, bound for either the Mediterranean or the eastern shores of North America. Like migrating birds, these vessels followed the pleasant weather and favourable winds. Having considered my options, I had decided to look for a sailing yacht heading north, rather than east.

Already in possession of the required visa for the United States, I decided this document was my gateway to explore this part of the world. Through my job on *PuraVida* I had become acquainted with crew from other boats. Among the sailing community, information was shared liberally, and I had a vague idea of which boats were heading in my preferred direction. This insight made it easier to choose and approach a vessel that promised to be a suitable match.

This time I had a specific boat in mind. She had stood out to me while docked close to *PuraVida*. A classic wooden yacht built in the 1930s, she oozed charm. Many of the fittings and carpentry were original, the varnished woodwork was in good condition, and the brass fittings gleamed. The yacht was not as fancy and luxurious as *PuraVida*, but it had character, and the captain was rumoured to be laidback and friendly. The boat had left our marina a little while ago and relocated to Nelsons Dockyard. I wanted to try my luck there first.

I briskly walked across to the other marina. Then, pretending to look at all the yachts, I dawdled back and forth, lingering unnecessarily. Even after all this time working and living on the yachts, walking up and asking for a job was still challenging. I could confidently approach a captain or crew member socially to ask a question about their yacht, but when asking about employment, I became shy. Reflecting on this irrational behaviour, I soon realised that the reason I lacked confidence when asking for work was because of my fear of rejection. With this insight, I could see that the outcome of these conversations did not matter. A 'no' was not a personal rejection, but rather an answer to my inquiry. Armed with this new awareness, I decided to conquer this awkwardness once and for all. I found a quiet corner and sat down. Closing my eyes, I drew a few deep breaths. When I opened my eyes again, I felt centred and focused, ready to get a job.

With a spring in my step, I approached my favoured boat and noticed a guy in his early twenties working near the bow, on the far end of the deck.

'Hey!' I called out loudly and waved at him. He looked up and came walking toward the stern of the boat.

'Hi, I'm Regina. I've seen your boat at the English Harbour marina. She's a beauty!' I smiled.

'Hi, Regina, I'm Dean. Yes, I love *Philomena*. She carries her age with grace. Which boat are you on?' he asked.

The young man had a fresh face, and a set of sparkly brown eyes peering out from under unruly, curled dark hair. He eyed me with a cheeky grin as he moved restlessly from one foot to the other, waiting for me to speak.

'*PuraVida*. We were docked near you. Listen, I hear you are heading to North America shortly, right?'

He nodded, hair bouncing and his grin widening as he drawled in a broad American accent, 'Yup. Headin' home. Can't wait!'

'Tell me, Dean, have you got a full crew for the delivery? I'm leaving my boat and would love to head north …' The question tumbled off my lips with surprising ease.

'No, we're not fully crewed,' he said. Suddenly, his attention perked up a notch and he looked at me with increased curiosity. 'We're still looking for a cook and stewardess for the trip. Ben, the captain, is not here right now. He should be back any minute. Do you have a local phone number I can give him so he can contact you?'

I handed Dean a copy of my resume and thanked him for his help. Rather than approach other boats, I took a break and settled down with a book and one of my rare Caribbean cappuccinos. Just as I got comfortable, my phone rang.

'Regina, it's Ben, *Philomena*'s captain. Dean said that you stopped by to see if we needed crew. Are you still in the area?' he asked, sounding friendly.

'Yes, I'm just at the coffee shop, I can come over now.'

'Don't rush. Finish your coffee and then come to the boat for a chat. Sound good?' Ben asked.

I said that I would be there soon, put my book away and willed myself to enjoy my coffee. That was a challenge now that I had an exciting meeting ahead of me.

As I approached *Philomena* for the second time, I saw a lanky guy with weathered skin and short grey hair on deck, talking with Dean. I called out and they both looked up and smiled. Dean disappeared below deck and the older man came to greet me.

'You're Regina, right? I'm Ben,' he said, smiling as he gestured for me to come aboard.

'Dean tells me that you work on *PuraVida* and are looking for a passage north?' he asked.

'Yes. I have been on *PuraVida* since the start of this year. I am going to be honest with you, Ben. I am looking for another boat because I am not entirely happy on that yacht anymore. The captain and I have clashed several times and I find it hard to work and live in a hostile environment. I am also not interested in the party scene and drinking and would love to work on a yacht with a more balanced crew,' I said, hoping I wasn't being too frank. At the same time, I could see no point in pretence. I was clear about what I wanted. I smiled and scanned Ben's face trying to anticipate his reaction.

He listened intently and, after a moment, smiled.

'You know, Regina. You may not be aware, but I quietly monitored you when we were docked over at English Harbour. I noticed you were up early every morning drinking your coffee in the cockpit, enjoying the peace and quiet. Then I saw you diligently doing your work. And you were always friendly towards everyone on the dock.'

Jumping Ship

Left speechless by his kind remarks, I remained silent while Ben continued, 'I've been in the industry for a long time and Simon is familiar to me. I understand why you choose to leave, and I'm happy to have you on board *Philomena*. The only problem is that the owner is running for the Senate in the US later this year, so I can't offer ongoing employment; we need US citizens for that. You're welcome to do the passage with us to Newport, Rhode Island, but that's where your journey on this boat will end. If that sounds okay, then welcome aboard!'

I smiled and excitedly nodded my head.

Ben must have sensed my enthusiasm and said, 'Look, *Philomena* is a relatively small yacht to employ four crew, but that's how I like to run my boat. Dean, who you've met, is the deckhand and he's been with us for the entire Caribbean season. I usually have a chef and a stewardess, and I am looking for both for the upcoming passage. The chef gets paid a little bit more than the stewardess, but you can choose which job you prefer.'

When Ben quoted the salary, which was less than half of what I had been earning on *PuraVida*, I paused. Due to my frugal lifestyle, I had saved most of my wages on *PuraVida*. For once I was in a financially stable position. I quickly regrouped and decided that I wanted to sail on this wonderful yacht and Ben and Dean both seemed easy to get along with. All things considered, this was a wonderful opportunity.

'Ben, I can cook and am happy to do so, if need be. But I prefer the stewardess job for the passage. The pay you're offering is considerably less than what I currently make, but it will be an honour to crew on *Philomena* for the passage. I understand that I will need to find another yacht once we get to the US,' I said, happy with my decision.

'All right, Regina. We have a deal. I would suggest that you tell Simon this weekend. You are welcome to move aboard *Philomena* anytime from Monday onwards. I'll give you my number so Simon and I can arrange the sign-over at immigration.'

I appreciated Ben's understanding and kindness. He seemed motivated to facilitate a smooth transition and I was grateful for his maturity. I was not looking forward to telling Simon about my plans, but I would have to face him soon.

'I plan to leave in about a week's time, depending on the weather,' Ben said. 'We will head to St Maarten to provision. We'll either find a cook here before we leave or pick up the last crew member there. Again, depending on long-term forecasts, we might stop by in St Barths for a few days. From there we will sail to Bermuda for another brief stop to refuel and provision. After that, we will look for the Gulf Stream and hopefully hitch a comfortable ride north. The entire trip should take between a month and six weeks,' he explained.

I appreciated the way he explained everything to me so clearly.

'Okay, Regina, I have to go. I'll hear from you sometime on Monday about the sign-over.' He smiled, extending his hand. 'Enjoy your weekend and I look forward to you joining us on *Philomena!*'

I virtually ran back to *PuraVida*, only to find an empty boat. Simon and Enzo were either visiting crew on another yacht or hanging out in the bar, which suited me. Reaching for a few clothes to last the weekend, I stuffed them into my small daypack and left a note saying I would be back Sunday night. Walking towards the main street, I called Jay.

'Hello you. Tell me, are you working?' I asked. He usually worked Monday through to Saturday, but I figured he would finish soon.

'Yes, Regina. We just dropped off some fruit and vegetables in town and are heading back to the workshop. Are you coming to All Saints?' His voice was hopeful.

'I am catching a bus in English Harbour now and will be waiting at the house when you get home. We can go out and get dinner later if you like?'

I hopped on the next dented and scratched little bus that came barrelling along. As I took my seat, I was suddenly aware that this was one of the last times I would ride on the local transport. I looked at the other passengers and tried to soak up every detail. The latest local party hit blared out from rattling speakers. A lady with dreadlocks firmly wrapped and piled high on her head was loudly talking on her mobile phone. The young bus driver was debating a local issue with a passenger while racing down the road, occasionally screeching to a halt to collect passengers. Two grey-haired ladies, adorned with fancy hats, were discussing family matters. An old man was looking out the window. Following his gaze, I saw colourful little wooden houses. Clothing and linen were pegged on laundry lines that stretched from tree to tree. A barefoot child was laughing as he chased a tyre rim with a stick down a gravel path. People had gathered on a corner for an impromptu afternoon chat. Tiny shops with metal bars protecting their window fronts were advertising an astonishing array of cheap treats, household goods and local spirits.

With a pang, I realised I would miss this little island nation. I had grown to love its chaos, liveliness, sounds and smells. And its people, with their animated banter, beaming smiles and sultry dancing. Overall, I had visited and lived in Antigua for more than a year. During this period, the country and its people had left a lasting imprint on my heart.

In the same way that I had absorbed the bus ride, I walked through All Saints with my eyes and heart wide open. Jay and I had often ordered takeaway from the Chinese place next to the bus stop and I waved at the owners on my way past. I turned right at the big old tree. Down the road, I greeted the ladies chatting in front of a house. Turning left onto the potholed track, I remembered the first time I rode home on my new motorbike. Reaching Jay's yard, I recalled how shy I had initially felt in his shack. He had painted the little house yellow for me and laughed at my embarrassment when I had to dash across the yard for a shower, wrapped in nothing but a towel.

I opened the front door and scanned the room. Though still unpainted, the inside walls were now decorated with pictures of us stuck to the recycled wood panels. The tiny kitchen was home to the antiquated and rusty gas stove. A few wobbly shelves were filled with our calabashes, some spoons and forks. There was still no fridge, fan or electric light. In the bedroom, Jay's ever-present pile of clothes was on the floor and the mosquito net I had purchased was already sporting impressive holes.

I lay down on the bed we had shared, closing my eyes and allowing memories to flow. Reflecting on the upheaval, pain and success I had experienced since leaving Australia, I did not want to change a thing. I had learned a lot about myself, having grown and survived alone in a foreign country. Most importantly, I had lived and loved fully. I was grateful to Antigua and to Jay for their contribution to who I was now.

I took a seat on the verandah and waited for Jay's return. I saw him from afar, sauntering along the road towards me. Regardless of my understanding and wish to leave, I felt sad knowing the time had come to say goodbye.

As soon as he spotted me, he beamed and called out, 'Regina!' The neighbours within a few streets would have been alerted to my presence.

I laughed. 'Jay!' I called back mischievously.

He reached the house, removed his smelly boots and placed them on the verandah. Then we walked inside. Once more, I found myself enveloped in Jay's strong arms and felt his soft lips on mine.

'Let's sit down for a moment. I need to tell you something.'

'Babes, did you find a boat?' he asked, one step ahead.

'Yes, I have, Jay. A really good one, too.' As I spoke, I began to relax. I felt relieved that Jay was happy for me. We were both mourning our relationship yet at the same time honoured our separate futures.

'The captain is a bit older and is friendly and calm. Do you remember when we went to look at the classic boats?'

Jay nodded.

'It is one of those yachts. It's much smaller than *PuraVida*, but beautiful. I am going to sail to North America, can you believe it?'

I took a breath and focused on his eyes, now serious. 'We are leaving next weekend, Jay. So this is our last weekend together. I want this to be a special time with you. Are you with me?'

'Yes, babes. Let's have a good time!' He smiled, and though still a little sad, I could see that he was trying.

After a refreshing bucket shower together we ventured out, taking a bus back to English Harbour. Jay knew a band that was playing in one of the bars. We ordered drinks and once the band started, took to the dance floor and let loose. The place was packed, but for Jay and me this was a time when, as in our early days, we only had eyes for each other. We laughed and danced the night away, bodies steaming from the exertion, minds happy and light.

Sunday morning started with a breakfast of juicy mangoes, oats and powdered milk. We ate out of the calabash bowls while drinking sweet herbal tea. Life here was simple and wholesome. I was at peace.

'Jay, are we going to Shirley Heights this afternoon? One last time?' An unnecessary question I thought, expecting a solid yes.

'No. I do not want to go today,' he said, eyes sorrowful. 'Regina, I am sad you are leaving. I don't feel like going this week.'

'Okay,' I said, trying to swallow my disappointment. My own sorrow lingered beneath the surface. 'I understand. Let's have a quiet evening instead.'

My final day in All Saints was sombre and quiet. Aside from a short walk along the pastures, we spent most of the day lying in bed, snuggling and embracing each other.

'Regina, I will come to Nelsons Dockyard and visit you on the boat.'

I had anticipated this. Taking a deep breath, I replied with a heavy heart. 'No, Jay. I don't want you to visit. I want us to say goodbye today. Next week I will settle into my new job and I want to focus on the boat. This is a new start for me, and I do not want a reminder of us there.

'Do you understand?' I said, feeling harsh and guilty. At the same time, I knew I did not have the energy for yet another sad and emotional separation. I wanted to say goodbye today and softly transition into my next chapter. The less distraction, the better.

'Babes. It's all right. I will miss you and hope one day you will come back.'

I approached Simon immediately after breakfast the following morning. 'Do you have a moment?'

He looked up from his news report and nodded. 'Yes, what's up, Regina?'

'Simon, I have decided to leave *PuraVida*. I am not happy with the situation on board and decided to look for another yacht. I found one last weekend and can move on anytime from today onwards,' I said calmly.

There was silence and Simon stared at me, flabbergasted. I briefly wished I had given a more eloquent explanation.

'What? You decide this now, just before we are to head off to the Mediterranean? Thanks for leaving me in the lurch like this!' he said, voice dripping with sarcasm. 'Now we're a crew member short. No idea how I am going to find someone else so quickly.' Simon's voice rose as his face turned crimson, but by now I was accustomed to his outbursts and knew not to take them personally. Once he stopped for breath, I interjected.

'Simon, I am sorry for the inconvenience. But I'm not happy onboard. Plenty of crew here are looking for a new boat, I am sure you will find someone good.'

After a short negotiation we agreed that he would sign me over to *Philomena* that afternoon, and I would move my belongings at the same time. I quickly threw my belongings back into my bags and said goodbye to Enzo. Simon and I walked to Nelsons Dockyard in awkward silence. Ben, my new captain, diffused any remaining tension at the immigration office. When Simon and I shook hands we parted with the promise to catch up for a drink before our departure.

Once again, I was a stranger on the dock, waiting to climb aboard a new boat and make it my home. In my cabin I quickly unpacked. For a moment I marvelled at my situation. I had first packed my bags fifteen months ago. Here I was, many adventures and experiences later, continuing my voyage.

'Regina, when you're done, find me on deck and I'll walk you through your duties,' Ben called, snapping me out of my reverie. I quickly found a spot for the last few items and stowed my bags.

'All right, Ben. I'm done,' I called.

After briefly instructing on Dean how to continue with his job, Ben headed my way.

'Okay, Regina. Life is simple on board here, so I'm sure you will be done with your duties in no time. Down below – that's your domain. Basically, I want you to keep the interior nice and clean. You don't need to clean our cabins though, we're responsible for them. Vacuum or sweep the floors as required, wipe down the woodwork daily to keep it clean and fresh, and clean the bathroom and toilet once a day. Whenever we spend more than a day in port, you will collect laundry and send it out to be serviced. That's pretty much it.

'Now,' he said, 'Regina. I support the philosophy that once you finish with your assigned work, you are free for the day. So, you can basically suit yourself, when and how quickly you choose to do your jobs.'

'Ben, is this really all I have to do?' I said, looking at him in astonishment.

He smiled.

'Wow! That's a fantastic arrangement. I think I might finish my days very early.' I looked at him again, not ready to believe my luck.

'I figured,' he replied, laughing openly at my surprise. 'But that's okay. As I said, it's totally up to you.'

He showed me where the cleaning supplies were stored, and I immediately attacked my job list. Barely two hours later, the interior was sparkling and I put the cleaning supplies away. I was bubbling with joy. The rest of the day was mine!

My final week in Antigua was balm for my soul. I felt safe and secure on *Philomena*. Ben and Dean were warm, friendly and calm, honouring our space and privacy. In my spare time I would read in the shade of a palm tree and for the first time in a long while, I felt I could fully relax.

I spent a lot of time on Galleon Beach in my own company. I was sad about leaving Jay and reminisced about our time. I was certain the decision to move on was the right one for me and this short period allowed me to grieve, accept and let go.

After more than a year of constant travel, changes, new people, love, separations, and reconciliations, I felt exhausted. My mind yearned for a break to absorb all the impressions. As the days passed, a sense of peace and clarity began gently blossoming within me. I laughed as I remembered the fun moments, and quietly cringed at the awkward mishaps. But no regrets. I visited Henry and Maude one last time and told them about my new boat and my plan to leave for good. They were happy to see me enjoying the yachting industry and pleased with my choice of boat and captain. After a few days I ventured back into English Harbour and called in on *PuraVida*. Simon and Enzo were all smiles. I was glad that the upset had passed, and we shared a beer in the cockpit. Simon mentioned having recruited a suitable replacement for me.

I also called Jay and despite my earlier reluctance, we did catch up again for one last afternoon. He wanted to hear about my new boat and captain and was at peace with my looming departure. He wished me luck and hugged me tightly.

'Regina, call me whenever you feel like it!' With a last smile Jay turned away and boarded the bus.

With a heavy heart I watched him take a seat and waved as the minivan pulled away. Self-consciously I wiped away a few tears and turned to walk back to my boat.

A few days later, early in the morning, the two remaining crew came aboard. We were amid pre-departure preparations.

'Regina, this is William and Sheldon. They are the two varnishers I told you about. Both have done the passage to and from Newport many times on *Philomena*,' Ben explained. 'Guys, this is Regina, the stewardess for the passage.'

I smiled at the two tall and dignified guys and we shook hands. I had observed the local varnishing teams on several boats in the marina and was intrigued by their painstaking work. They always added a friendly presence to the dock.

Once they'd thrown their bags into their cabin, they came back on deck to help get the boat ready to sail. Shortly after, Ben cranked up the old diesel engine. Once the motor was warm, he instructed us on how we would leave the dock and with a short nod, pushed the lever into gear. Gently *Philomena* shuddered and moved forward. The lines were released and we set off.

'See you next season!' people called and waved from the dock as we pulled away.

Slowly we made our way between the anchored yachts. I helped by coiling up ropes and stowing away fenders. Once out of the bay, Ben called to hoist the sails and the guys got busy on the foredeck. I stood at the stern observing the men flexing their muscles as they attempted to hoist the crisp white sails. On this yacht, rigging and deck fixtures were old school, involving a lot of strength and physical labour. Finally, when the sails reached the top of the mast, wind started to fill the canvas. Once everything was trimmed and we were on course, Ben cut the engine. The sun peeked through a gap in between the sails. Beneath us I heard the softly swooshing sound of our wake.

From the stern of this elegant and timeless yacht, I looked back at Antigua. It harboured a big chunk of my heart. I watched as the mountainous outline of the island grew smaller and smaller. When it finally disappeared beyond the horizon, I said a silent, final goodbye to Jay, the country and its people. I had immersed myself fully in this chapter. I had lived and loved, been challenged and gained insights, struggled, and willed myself to continue.

I took a deep breath, realising how far I had stepped out of my comfort zone compared with my previous sheltered life in Australia. Courage, curiosity and strength were what propelled me and what I needed to create a life in line with my dreams and aspirations. The result, in my eyes, had been completely worth it. My journey had been scary, awkward and confronting, and at times my life seemed to evolve like a random, meandering track rather than a straight pathway. I had set out on this journey with a different outcome in mind but over time had come to accept and embrace the challenges and experiences I encountered. I learned to lean in and trust the unfolding of my life. Now I understood, when moving towards my future, that simply commencing the journey, one footstep or one decision at a time, was sufficient. After that, all I had to do was relax and allow the path to reveal itself. I felt strong and confident about heading to the United States and facing the unknown there. While I still longed for reconciliation and approval from my parents, I knew that the answers to my inner emptiness would come neither from another person, nor from a particular location on this planet. I had to look within myself for that. I finally understood that the only person responsible for my life was me.

As I headed onward, I pledged to assume full responsibility for my choices, and for the creation of my unique personal story. I still did not have a home, nor did I yearn to put down roots, so my decision was to embrace this nomadic life with abandon. I vowed to go out and experience life with an open heart, and to be vulnerable. I would continue to be diligent about learning about myself and to live from a place of integrity. Going forth, this was my contract with myself, and the clarity I had been looking for all this time. It was my calling and my purpose.

For now, I turned to face the sun. The wind brushed my face. I smiled and allowed the freedom of the open sea to touch my heart. Our course was set, and the yacht was dutifully pushing us north. Leaning against the guardrail, I wondered what was in store for me on the distant shores ahead.

More change, of course!

YACHTING GLOSSARY

Bilge Space beneath and in between the floorboards and the hull.

Boom Pole underneath the mainsail, usually reaching across the cockpit area.

Bow Forward area of the yacht.

Cabin Rooms onboard.

Companionway Usually a staircase, leading from the cockpit down into the cabin.

Deck Top outside area.

Dinghy/Tender Small vessel used to travel from the yacht to/from the shore.

Foredeck Area of the deck forward of the mast, reaching to the tip of the yacht.

Galley Kitchen.

Guardrail Stainless-steel fencing enclosing the deck.

Gybe Changing sail direction, as the stern of the yacht passes through the wind.

Halyard Sheet attached to the top of the sail; used to hoist it to the top of the mast.

Hatch Window built into the hull or onto the deck, for light and airflow.

Head Toilet and/or bathroom.
Heel, heeling Tilting of the yacht, caused by wind angle and force of wind.
Helm, helming Steering wheel, steering the boat.
HF (radio) Radio for long-distance communication (high frequency).
Hoist, hoisting Raising a sail up to the top of the mast.
Hull Body of the yacht.
Jib Sail at the front of the boat, reaching from the mast down to the bow.
Mainsail Big sail attached to the mast on one side and to the boom on the bottom.
Mast Pole in the centre of the yacht's structure, designed to hold up the sails.
Navigation Station Alcove containing all the navigational aids, computer and charts.
Port Port side is the left side of the yacht, facing the bow aboard.
Porthole Circular window in the hull.
Rigging Construction that holds the mast in its upright position (includes shrouds).
Saloon Living room of a yacht.
Self-tailing winch Winch with a mechanism that holds the sheet in place.
Sheets Ropes or lines on board; attached to a sail they are used to hoist or trim the sail.
Shroud Wires connecting the top of the mast to the deck, stabilising the mast.
Spinnaker Large lightweight sail used instead of a jib, with wind from the stern quarter.

Yachting Glossary

Starboard Right side of the yacht when facing the bow.

Stern Rear area of the yacht.

Tack Changing sail direction, the bow of the yacht turning into the wind.

Tailing winch Winch where tension on a rope is kept by manually holding on to it.

Topsides Two sides of the hull.

Trimming Adjusting the sail according to wind angle and force, for best performance.

VHF (radio) Radio for short-distance radio calls (very high frequency).

Winch Cylindrical component on deck; a winch will trim the sail by tensioning sheets.

ACKNOWLEDGEMENTS

When I set out to write this book, I had no concept of how much time and effort the project was going to swallow up. This was likely a positive, for had I known the hours-upon-hours of work involved, I probably would have abandoned it long ago. Over some periods the manuscript lay dormant and I often wondered if it would ever see the light of day. Well, it did. Because I am stubborn and child-free and have the luxury of time to spare. This work shall be the only birthing process I endure. *Now live on, baby! I've paid my dues.*

But most importantly, the book is here today because of kindness. It was the countless small gestures, timely words of encouragement and support that kept me going.

Helene Young. It was you who instructed me to sit down and write 1,000 words a day. It wasn't until you pointed out the obvious that I became serious. Thank you. And again, for your kind offer to read my manuscript. I am humbled and immensely grateful for your generosity and support.

Isolde Martin. You were the first person to set eyes on the earliest (and cringeworthy!) draft of the manuscript, and I appreciate your gracious feedback immensely. Your generous assistance and encouragement early on instilled hope and trust in me to persist on my writing and publishing journey.

June Alexander. It was by pure chance that I stumbled upon your website, and I am thankful for the algorithms that placed you in my trajectory. It was magic to see you carefully editing my words, gently smoothing out abrasive parts and elevating what deserved to shine. Thank you for encouraging me over and over to pursue publishing.

Bernadette Foley. It was your skill, care and experience that turned my manuscript into a polished and quality book. I watched you do this with grace, calm and great professionalism. Thank you for keeping it all on track at times when I felt flustered.

Hazel Lam. I feel incredibly lucky that you were available and willing (!) to work on this project. The book looks fabulous, inside and out, and I am absolutely stoked with the result. Thank you!

Nicole Webb. You brought peace of mind to the process by taking care of the publicity aspect. Thank you for sharing your skills and insights, and for making my story accessible to a much greater audience.

Mum. When I was little, I remember feeling that it was you and me against the world. You were the centre of my universe, the person I admired most and the authority I persistently rebelled against. You stood firm in your truth and in your love for me, and I knew, even during turbulent times, that you would always be there for me. I.H.D.G.G.F.G.

Dad. We didn't always see eye to eye, and it took work to create our bond later in life. But we did. We talked, learned from each other, appreciated our differences, and healed our connection. This I will value forever. Wherever you are, thank you for accepting my wild and unconventional choices, for your love and the warm and cuddly hugs. I miss you and you are forever present in my heart.

Acknowledgements

Thomas. You were the rock in the family equation, and I am grateful for your steady and loving presence. You are my bonus dad and I feel blessed to have you in my life.

Sven. Thank you for the time we shared together, the memories we created and for being a cherished friend. I value our friendship more than you are probably aware of. And thank you for sharing your beautiful family with me. I love you all deeply.

Leo. Thank you for catching me when I truly needed it. I will always be grateful for the love and support you have so generously extended.

Evelyne. Our history and the genuine connection we share mean the world to me. I am grateful for your love, the unwavering support, and the countless belly laughs.

Jo. My Sagittarius sailing soul sister. We met on a yacht many years ago and I am grateful we still get to dream up extraordinary adventures.

Morgan. You are my distant anchor whenever I need to seek shelter during a storm. Thank you for who you are and for being there.

To the all the special women in my life. I look up to you. You inspire me, give me strength and make me laugh. I hold you dear in my heart.

To the ASA and QWC. I am grateful for the resources, support and communities you provide.

To all the writers, published or 'yet-to-be'. I thank you for your time and the kind and genuine advice. It is amazing to feel held in such uplifting company.

I wish to extend my love and gratitude to the people who inspired my story. Your presence touched, challenged, enriched and changed me. Without you I would not be who I am today.

Thank you. Every now and then I wonder if you, like me, find yourself quietly chuckling and reminiscing about this time. 'What a blast it all was!'

Regina Petra Meyer was born and raised in Switzerland and worked as a travel agent for several years. Her curiosity was piqued by coordinating trips for her clients to all corners of the globe, and eventually she packed her own bags and adopted a globetrotting lifestyle. Regina has adventured across all continents, enjoys meeting people and trying new foods – providing she can distinguish what's on her plate. She has lived and worked in Antigua in the Caribbean, the USA, New Zealand, and currently calls tropical Cairns, Australia, her home.

Regina has no children, remains unmarried, and cherishes the freedom her life offers. Alongside her love of exploring the world, she is equally curious and passionate about her inner journey and evolution. When she's not writing, Regina helps people to become empowered, to embrace courage and follow their dreams.

Regina's memoir *Change of Course* is her first book.

For more information visit Regina's website
reginapetrameyer.com

You can connect with Regina on the following platforms:

🅕 facebook.com/reginapetrameyer
🅘 instagram.com/reginapetrameyer
🅖 goodreads.com/reginapetrameyer

A last note: If you enjoyed reading *Change of Course* please rate and review the book on your bookseller's platform and feel free to recommend it on your social media channels. Authors rely on your engagement and word-of-mouth is the best advertising yet. *Thank you!*

www.ingramcontent.com/pod-product-compliance
Lightning Source LLC
Chambersburg PA
CBHW051534010526
44107CB00064B/2726